Administering USENET News Servers

A Comprehensive Guide to Planning, Building, and Managing Internet and Intranet News Services

James E. McDermott
and
John E. Phillips

With a Foreword by Rich Salz

ADDISON-WESLEY DEVELOPERS PRESS
An Imprint of Addison Wesley Longman, Inc.

Reading, Massachusetts • Harlow, England • Menlo Park, California
Berkeley, California • Don Mills, Ontario • Sydney
Bonn • Amsterdam • Tokyo • Mexico City

Library of Congress Cataloging-in-Publication Data

McDermott, James E. and Phillips, John E.

Administering Usenet news servers : a comprehensive guide to planning, building, and managing Internet and Intranet news services / James E. McDermott.

p. cm.

Includes index.

ISBN 0-201-41967-X

1. Usenet (Computer network) 2. Client/server computing. 3. Internet (Computer network) 4. Intranets (Computer network) I. Title.

TK5105.875.U83M353 1997

005.7'136—dc21

97-3462

CIP

A-W Developers Press is a division of Addison Wesley Longman, Inc.

Sponsoring Editor: Mary Treseler
Project Manager: John Fuller
Production Coordinator: Melissa Lima
Text design: Vicki L. Hochstedler
Set in 11-point Minion by Vicki L. Hochstedler

1 2 3 4 5 6 7 8 9 -MA- 0100999897
First printing, April 1997

THIS BOOK IS DEDICATED TO THE FOND MEMORY OF FRANCES M. DOUGLAS, WHO INSPIRED ME IN BOTH MY WRITING CAREER AND MY LIFE.

J. E. M.

I WOULD LIKE TO DEDICATE MY PORTION OF THIS BOOK TO MY WIFE LYNE FOR ALL HER LOVE AND SUPPORT; AND ALSO TO MARC BOUCHER FOR TEACHING ME UNIX.

J. E. P.

Contents

Foreword

USENET has always been the "problem child" of the major Internet services. E-mail is easily understood because of its direct parallel to conventional memos and postal mail. And almost everyone has seen a Web browser—most people use one regularly; those who haven't can think of it as a book with fast cross-references.

USENET is different. It's more like a bulletin board and a set of Post-it notes. Actually, it's several thousand bulletin boards, each labeled with a name and a one-line description that tries to focus the discussion. If I want to say something about the Java programming language in USENET, I find the *comp.lang.java* board, take a Post-it, and write my message. Later on, someone else can come to the same board, see my note, and stick up his or her reply. Others may see the first two notes, comment on them, and post a succession of additional notes that comment on what's been said before, that correct errors, that correct errors in the corrections, and so on. My original note will probably fall off and become lost, but the exchange of notes—the discussion—continues.

Now, here's where it gets weird. Instead of there being just one copy of each bulletin board, organizations have their own copy of the boards they are interested in. While there is consensus on a few hundred "main" boards, there are thousands of boards carried by anywhere from a half dozen to several thousand sites. Each site exchanges the contents of the boards that it carries with friendly "neighbor sites." Even more impressive, when I write an article and it gets sent to a "well-connected" site, that article can be available to about half of the Internet in a few hours; by the end of the day my article will be available nearly everywhere. Teddy Roosevelt's statement is out-of-date: USENET is now the world's bully pulpit. Hundreds of thousands of people at tens of thousands of sites use thousands of newsgroups: The amount of data that is getting shipped around, and copied, is staggering. A gigabyte disk will fill up in a few days.

USENET and the Web are complementary. The explosive Internet growth (largely caused by the Web) has meant an explosion in the number of sites that want, or need, to run USENET. Businesses use it as an official support channel to their customers; professors use it to distribute curricula; and people the world over use it to "talk" about shared interests. As USENET has grown, it has become much less elitist. When I first released INN a few years ago, it wasn't unreasonable to require system administrators to read a few hundred lines of configuration information and to be intimately aware of the details of their C compiler and system libraries. Site management wasn't an issue, since most people using it were already running USENET or had just "graduated" (often literally) from a site that was. Nowadays, the news administrator might be a small ISP businessman who knows more about A/R than K&R. Any prior exposure a user has to USENET is often as a paying customer of another online service, so he or she will be completely unaware of such practical issues such as disk space or "server throttling."

Many of us long for the "good old days" when Dennis Ritchie would write on ANSI C drafts, Dave Korn would post ksh bugfixes, John Nagle would explain TCP timeout issues, and so on. Programmers are a small minority of the populace, and as more of the general public join USENET, programming takes an appropriately smaller amount of space in the news spool area.

USENET is now different from the rest of the world. It has its share of arguments and intolerance, and much of what people write is wrong or just plain dull. But there is real communication happening on USENET, and that's a good thing. We can't get along, and stop fighting, until we sit down and talk. USENET does help make that possible. Am I really saying that USENET helps to make the world a better place? Yup. It's a difficult job, but if you want to get involved, this book will help.

Rich Salz
April 1997

Preface

This book came about after a conversation with John Phillips, a friend and Internet consultant who, after building his nth INN news server, commented that there was not a lot written about news servers. He had gleaned some information from FAQs, RFCs, the INN manual, and so on, but he had learned an equal amount through trial and error, newsgroup postings, word of mouth, and general Internet folklore.

I had taken a hiatus from Newbridge Networks Corporation to pursue a writing career, and was looking for something to write—preferably for money. A scan of offerings of the the more prominent publishers confirmed John's suspicions; specifically, there seemed to be no current books on INN, the most prominent UNIX netnews software in use. There were books on USENET newsgroups and how to use them, but as far as building a news server you were pretty much out in the cold. I knew very little about the inner workings of the Internet (I could barely spell *IP* at the time), but I had played around with the Web and e-mail and had had some exposure to News. So, armed with more optimism than sense, I decided I would write a book on USENET News servers. I approached Addison-Wesley Developers Press with the idea and started a dialogue with then-editor Kim Fryer, which ultimately resulted in a book contract and a summer and fall lost in writing. In the process I decided to add the newer DNEWS software to the book since it was becoming popular for PC-based news servers.

Looking back, I see that my initial motivation was to further my freelance writing career by getting a book deal. John's motivation was far more altruistic, as he believed the book would have value to the Internet community from both a constructor's and a news administrator's point of view. John generously supplied the core technical information along with access to many of his UNIX colleagues, who themselves gave generously of their time and talents. For myself, I have become somewhat less mercenary and now see the book as a creative work. Writing is like that if you want to do it well. You have to write for more than the money. There has to be a real passion for the result—an almost pathological desire to see it on a bookstore shelf. However, now that the book is finished, I finally understand the expression "It is better to have written!"

James E. McDermott

April 1997

Acknowledgments

Obviously, you don't write a book like this without a great deal of direct help and moral support from many people. First off we'd like to recognize the tolerance and understanding shown by both our families throughout the writing of this book, and to apologize for our inaccessibility and our sometimes noisy late-night sessions.

We would like to acknowledge the contributions of the following people: Paul Kern, Anne Bennett, Jim Morris, Bruce Jones, Axel Jones, Kent Landfield, Lewis S. Eisen, Peter Thonis, Hugh Ellis, Robert Zakon, Igor Chudov, Russell McOrmond, Mark Moraes, Pushpendra Mohta, Tom Podnar, Ron Newman, Lars Ingebrigtsen, Chris Pugmire, Rainer Paduch, Susan Stuart, Chris Lewis, Mark Douglas Lowes, J. D. Falk, Rob M. Fleischman, James A. Brister, Dave Barr, and Michael Grubb.

In particular, we'd like to highlight the contributions of James Mathiesen of D.E. Shaw and Company, who not only acted as a technical reviewer for the book but also helped tremendously in sorting out key details on INN. To say James gave generously of his time would be an understatement, as he was always available to answer a phone query or to respond to a panicked e-mail message. We also thank David Jones of Mosaid Technologies, who also acted as a technical reviewer and kept us on our toes regarding style and content; and Rich Salz, who lent his time and credibility to the book by way of his excellent foreword.

A thanks to all those who wrote helpful applications, scripts, and essays, and those who maintain USENET-related sites. Wherever possible we've tried to mention them "in-situ."

All equipment used in the creation and testing of our news servers was generously donated by Hardware Canada Computing. A special thanks goes to Guy Bond of Cisco Systems, Inc. for his technical assistance. We also thank the Internet Software Consortium and Netwin, Inc., for the netnews software used in the news servers.

Finally, a general thanks to the people at Addison-Wesley Developers Press who have proven just what experts they are in guiding relative newcomers through the book-writing process. Specifically, thanks to project manager John Fuller and the rest of his production team—desktop compositor Vicki Hochstedler, copy editor Maggie Carr, and production coordinator Melissa Lima—and of course to acquisitions editor Mary Treseler, who joined the project midflight and never missed a beat.

Conventions

This book uses a number of unique text highlights to help separate the various types of information such as filenames, user entries, and so forth from the regular text. Special eye-catching icons are also used to focus the reader's attention on key information. Table 1 provides a list of these conventions.

Table 1 Book Conventions

Convention	Explanation
bold	user entries required
underlines	indicate files or directories
italics	used to highlight a word that is not to be taken literally
	This icon is used to flag an important piece of information.
	This icon is used to indicate a value that likely will have to be changed on your system.

PART I

INTRODUCTION

1 The Internet Today

The Internet is the amalgamation, and in some cases absorption of numerous separate network entities such as NSFnet, ARPANET, USENET, and commercial packet networks such as Tymnet, but it was NSFnet that defined the way forward for the Internet as it exists today. NSFnet, which was founded by the National Science Foundation in 1986, allowed and even encouraged networks from other public and educational institutions to connect to its small but widespread network. It originally consisted of only five supercomputers connected by 56Kbps (kilobits per second) leased lines using TCP/IP as the transmission protocol. Connections to one of these *backbone nodes,* was usually done through a dial-up connection and the UNIX-to-UNIX Copy Protocol (UUCP), since dedicated lines were very expensive at the time. These sites, in turn, may have had other sites connected to them by dial-up connection, so the early topology was a weblike mesh—a very flat structure—with a single central backbone. A site might be directly connected to a major NSF backbone node or might have to "hop" through numerous computers in a sequential addressing scheme to get to its destinations. In those days it was easy to get UUCP connection maps showing how various hosts were connected so you could avoid extraneous hops and make the optimal connections.

Each site appearing on these computer-generated maps was described by entries containing the key information on the site such as host name, machine, organization, latitude and longitude, e-mail, and so forth. Table 1-1 shows a typical entry.

Table 1-1 Typical UUCP Data Entry

#N	blizzard
#S	SUN Sparcstation 2; SUN OS 4.1
#O	Phillips Consulting Group
#C	John Phillips
#E	blizzard!jep@pcgbase.com
#T	+1 904 111-1111
#P	Daytona Beach FL 32720
#L	31 01 50 N / 81 20 00 W city
#R	
#U	edus ki4pv moksha bhag
#W	blizzard!jep (John Phillips); Sat April 20 09:19 EST 1992
#	
blizzard	

These maps, though complex and detailed, were nonetheless public and freely exchanged. See Figure 1-1 for a partial UUCP map for the USENET community in the New York area circa 1993.

Other networks, connected in by using gateways, machines that processed and translated the many different protocols that were rampant at the time.

While the government and telecommunications giants only talked about a nationwide information superhighway, and standards committees bogged down in technical debates, the Internet happened—not just nationwide but worldwide. This "accidental superhighway" is a global phenomenon that today connects over 3 million computers to over 30 million people, and the growth is accelerating.

Figure 1-1 A typical UUCP map.

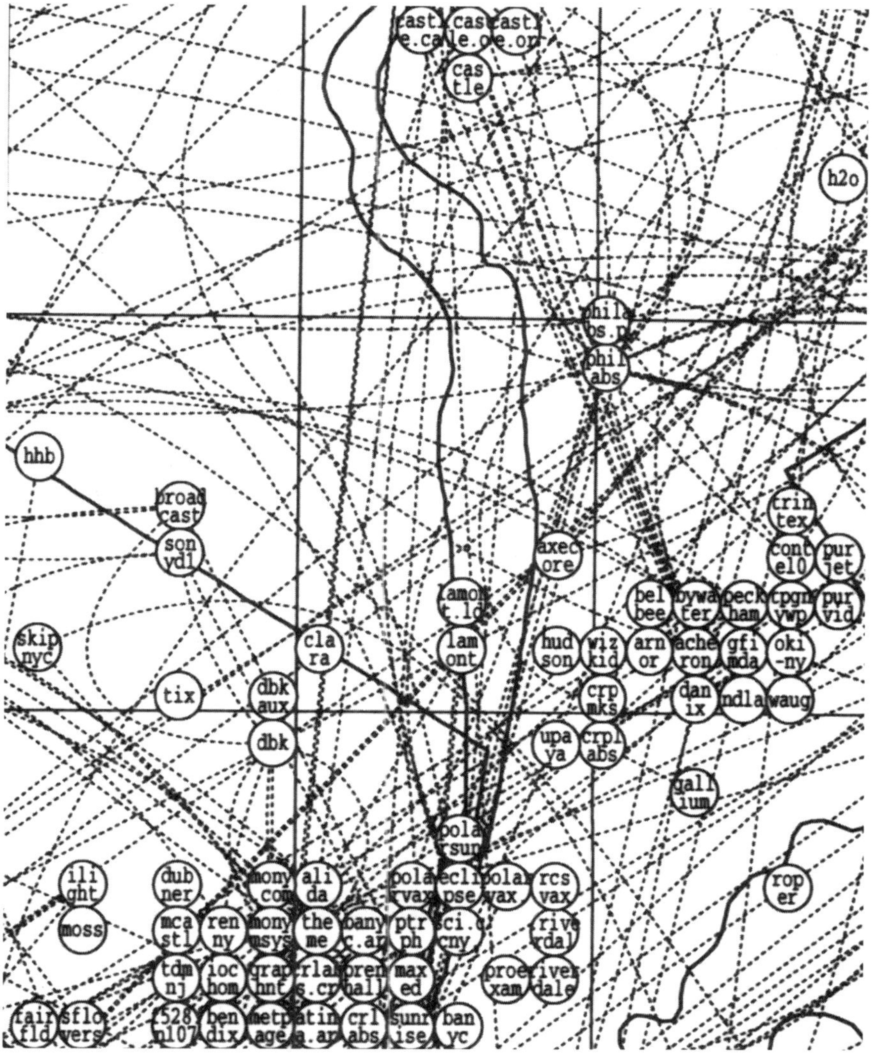

PHYSICAL TOPOLOGY

Through the late 1980s and early 1990s, dedicated, leased lines carrying the TCP/IP protocol and other protocols such as X.25 largely replaced dial-up UUCP between sites, and the Internet topology began to change. More and more universities and research institutions joined in the process and, in so doing, increased awareness of the Internet. Soon its popularity soared, and commercial enterprises began logging on as once strict usage policies were relaxed or went unenforced. As significant commercial traffic began flowing through the NSFnet backbone and through educational sites, the National Science Foundation, which funded NSFnet, could no longer justify spending public money on what was becoming a commercial enterprise. As a result there was a proposal for sweeping changes to the infrastructure to allow the NSF backbone to restore its original mandate of being a network for researchers and learners.

THE MODERN-DAY INTERNET TOPOLOGY

In the spring of 1995 the architecture of the American Internet underwent a major change from a single dominant NSFnet backbone to a series of commercially owned backbones running coast to coast. Largely because of these changes, the Internet is now a much more hierarchical arrangement with a number of massive backbones managed by Network Service Providers (NSPs) and a small number of super pipes to cross oceans and continents. Fanning off these backbones are spurs that support connections from Internet Service Providers (ISPs), governments, universities, and large corporations. Below these spurs are many more branches—smaller ISPs, companies, and individuals.

The backbones themselves are joined together at Network Access Points (NAPs) where powerful routers handle many terabytes of data per hour. Figure 1-2 depicts the generalized architecture of NAPS, NSPs, ISPs, leaf

Figure 1-2 Today's Internet architecture.

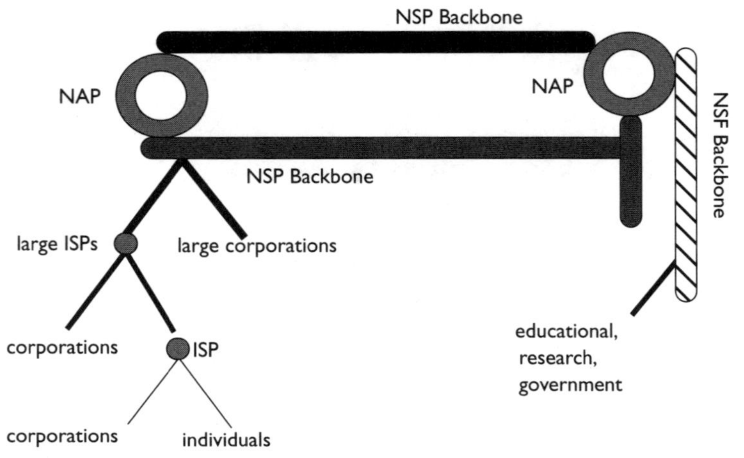

nodes, and so on. Figure 1-3 shows the location of these NAPs and is courtesy of CERFnet, a large NSP.

Figure 1-3 Network Access Points (NAPs) for North America. (Illustration courtesy of CERFnet, www.cerf.net)

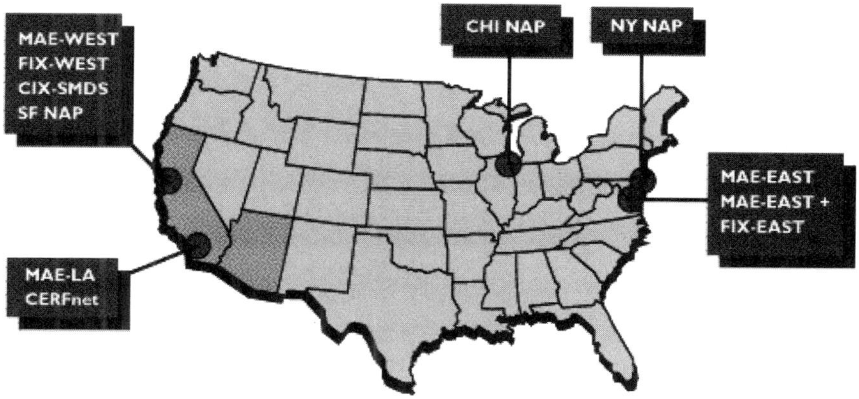

Figure 1-4 shows the CERFnet backbone as of August 1, 1996. Note the NAP connections.

Figure 1-4 CERFnet Nationwide backbone showing NAP connections. (Adapted from an illustration provided by CERFnet, www.cerf.net)

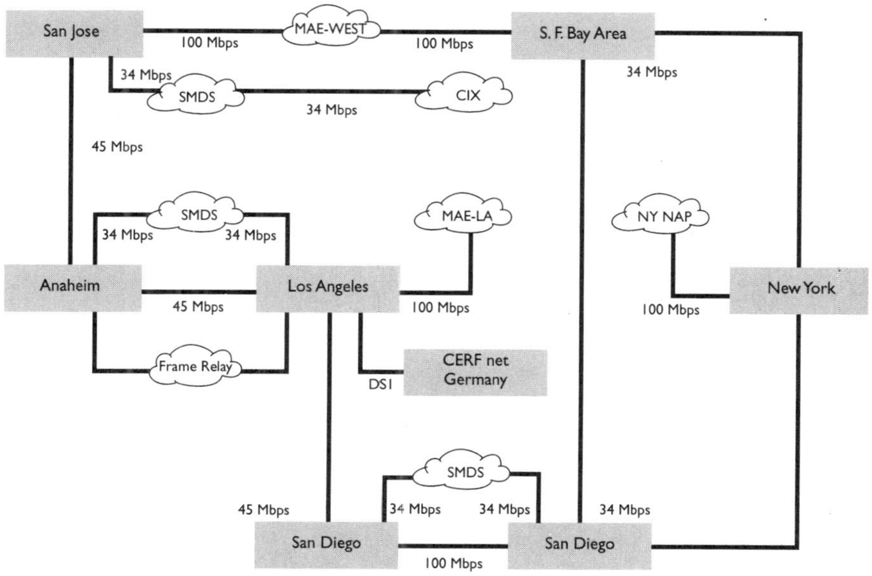

MANY PLAYERS

There are numerous NSPs with varying degrees of geographic coverage, NAP connections, and capacity. For example, Table 1-2 lists some of the major providers routing traffic through the busy New York NAP on September 29, 1996.

Table 1-2 New York NAP Internet Interconnections

@Home Network	Global SprintLink
Advanti	EUNET
AGIS	IDREN
ANS	IDT
ANS_Cisco	IIJ
Apex	MCI
AT&T	Nysernet
BBN Planet	SprintLink
CERFnet	UUnet
Digex	vBNS
ESNET	

Many providers publish their network topology maps. Check their Internet site or contact them directly for a copy. The information these maps carry can be invaluable in determining performance problems due to low-bandwidth pipes and NAP bottlenecks. For instance, at the time of writing, two major Canadian backbone networks joined only at a U.S. NAP. This degraded communications between companies using these two separate providers.

TRAFFIC VOLUMES

The traffic through these NAPs is incredible. Fig 1-5 shows the volume of incoming and outgoing traffic for one day through the New York NAP.* Note that the outgoing traffic is significantly less than the incoming traffic. This phenomenon results from dropped packets owing to congestion, but dropped packets do not necessarily signify lost data since TCP/IP is extremely robust. Still to some, the dropped packets are a portent of the future collapse of the Internet, especially considering its phenomenal growth rate.

*Statistics courtesy of CERFnet.

Figure 1-5 Typical daily traffic through the New York NAP. (Illustration courtesy of CERFnet, www.cerf.net)

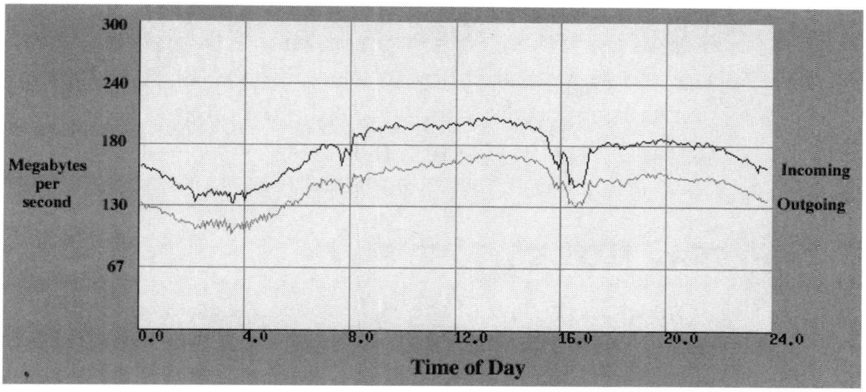

As grassroot traffic increases, the NSPs will have to build more capacity to handle it and, in turn, the NAPs will experience more traffic. The NAPs will have to counter with greater capacity to handle this traffic. Is there a technological limit? Probably not; more parallel processing can be added, NAPs can be segmented, more NAPs can be added, more alternate high-speed backbones can be established, and so forth. All these techniques and many more can be employed to improve the Internet's performance and reliability. The problem is more a fiscal one—a financial limit. Who will pay for these upgrades? The answer is probably the end user. Some experts are predicting the end to low-cost, flat-rate Internet access and a rise in prices for corporate access. Others are insisting that as the telephone and cable companies get involved, prices may go down and performance will improve.

One thing is clear: The Internet is growing and growing faster than predicted. One other thing is crystal clear: The Internet, in one form or another, is here to stay.

LOGICAL TOPOLOGY

Although a physical knowledge of the Internet can be useful especially when it comes to choosing an ISP, a logical familiarity is more instructive, especially from a USENET News perspective, since most users perceive the Internet logically. In other words, they analogize what is really happening in order to better understand it. Consider television. When we flip through the 500-channel television universe, we're not interested at all in how the signal gets to our sets or which frequencies are being used to carry the signal. We merely select a channel number. But even selecting a channel gets tedious when there are so many to choose from. Now with the newer remote control gizmos you can select ESPN, NBC, CNN. People tend to like names as opposed to numbers, and most Internet users handle navigation the same way. To get to the domain pcgbase.com, they type in this name or often just click on a selection presented by a Web search engine.

THE HOSTS.TXT FILE

From the early days of the TCP/IP based networks, designers recognized people's preference for names over Internet Protocol (IP) numbers. An early implementation of this name/number translation was the creation of a single, maintained file (HOSTS.TXT) that contained registered host names and their equivalent IP numbers. The file was located at Stanford University, and when a new host was added to the Internet community, this file was updated with the host name and corresponding IP number. Periodically, an Internet site would download this file in order to catch any additions or deletions. This worked fine while the number of hosts was relatively small, but as the Internet grew, maintaining this file became difficult, and constant downloads were required across the network to ensure synchronism. Another problem was the lack of screening for duplicate host names. This left many key sites such as mail hubs vulnerable to impersonation and service disruption.

DOMAIN NAME SYSTEM

The Domain Name System (DNS) was a major breakthrough, and it still remains the method of choice for host name translation. DNS provided a method of local name management as well as instant global access. DNS uses a distributed database with name/number translation information spread across the Internet to ease the processing load on any one site as well as to speed up response. The distribution is based on a hierarchical scheme similar to a typical directory structure. The root is divided into top-level domains conforming to a standard that has up until recently been stable. Below these top-level domains are second-level domains, third-level, and so on as required.

Each domain level contains DNS records of name/number translations information for that domain. For example, if the host name was *bart.alermax.com*, it is in the *alermax.com* domain, and the information on its IP number would be held at the site designated to hold *alermax.com* domain information. Domains themselves can be further broken down into subdomains.

Fig 1-6 shows the domain name hierarchy with an example of a machine named *bart* in the Alermax company. The fully qualified domain name of the machine bart is *bart.alermax.com.* Also shown in Figure 1-6 are a few examples of country designations that subsequently break down into state, province or territory, and so forth. Country designations are top-level domains and adhere to an ISO standard.

Figure 1-6 The Domain Name System (DNS) hierarchy.

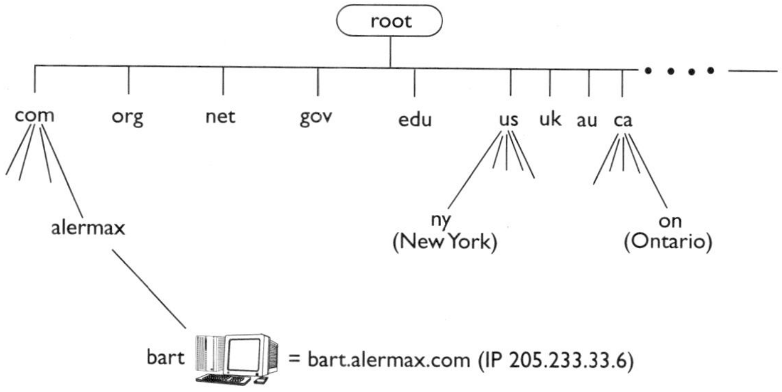

To handle the load for any particular top-level domain, the Internic, the governing body for DNS, has spread the naming database among a number of servers located at many different locations around the Internet.

DNS is a distributed database and a perfect example of a client-server network application. For example, if *bart* wants to talk to the machine *homer* (fully qualified domain name is *homer.alermax.com*), the DNS client (called a resolver) on *bart* sends a request to its DNS server. Because *homer* is in the same domain as *bart*, the information to resolve *homer.alermax.com* is already in the local DNS database. The IP number for *homer* is returned to *bart*, who is then able to set up communication with *homer*.

If a host's name/number information is not kept in the local DNS server (say the host name was *lisa.waterloo.ca*), the sequence of DNS queries would be something like the following (refer also to Figure 1-7):

- *Bart's* resolver requests *lisa's* address from the local DNS server.
- The local DNS server retrieves the IP number of the *.ca* name server from *root.*
- The local DNS server then retrieves the IP number of the *waterloo.ca* name servers from the *.ca* name server.
- The local DNS server then retrieves the IP number of *lisa* from the *waterloo.ca* name server.
- The local DNS returns *lisa's* address to *bart.*

DNS servers cache information. As a result, when looking up *lisa,* the local DNS name server might already know *lisa's* address. This avoids repeating the name resolution chain each time *bart* wants to connect to *lisa.*

This is a simplistic walk-through. The DNS scheme has other, more advanced capabilites that are not covered here. (The bibliography gives some references for further reading.)

Figure 1-7 DNS name resolution.

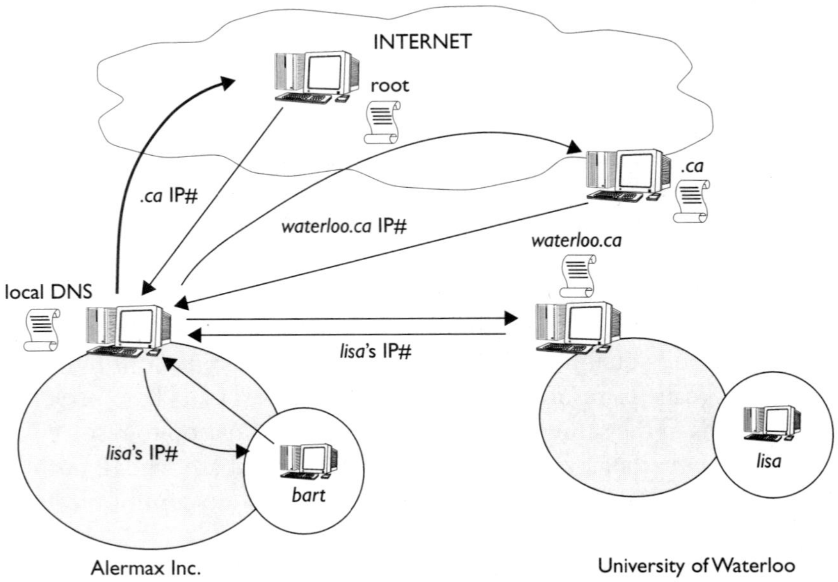

2 The History of USENET News

Every hour of every day news servers that make up the USENET News network flood the global Internet with millions of bytes of data representing thousands of individual news articles on topics ranging from software bug fixes to hobbies. From humble beginnings with two remotely connected computers, News has become a mainstay of both business and personal communication, as important as e-mail, and accounting for nearly half of today's Internet traffic. This chapter will explain what News is, where it came from, how it works, and who makes it work.

Capsule Summary

USENET News is a collection of servers on the Internet that, by mutual agreement, propagate news articles to each other. The news software on these machines segments these articles by topic into *newsgroups*. In many ways, USENET is like a very large bulletin board system (BBS), wherein comments posted by one are seen by many. But there are significant differences. For example, readers subscribing to selected newsgroups receive only articles associated with those newsgroups. Subscribers can post responses to existing news articles or post their own original news item. Another difference is that, unlike the BBS where there may be only one main server housing the database, there are literally tens of thousands of copies of the news database scattered around the globe. This makes the scheme self-healing, in case a server goes down, and allows broad participation.

News servers have traditionally been located at institutions, very large corporations, and government departments because considerable financial commitment and senior technical expertise were required to connect to the Internet. Lower-cost equipment and substantially cheaper bandwidth have made possible a much broader participation. As a result there has been an explosion in news traffic with the number of newsgroups eclipsing 20,000 and the number of participants estimated in the millions.

WHY NOT JUST USE E-MAIL?

A mailing list of recipients and their e-mail addresses is often used to distribute information to a large audience over the Internet. The sender uses mailing lists to send a copy of a message to each person on the mailing list. This works well for a small list but becomes inefficient when the list grows large, since sending the same message to multiple recipients consumes bandwidth and CPU resources. Maintenance of the list is also a concern. E-mail addresses may become invalid, making the message undeliverable. This causes mail to pile up on the disk or be bounced back to the originator. On the recipient's side, there are issues with locating lists or even knowing they exist, as Figure 2-1 illustrates.

Figure 2-1 Mailing lists.

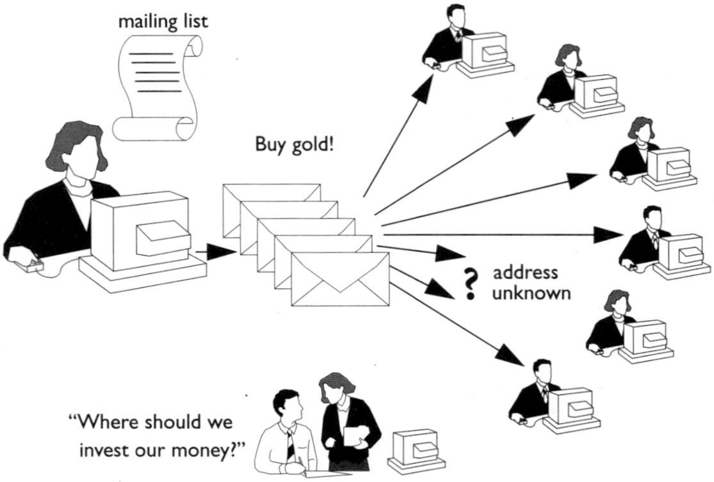

USENET News avoids these problems by posting messages (as articles) to the USENET News server network and letting interested parties find them by searching the newsgroup hierarchy. One of the advantages of this approach is that only one copy of an article needs to be posted to each server, regardless of how many people, connected to the server, wish to read it. Also server addresses stay relatively static since servers move less frequently than people do. The server manages the news articles automatically, and articles are either archived or expired after a given amount of time. As a result, unread or obsolete articles don't accumulate on a disk as undelivered mail messages can.

SOME HISTORY

The term *USENET* is derived from "Users Network," one of the early Internet network entities. Like most things Internet, the roots of USENET News are at the same time both simple and complicated—simple because in the late seventies three graduate students, armed with homegrown software, established the first news servers; complicated because over the years both the software and the underlying processes of the early days have evolved dramatically owing to the easy availability of source code and the efforts of countless dedicated volunteers. To get a perspective on the current state of affairs, it's helpful to look back to the early roots of USENET News and the major changes it has undergone.

THE EARLY DAYS—ANEWS

In 1979 graduate students Tom Truscott, Jim Ellis, and Steve Bellovin created a shared electronic bulletin board between Duke University and the University of North Carolina. Built around the new dial-up protocol UUCP, a suite of programs that performs UNIX-to-UNIX copy using standard telephone lines and modems and script software written by Bellovin at UNC, the system allowed people in both universities interested in UNIX topics to read and post comments. Thus the two machines, *unc* and *duke* were the first news servers, and, in a very real sense, the three graduate students are the main founders of USENET News (see Figure 2-2).

Early adopters quickly saw the value of news servers as a communications medium, and the news traffic grew dramatically. Unfortunately, since the original software was script based, the overall system was not too efficient, so a series of improvements was undertaken to enhance performance. Bellovin rewrote the scripts in C, Daniels and Truscott made further enhancements, and they produced the ANEWS version.

Figure 2-2 The first USENET connections.

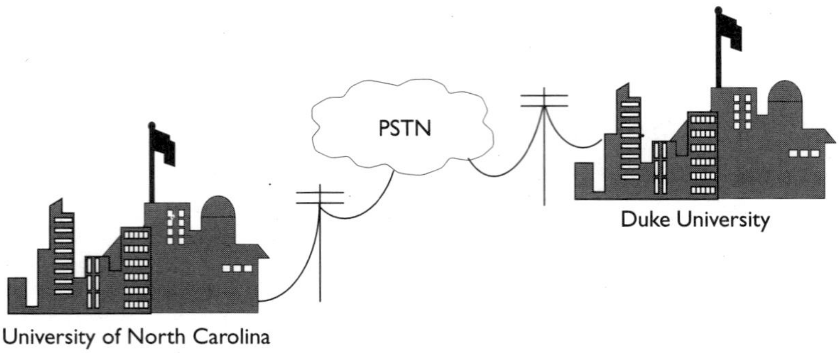

BNEWS

By 1981 USENET News had become a victim of its own success, and the ANEWS software, which was intended to handle a few articles a day, was quickly overwhelmed. To handle the prevailing news volume and to allow for future growth, a new version of software called BNEWS was created. BNEWS was written primarily by Mark Horton at the University of California at Berkeley and high school student Matt Glickman. It went through a number of rewrites by the creators and Rick Adams at the Center for Seismic Studies. The new software complied with the RFC 822 message format standard and was better at handling the volume of news traffic. By 1986 this version was under pressure, owing in large part to the underlying limitation of its UUCP underpinnings.

UUCP AND NNTP—A PARADIGM SHIFT

Since UUCP handles News in store-and-forward batches (see Figure 2-3), the success of the approach increased the volume of news to such an extent that the resulting long-distance costs became prohibitive. Part of the reason lies in the fact that the store-and-forward technology had no way of preventing the transmission of duplicate articles.

The Network News Transfer protocol (NNTP) grew out of independent work in 1984–1985 by Brian Kantor at University of California at San Diego and Phil Lapsley at University of California at Berkeley. Primary development was done at U.C. Berkeley with help from Erik Fair, Steven Grady, and Mike Meyer, among others. The RFC 977 protocol was the result of their collective effort.

Figure 2-3 A typical UUCP exchange.

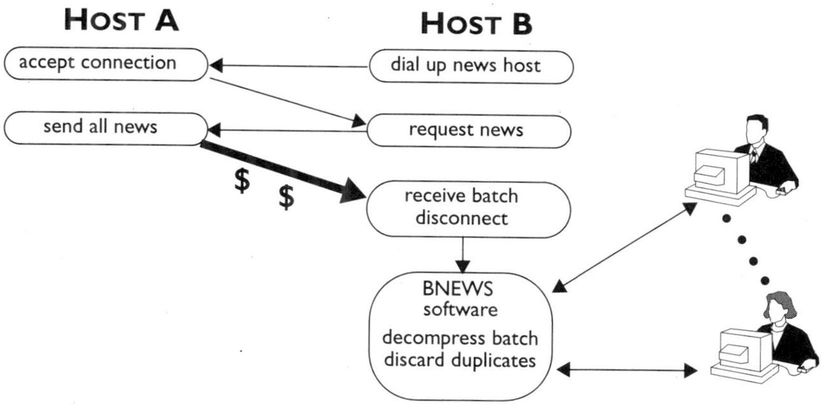

(Host A creates and compresses news batch for Host B; that is, it acts as a news feed.)

NNTP would largely replace UUCP for the high-speed propagation of news between servers. The new protocol allowed hosts to exchange articles by TCP/IP connections rather than by using the traditional modem-based UUCP. Pushing news over the leased TCP/IP connections between sites greatly facilitated the growth of USENET News just when the long-distance UUCP dial-up costs were becoming a big burden on many administration budgets. NNTP's main role was to handle the exchange of news between servers. The news server itself still required news server software such as BNEWS to disseminate news to and from the attached news community. NNTP also permitted users to read and post news from machines not running the USENET News software. Unlike UUCP, which batches articles into one large compressed file, NNTP intelligently and interactively deals with the receiving host on an article-by-article basis, sending only those articles required. Overall, NNTP produces a more efficient and therefore a faster news system.

In most cases where Host A feeds Host B, Host B also feeds Host A. The exchange is depicted in Figure 2-4 as follows:

- Host A maintains a log of articles it has received that, according to its configuration, Host B would also wish to receive.
- Periodically (every few minutes, hours, or days), Host A connects to Host B.

- Host A sends an Ihave message-id command. If host B already has received the article from another news server, the command is refused. Otherwise Host A sends the article.
- Host A sends more Ihave message-id commands until all articles are sent.
- Host A sends a Quit command and ends the connection.
- Local news readers on Host B can access the new articles.

The NNTP protocol reduces the transfer of unnecessary articles. Host A, in this case, can note whether Host B is in the article path (covered in Chapter 3) and, if so, not offer the article. Host B could receive feeds from multiple sites but is concerned only with the overhead to transfer the article once.

Figure 2-4 A typical NNTP exchange.

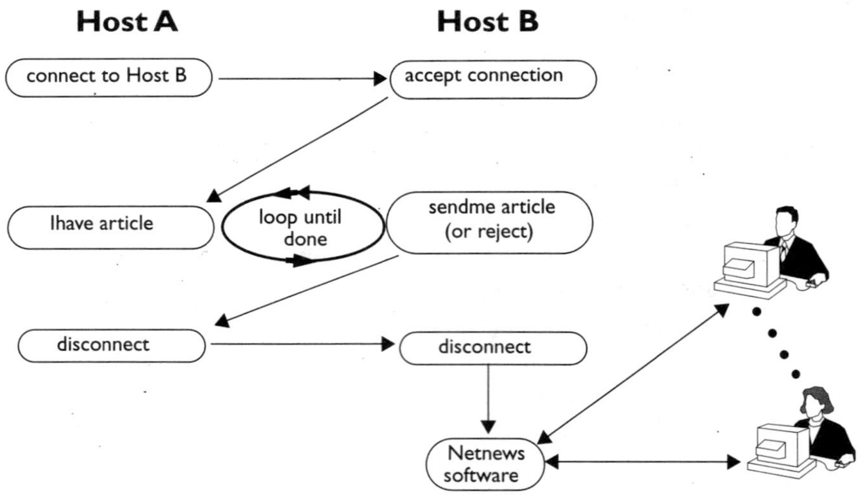

CNEWS

To speed up news exchange and processing, Geoff Collyer and Henry Spencer of the University of Toronto developed CNEWS, a thorough rewrite of BNEWS. Another driving force in the development of CNEWS was that the much modified BNEWS had begun to develop multiple streams of releases, often incompatible with one another. The CNEWS software was released in the fall of 1987, and although still in use today, it is batch-oriented and lacks the needed scalability to address today's larger news volumes. Today, it has largely been replaced by InterNet News (INN).

INN

Rich Salz of Bolt, Beranek and Newman, Inc. developed INN and released it for public use in August 1992. Salz designed INN to run on UNIX hosts that have TCP/IP connections and to use asynchronous, rather than batch, processing. However, INN does provide full UUCP support. INN integrates NNTP into its main software thus obviating the need to maintain both packages separately, as in the case of its predecessors. INN is free for downloading off various file transfer protocol (FTP) sites (as well as on the enclosed CD-ROM).

DNEWS

DNEWS is easy-to-use, commercial news software developed by NetWin Inc., a New Zealand software company. DNEWS was designed to handle both a traditional Ihave-style feed and a sucking feed. A sucking feed pulls only those newsgroups that are actively being read by the news-reading community; using a sucking feed can result in lower bandwidth and disk space demands. Figure 2-5 shows a timeline for USENET News.

Figure 2-5 A USENET News timeline.

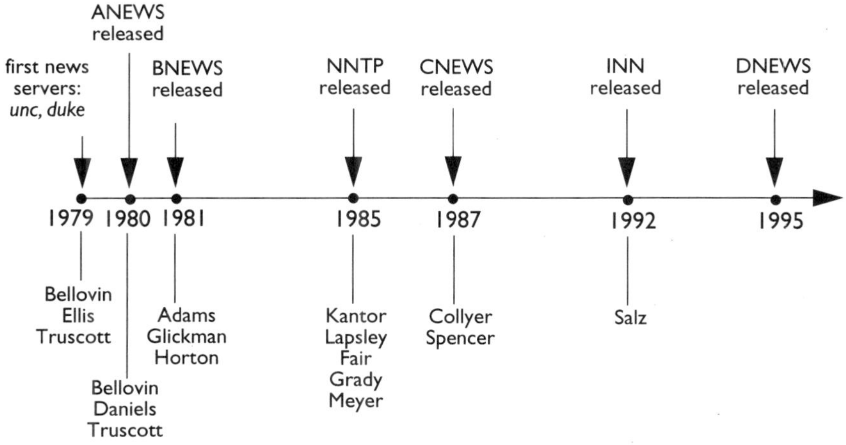

3 A News Primer

The News Article

A news article contains two important components, the *header* and the *body.* The header contains all the administrative details such as the article's source, its destination, a descriptive title, and much more. The body contains the actual text of the article. The optional *signature* contains personal information about the sender, witticisms, and other information. RFC 1036 dictates the syntax and content of the header and also suggests guidelines for the body content, although generally most content in the body section is freeform. Here is a typical news header:

From: Wed Jul 10 12:02:14 1996
Path:news1.istar.ca!tor.istar!news.inforamp.net!news.nst n.ca!newsflash.concordia.ca!utcsri!rutgers!sgigate.sgi.co m!esiee.fr!jussieu.fr!math.ohio-state.edu!deshaw.com!do-not-use-path-to-reply
Date:Wed, 10 Jul 1996 07:00:14 GMT
Supersedes: <Du7q45.74B@deshaw.com>
Expires: Sun, 14 Jul 1996 04:00:00 GMT
Message-ID: <DuBFGD.BBp@deshaw.com>
From: netannounce@deshaw.com (Mark Moraes)
Subject:Welcome to Usenet!
Newsgroups: news.announce.newusers,news.answers
Followup-To: news.newusers.questions
Approved: netannounce@deshaw.com (Mark Moraes)

Expires: Sun, 14 Jul 1996 07:00:14 GMT
Lines: 82
Xref:news1.istar.canews.announce.newusers:973
news.answers:46985
Archive-name: usenet/welcome/part1

Modern news reader software reorders and hides information to make it more readable. The following message was formatted by the news reader function in Netscape Navigator:

Subject:Welcome to Usenet!
Date: Mon, 8 Jul 1996 07:00:05 GMT
From: netannounce@deshaw.com (Mark Moraes)
Newsgroups: news.announce.newusers, news.answers
Followup-To: news.newusers.questions
Archive-name: usenet/welcome/part1
Last-change: 5 Dec 1995 by
netannounce@deshaw.com (Mark Moraes)

Changes-posted-to: news.misc,news.answers
Welcome to Usenet!
The newsgroup news.announce.newusers contains a lot of introductory information about Usenet. All new users should read and fully understand all the documents in news.announce.newusers before trying to post messages to Usenet or create new Usenet groups.

A distribution attribute, contained in the header, controls newsgroup propagation within geographic or organizational boundaries. Designations such as "world" imply global distribution, whereas "can" designates distribution only within Canada.

In practice, most sites no longer check incoming distributions. If they do, they are extremely permissive, allowing almost anything (world, na, usa, ne, inet, etc.) to come in. Often the distribution field is used only to prevent restricted internal groups from being propagated off-site.

NEWSGROUPS

Newsgroups are, in theory, focused bulletin boards where interested parties can discuss and exchange ideas on a single topic electronically. The USENET community defines eight top-level hierarchies. A hierarchy of finer detail exists within each of these main categories (see Table 3-1).

Table 3-1 Newsgroup Hierarchy

Name	Subject	Example
comp	Computer topics	*comp.unix*
humanities	Nonscientific academic debate	*humanities.amnesty*
misc	When a newsgroup doesn't exactly fit one of the other six	*misc.jobs*
news	USENET News and news software	*news.admin*
rec	Recreation and hobbies	*rec.pets*
sci	Established science disciplines	*sci.chem*
soc	Social issues and topics	*soc.singles*
talk	Debating and discussion forum	*talk.politics*

There are also numerous other top-level newsgroups such as regional hierarchies grouped by their DNS reference, private corporate newsgroups, and commercial news sources such as ClariNet News.

When articles within a particular newsgroup begin to get too specific, a new newsgroup is often created within the original newsgroup as a subgroup. For example, *rec.outdoors.fishing.fly* might have spawned from *rec.outdoors.fishing* when readers interested in fly-fishing started to dominate the parent group on general fishing.

When a user posts an article, it may elicit a response (or a number of responses). The response gets posted, which in turn may elicit a response of its own. This activity creates a message thread. A *thread* is a back-and-forth conversation, and most news reader software can navigate threads easily.

A lot of off-topic articles get posted to newsgroups, but the hierarchy and naming convention paradigm holds and works well enough. Creation of a newsgroup under one of the eight recognized headings requires subjecting the newsgroup proposal to a formal vote by the news administrators that operate the news servers. The news administrators enforce their authority by refusing to carry unauthorized groups. All in all, this is a relatively civilized process. On the outskirts of this civilization, however, lies the USENET equivalent of the Wild West—the *alt* group.

THE *ALT* HIERARCHY

The *alt* designation, which stands for "alternative," is aptly chosen. Here reside some of the most disgusting, controversial, and silliest newsgroups ever conceived. In some instances a newsgroup title alone can be enough to disgust or inflame the average user. Creating a newsgroup in the *alt* newsgroup requires little formality, and, in some cases, can be done automatically by sending a control message to every USENET news server in order to create the new newsgroup.

NEWS IN MODERATION

A newsgroup may be *moderated,* in which case submissions are not posted directly but are diverted to a *moderator* for consideration and possible posting. Moderators are typically human as opposed to software, although at times moderators can seem inhumane when they reject articles.

THE NEWS SERVER

The news server is the essential building block of USENET News. It can be built on almost any platform—UNIX, Windows NT, Macintosh, and many others. To date, the majority of news servers have been built on the UNIX operating system because of its inherent scalability, built-in networking, and traditional relationship with the Internet. Recently servers built on the Windows NT operating system have also become popular.

The primary role of the news server is to receive and send news to and from other news servers. Once the server receives news, it maintains a central database of news articles for clients to access. It also handles and controls the propagation of locally posted articles (see Figure 3-1). The server is also capable of piping news to and from e-mail accounts. This feature allows a road warrior to still read key postings and post responses while on the road. The final task of the server is to delete or archive old news articles.

Figure 3-1 The news server.

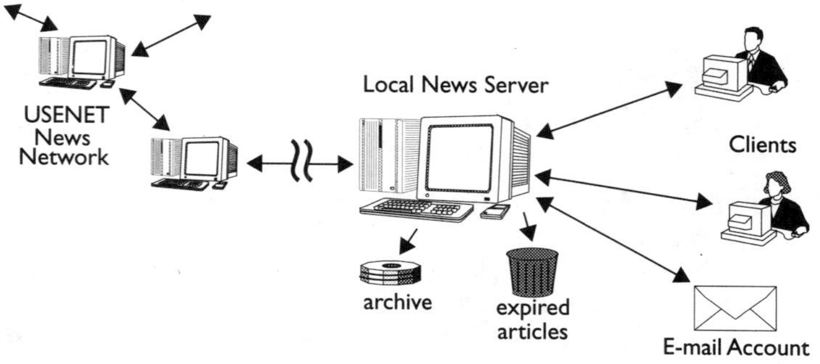

THE NEWS READER

The client software installed on the user's desktop is referred to as a news reader. It provides many features for reading and posting news. These features include the ability to filter and display news and to navigate news threads. The software also manages follow-up postings, the posting of original articles, and the subscription to newsgroups. The news reader can also automatically process numerous file types and launch helper applications to play or view multimedia files. This facilitates Intranet collaborative workgroups.

The first time a news reader connects to a news server, the server sends a list of available groups. From this list the user selects the groups he or she wants to read. From this point, the user sees only unread articles from subscribed groups.

THE NEWS FEED

The first step in getting news for an organization is to procure a news feed. Some news feeds are free of charge, but many such as UUNET are commercial and charge a fee to provide a news feed. Most Internet Service Providers (ISPs) also offer their customers a news feed for a nominal charge.

To be able to offer its connected community the broadest coverage of newsgroups, the news server will often get news feeds from a number of other news servers. A balance needs to be struck between cost and what the clients want. In addition, the more newsgroups received, the more bandwidth consumed by news at the expense of other forms of traffic in the news server. This can cause an even greater bandwidth problem since the USENET News community expects the server also to propagate the newsgroups it receives. It is this cooperative one-to-one or one-to-many propagation that accounts for the efficient global coverage of the USENET News.

Regardless of which way the politicians and Internet vanguards drag the Internet's destiny, News will continue to be a major contributor to personal and professional growth, and the news server will remain its quintessential element. The rest of this book covers the planning, construction, and administration of news servers.

PART II

PLANNING

This section takes a rational look at the planning side of news server implementation and is intended primarily for the information technology (IT) manager or equivalent who has to do the internal selling, make the decisions, and plan all aspects of the implementation.

The creation and rollout of the news server can and should be considered a project; that is, there are specific goals, a budget, a list of tasks to be completed, and, most important, completion criteria. Decisions made during this phase can have a profound effect on the subsequent use and management of news.

In the past, many news servers were created in a seat-of-the-pants fashion. Often there were no clear goals, except to be able to read a favorite newsgroup. Little or no thought was given to the impact of the news server on the corporate network or the company culture. This was perhaps understandable in the early days of the Internet when information was scant and software was being rewritten as it was being used. Today, with stable software and a wealth of history to draw on, the project of implementing a news server can be thoroughly planned and successfully executed.

4 Bringing News Inside

Most companies that have an Internet connection use an ISP. The ISP will also provide e-mail, World Wide Web (WWW) access, as well as some form of news-reading capability. Initially the ISP houses the news server. News readers residing within the company read news from and post news to this news server using the corporate access bandwidth. Figure 4-1 shows a typical connection, although many companies still do not employ any form of security firewall. (These issues are covered in greater depth in the chapter on network topology.)

Figure 4-1 An ISP-based news server.

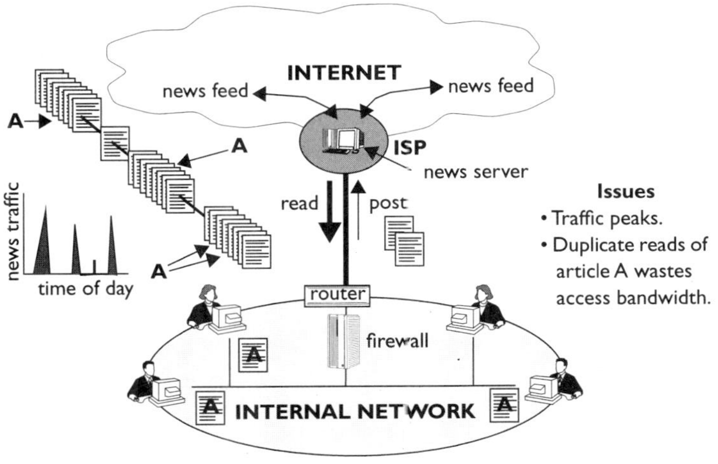

Connecting to your ISP for reading and posting news works well in the beginning when news usage is small within your company or organization. As news becomes more popular—and it will—the amount of bandwidth consumed by news traffic can seriously impair the company's other services. This is especially true when you take into consideration that news and other services have similar peak traffic patterns. A bigger access pipe is a possible solution but usually an expensive one. There are other problems with locating the news server off-site, such as security, that can be addressed only by creating your own news server and bringing news inside.

Bringing news inside the company involves setting up a news server on the company's internal network—usually behind a packet filtering router or security firewall. This server can be built on a dedicated machine or can coexist with other services such as e-mail and the World Wide Web on the network. In addition to the server, news application software, often called *netnews* software, has to be installed and configured. Due to the stored nature of news, a large capacity disk will be required. Once news is inside, the Help Desk or equivalent will have to maintain it, a job previously handled by the ISP. This all translates into time and effort. All these issues are covered in more depth later in this section. Figure 4-2 maps out the architecture when an internal news server is placed on the corporate network.

Figure 4-2 An internal news server.

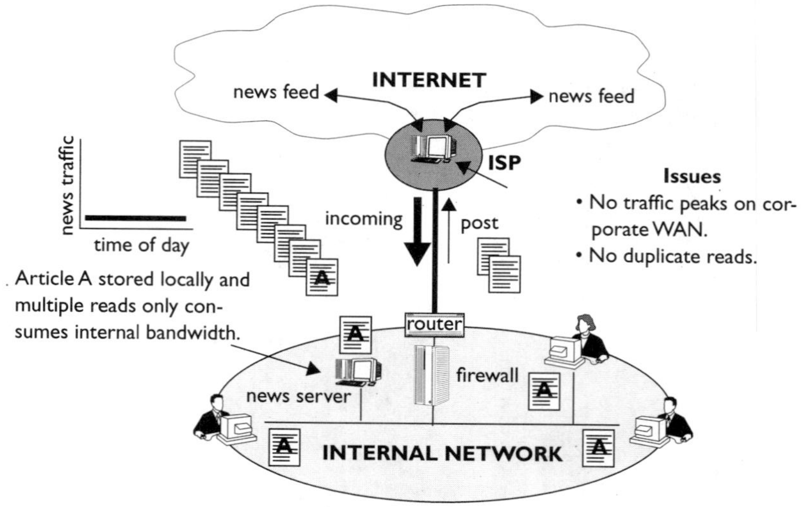

THE BENEFITS OF AN INTERNAL NEWS SERVER

Bringing news inside will cost money and consume resources, so it's important to be clear on the benefits it will bring to your company or organization.

BANDWIDTH OPTIMIZATION

The main advantage of installing an internal news server is the reduction in peak traffic over the access bandwidth since the news server spreads the retrieval of articles over the entire day. The corporate access bandwidth is therefore not held hostage to the similar habits of news readers around the company who simultaneously log on to news to read favorite newsgroups at certain times of the day.

Also multiple reads of the same article are handled more efficiently. Instead of 50 readers downloading the same article from the ISP's news server over the access bandwidth, the article is downloaded once to the server and then read locally. Intelligent segmentation and routing can ensure that news traffic doesn't interfere with other corporate traffic.

INTRANET NEWSGROUPS

Internal, or Intranet, newsgroups are rapidly becoming the biggest growth area for news. These newsgroups often contain sensitive company material, and for this reason they are not normally broadcast to the Internet community at large. They provide a facility to support collaborative workgroups whereby people in all areas of the company or within a department can communicate interactively. In an early section of the book it was mentioned that USENET News can distribute information more efficiently than a mailing list, and Intranet newsgroups are a powerful example of this idea at work. See Figure 4-3.

Desktop readers with appropriate helper application software can instantly view images embedded within an article. If a proper client-server model is employed within the corporate network, even workstations that don't have resident helpers can view embedded images by loading the required application from a zone server. The Intranet is a powerful method of communication for departments and project teams, but as long as news is off-site, your company or organization really doesn't have the option of creating secure Intranet newsgroups.

Figure 4-3 Intranet newsgroups.

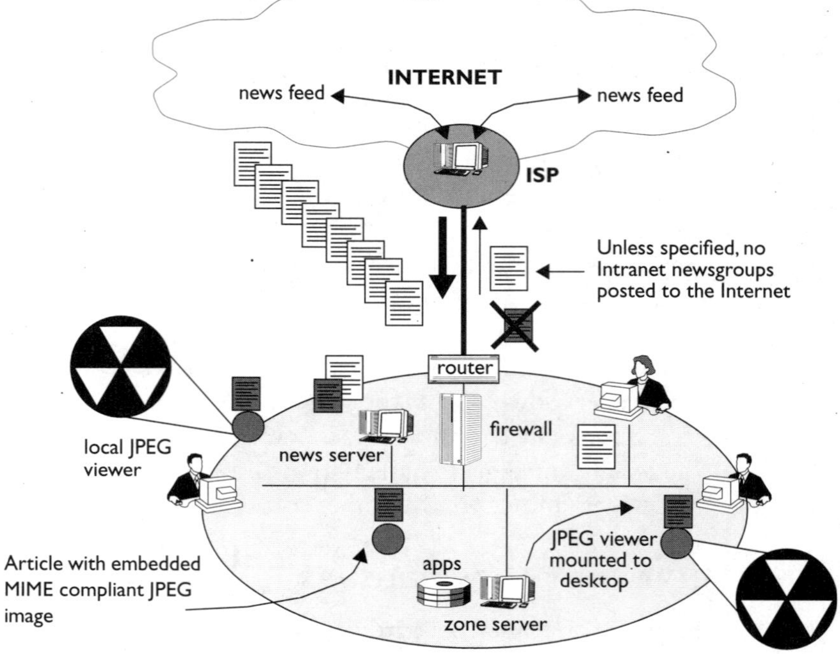

POLICY ENFORCEMENT

ISPs are generally reluctant to restrict usage, fearing they may get caught in an unwanted morality debate. Companies that create their own internal news servers can exert a greater degree of control over newsgroups, content, and usage. One very powerful self-regulating tool is the use of a *company.posted* newsgroup, wherein everything that gets posted to the world also gets posted locally in *company.posted.* A carbon copy is made and posted for all in the company to see (*company.posted* is covered in greater detail later in this book).

5 The News Feed

Where to Get the News Feed

In the early days of dial-up UUCP and low volumes of news traffic, the telephone company supplied the bandwidth to connect the USENET community. Local connections were essentially free. For a host machine in this environment, offering a news feed to another site was no big deal. Any communication charges were paid for by the downstream hosts. Administrators seldom raised an eyebrow when news feeds were given away.

With the advent of TCP/IP and larger volumes of news, the situation changed dramatically and fundamentally. Today dedicated lines for news can be very expensive and generally have to be justified on the basis of the benefit derived by the company or organization footing the bill. There never seems to be enough bandwidth, and to give it away for the purpose of offering someone else a news feed is hard to justify. For this reason you can probably forget about getting a full news feed as a favor.

Your ISP

Your most likely source for a news feed will be your ISP. Most ISPs take either a partial or a full news feed from their provider (an NSP or Network Service Provider, unless they happen to be one of the major players such as UUNET) and are usually willing to pass it on to their customers for free or for a nominal charge. If you go this route, you will be limited to the news coverage being supplied to your ISP by its supplier. This may be only a partial feed.

Occasionally ISPs are able to get additional feeds so they can offer their customers better news coverage. But ISPs can suffer from the same syndrome as the company looking for a news feed. Unless news is packaged with Internet access (arguably where the real money is being made in the Internet), many suppliers are reluctant to sell just news, especially since to provide news involves consuming scarce bandwidth and server resources. By all means try UUNET, MCI, Sprint, and other NSPs and major players, but don't be surprised if you have to buy Internet access to get a news feed.

SATELLITE NEWS FEED

The PageSat news service by NCIT Inc. is an innovative idea that exploits the fact that most news traffic is incoming. With this in mind NCIT developed a satellite-based news system that broadcasts a very full news feed (tapped from over 20 NSPs) to small satellite dishes installed on the company's premises (much like DDS TV for home television). The incoming news feed is connected directly to the corporate network thereby avoiding the Internet access bandwidth entirely. Articles posted to newsgroups are sent over the Internet access bandwidth to the Internet, but this traffic is low compared to the in-bound traffic.

COMMERCIAL NEWS

ClariNet Communications Corp. offers ClariNet e-News, an electronic newspaper delivered to your computer in the USENET News format. You get live news, computer-industry news, syndicated columns and features, financial information, stock quotes, and more in a USENET-style news feed. The ClariNet e-News service is not a news feed in the conventional sense but rather a repackager of news from various commercial news wires. Many ISPs also carry ClariNet e-News as part of their news offering.

COST

The typical cost for a reasonably complete news feed (the eight top-level hierarchies and some of the *alt*) ranges from $50 to $100 a month if obtained from your ISP. News feeds from some of the commercial news services mentioned earlier can run upwards of $500 a month and are usually targeted at ISPs and large organizations.

As discussed, free news feeds are becoming few and far between, owing to the cost of maintaining bandwidth. If your budget is small, consider getting a partial feed; maybe all you need is a half-dozen newsgroups—six newsgroups with total traffic of approximately 600 articles a day. You can probably get this for free through universities, local freenets, and so forth.

WHICH NEWSGROUPS TO GET

As mentioned, you can't have all of the newsgroups. A common set is the eight top-level hierarchies, excluding the *alt* hierarchy. Before deciding on the news coverage, consider the applicability, tolerance level, technical issues, and the use of sucking feeds.

APPLICABILITY

What news does your company really need to do its business? If you are in the real estate business, do you really need the *comp* hierarchy? Is the extra burden of carrying a full feed really warranted if it entices your employees to read the *alt.sex* groups on company time? On the other hand, if you are a market research company, you may want to have a sense of how far the borders of society extend.

TOLERANCE LEVEL

How sensitive are your employees apt to be to the objectionable material they may encounter through your news service? Because of pervasive cross-posting, you may find get-rich-quick schemes and shock articles with rude and provocative titles even in technical newsgroups. Take into consideration the best ways to minimize exposure to such offensive material.

TECHNICAL ISSUES

The amount of disk storage and the expiry cycle of articles constrain the amount of news you can offer. The amount of Internet bandwidth that news consumes also imposes an upper limit on what news you can handle. These issues are covered in more depth in Chapter 6.

SUCKING FEEDS

Full feeds can congest bandwidth, but a new idea called *sucking feeds* provides a possible solution. A sucking feed is an on-demand type of news exchange that greatly reduces the amount of news traffic between news servers. The sucking feed allows a news server to download dynamically only those news groups that are actually read. This innovation results in substantial savings in disk space and bandwidth, as well as enhancing overall performance.

WHICH NEWSGROUPS TO PROPAGATE

Until recently when you put up a news server you became a bonafide participant in the news propagation scheme. This means that just as you received a news feed from your upstream source (for example, your ISP) you were obligated not only to propagate postings back to your news source, but also to give others a news feed. The situation is markedly different today. Most internal news servers are termed *leaf sites.* They sit at the edge of the branching news tree and do not propagate the news feed to any other sites. All that leaves the news server are postings flowing back upstream to be propagated into the USENET universe by the ISP.

If you agree to give others a news feed, say a regional office, you should be aware of the bandwidth issues involved. As discussed later in Chapter 6, "The News Server," one reason many sites are reluctant to give away news feeds is that they may lose 64K or more of Internet access bandwidth to satisfy the downstream site, as illustrated in Figure 5-1.

You may wish to carry newsgroups of local or regional interest. Supporting these groups fosters goodwill among your fellow news administrators and takes only a small amount of bandwidth to maintain. The one requirement is that all participating sites agree to carry the newsgroups. Other sites may merely reject them or not be sent the newsgroups in the first place. This way, thousands of regional special-interest newsgroups can be shared without affecting the global USENET community.

Figure 5-1 Supplying a news feed.

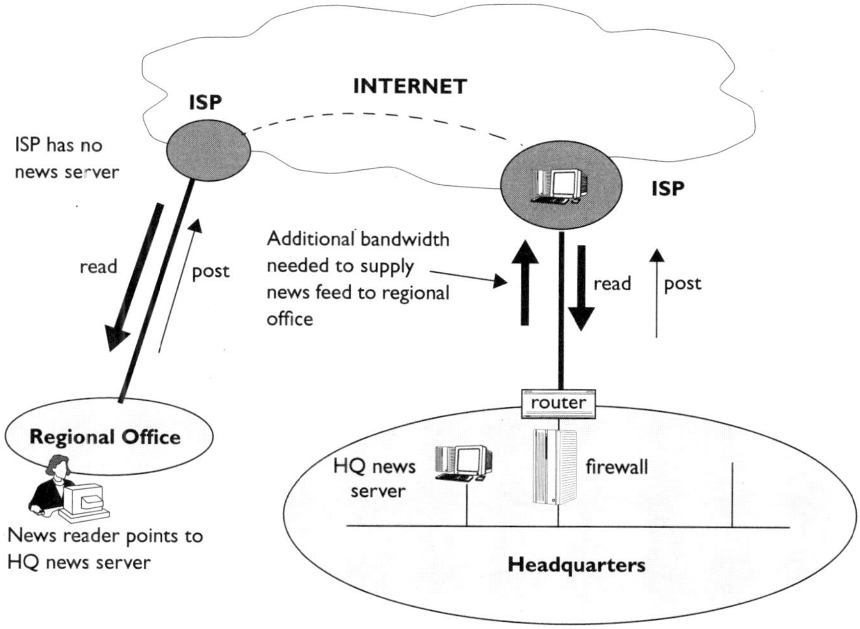

6 The News Server

Server Requirements

This chapter focuses on the four basic factors to consider in putting together a news server: the disk storage, RAM, CPU, and LAN (local area network) connection (refer to Figure 6-1). Understanding the role of each factor will be essential in making the optimal choice in terms of cost versus performance.

Figure 6-1 Major components of the news server.

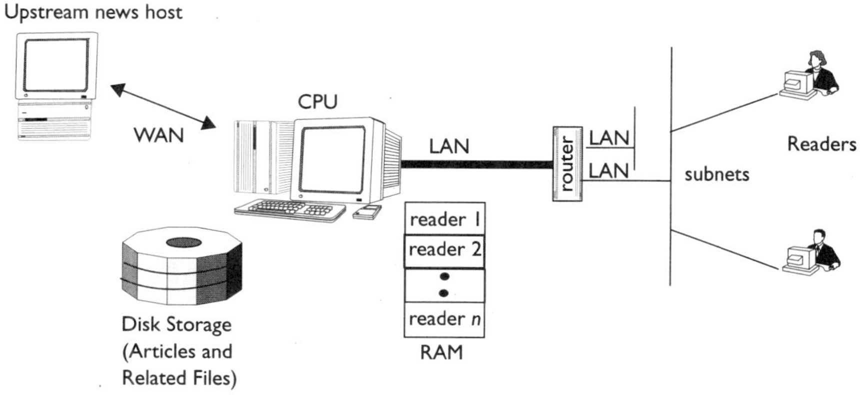

DISK STORAGE

Currently, if you get most of the newsgroups, about 400MB of news per day will come through your news server. News articles must be stored for a reasonable amount of time so people have a chance to read them. Depending on the number of newsgroups you receive and the amount of time you retain the articles, you will need anywhere from 1GB to 20GB in order to keep up with the traffic. Figure 6-2 shows the relative traffic of the top-level news hierarchies in a pie chart.

Figure 6-2 Relative newsgroup traffic.

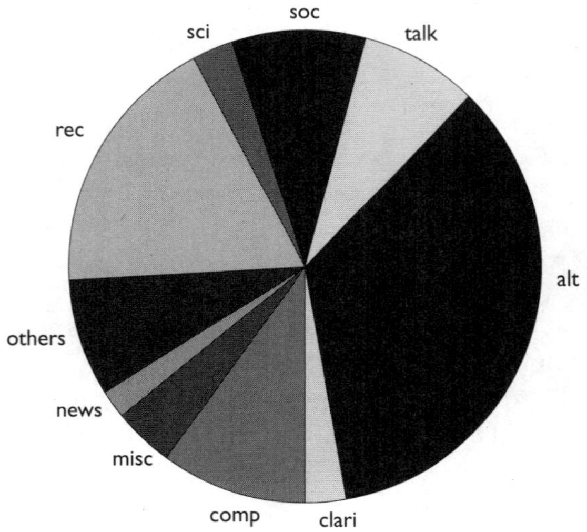

The hierarchy "other" shown in the pie chart is made up of regional, company-specific, and commercial newsgroups.

Table 6-1 shows the present and future storage requirements for four different scenarios. The table data were derived by using the "USENET Storage Space Calculator" found on the NetPartners Web site

(http://lykos.netpart.com/free/usenet.html).

The use of a news overview database increases the storage requirement by approximately 10 percent.

Handling news involves manipulating thousands if not millions of files. The issue is not just raw storage capacity, you need to consider how fast

Table 6-1 Storage Requirements (Rounded Off in Gigabytes)

Newsgroup Coverage	Today	In 1 Year	In 2 Years	Retention
All	4.5GB	6.0GB	7.6GB	7 days
All	9.0GB	12GB	15.2GB	14 days
All except *alt*	2.5GB	3.3GB	4.1GB	7 days
All except *alt*	5.0GB	6.6GB	8.2GB	14 days

files can be opened, closed, or deleted. A good disk input/output subsystem is necessary to carry out these operations efficiently.

Expiring news articles means deleting files. Depending on the operating system and disk subsystem, this process can be as slow as 100 files per second. The server typically expires up to 500,000 articles a day. Considering that the disk is expected to save incoming articles at the same time, this is not a trivial problem. Some file systems can create around 50 files per second and delete around 100 files per second. Newer file systems are capable of a tenfold performance increase. Press your vendor hard about disk input/output benchmarks.

It is also recommended that you don't create a file system larger than one backup tape. This allows unattended backups in the middle of the night.

RAM (Random Access Memory)

The NNTP protocol requires that the server deal not only with propagating news between servers but also with serving hundreds of simultaneus news readers.

The amount of memory necessary for dealing with the propagating side of news is relatively small. Using INN, the server requires about 10MB of RAM to process and handle a full news feed. Each reader connecting to the server requires memory, and the greater the number of simultaneous readers, the greater the memory demand.

The memory requirement adds up to a requirement of somewhere between 128MB and 192MB of RAM for a typical news server with full news feed and a hundred simultaneous readers.

NETWORK PERFORMANCE

Depending on your local network topology, the aggregate bandwidth required for all news readers to access news simultaneously may saturate a standard Ethernet. For this reason it may be necessary to consider a faster network technology such as FDDI, CDDI, or ATM for the news server segment.

CPU PERFORMANCE

As alluded to earlier, the CPU is not the key to news server performance. Even a 33 Mhz 486DX machine or a Sun SPARC2 can be used to create a small news server as long as the disk input/output system and memory issues are addressed. But if your news volume and readership have created the need for high-performance disks and a faster network connection, a higher-capacity CPU may also be required.

EXISTING SERVER OR DEDICATED MACHINE?

Companies or organizations considering installing a news server will need to decide between installing the system on an existing computer running other applications or on a dedicated machine. UNIX is inherently a multiuser and multitasking machine, and most UNIX-based servers can run a variety of applications. A lower-cost option for the news server is to build it on an existing machine, perhaps e-mail or the World Wide Web server, but there are some issues to consider if you choose this option.

SECURITY

In making a decision it would be wise to remember this important axiom: The greater the number of programs, the greater the chance for bugs and hence security holes. In a purely theoretical sense, every line of code that goes into a machine increases the odds that a bug or security hole may be created. It would never be advisable to build news on a firewall machine since the security role of these systems depends on their managing small amounts of very secure software. Netnews software certainly doesn't meet this requirement. On the other hand, news built on a DNS machine or on an FTP server might be an acceptable mix at least from a security standpoint.

PERFORMANCE

News can potentially degrade overall performance on the multifunction server and hinder the operation of other applications.

DIVISION OF SERVICES

By having mail and news on the same machine, you are creating a single point of failure for both applications. If news crashes, you may bring down the other applications as well. Also, software upgrades may require that the machine be brought down during the transition, which would affect all services.

CHOOSING HARDWARE

Although almost anything can be made to work, there are some setups that have proven to be successful as shown in Table 6-2. Systems 1 through 4 are full-feed, low-retention news servers with a large news-reading community. System 5 is arguably a low-end system, but it works well enough for partial news feed and short article retention.

Table 6-2 Successful News Servers

System	Platform	Operating System	RAM	Hard Disk
1	Digital Alpha 2100 model A500MP, one CPU	DEC OSF/1 2.0b	192MB	16GB 2 spindles
2	SPARC 20 model 712	Solaris 2.5	192MB	32GB 4 SCSI buses 16 spindles
3	SPARC 10	SunOS 4.1.4	128MB	4GB 4 spindles
4	Pentium-based PC	LINUX	128MB	16GB SCSI, multiple spindles
5	486-based PC	LINUX	64MB	4GB SCSI, 2 spindles

HARDWARE SUPPORT

Most hardware support can be broken down into two types, either on-site spare components or support contracts. You will have to decide which is better for you. If you depend on support contracts, make sure you understand the contract completely. Here are some things to consider:

- When the vendor promises a four-hour response time, does that mean a return phone call or a site visit within four hours?
- If service personnel arrive at 4:30 P.M., will they leave at 5:00 P.M., or does the contract include a work-to-completion clause?
- Will the vendor have access to replacement parts, or will parts have to be ordered?

If your company has planned its purchases carefully and standardized on hardware, you may be able to reduce the number of spares required. For example, one disk drive may provide sufficient spare capacity for multiple servers.

SOFTWARE SUPPORT

If you are using a commercial operating system, make sure you have a copy of the license on file. Also, you will usually save money in the long run if you keep the software under a support contract that will allow you to receive upgrades and have access to online patches.

7 Network Topology

Bringing news inside will affect the traffic volume and patterns on the company's Internet access bandwidth and internal network. As a result a number of questions will come up. Is the current access bandwidth sufficient? Which network architecture is best for securing the news server? What is the best way to handle regional news distribution? This chapter explores these issues and provides an overview of the types of access services commonly available on the market.

Internet Bandwidth

Most companies today use some kind of digital connection to their ISP for Internet access. Access using analog modems, although still employed for personal use, is not sufficient for corporations. There are two categories of physical connections: dial-up and leased line.

Dial-up connections rely upon standard telephone lines. Calls are set up and torn down as needed. This type of connection requires some kind of modem at each end. Standard telephone lines were never designed to carry data signals, and therefore the transmission speed is limited by line quality. Common examples of dial-up modes include analog modem, switched 56, and ISDN. Figure 7-1 illustrates a typical analog dial-up connection.

Figure 7-1 Dial-up Internet access.

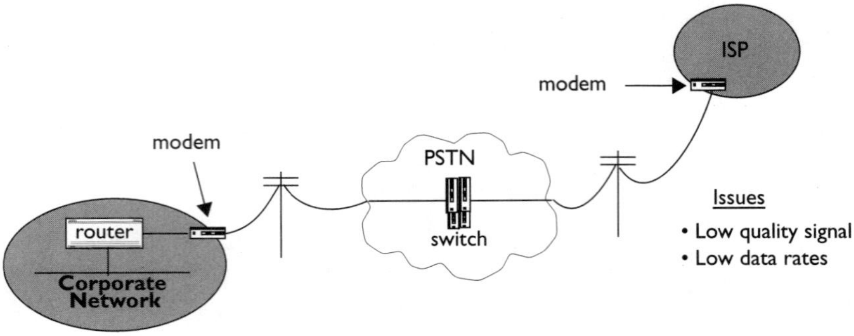

A leased-line connection is a specially constructed signal path from your site to the ISP, terminated at either end by a special data interface called a *Data Service Unit/Channel Service Unit* (*DSU/CSU*), essentially a digital modem. Figure 7-2 illustrates a typical connection. Since the connection is up 24 hours a day, there is never a busy signal. Also because the lines are designed to carry transmission signals, high transmission rates can be achieved and maintained.

Figure 7-2 Leased-line Internet access.

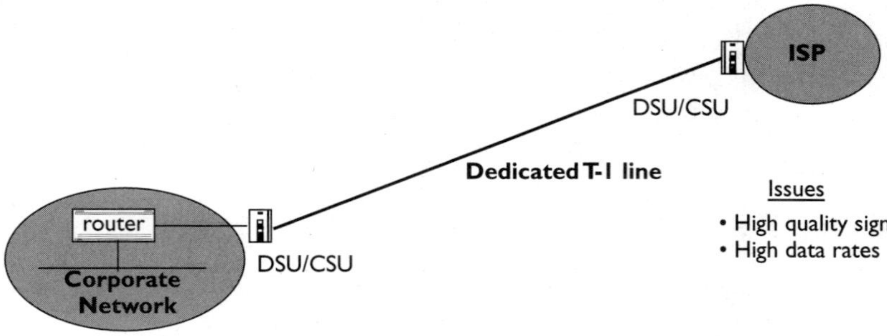

ANALOG MODEM

The analog modem is the traditional way to connect computers using a dial-up connection over normal twisted-pair copper telephone lines. Until recently the maximum rate of data transmission was 9.6 Kbps (kilobits per second), but with the advent of cheap, sophisticated, digital signal processor (DSP) devices, modems have become readily available for rates up to 28.8 Kbps and beyond.

SWITCHED 56

Switched 56, as the name implies, yields a digital data connection of 56 Kbps. Once the digital standard for computer communications, switched 56 service has largely been replaced by ISDN for dial-up applications. In places where ISDN is not available, switched 56 can still be a viable alternative. Yet with the advent of 28.8 Kbps modems on regular telephone lines, the special equipment, installation costs, and the higher monthly rates of switched 56 may be difficult to justify.

ISDN

The idea of ISDN has existed for many years, but it was not widely deployed for a long time, hence the long-standing joke that the abbreviation stands for It Still Does Nothing. In fact, the abbreviation stands for Integrated Services Digital Network, and today does a lot—and, indeed, could very well stand for Internet Services Done Nicely. So-called *basic rate* ISDN service consists of two bidirectional 64 Kbps digital channels called B (bearer) channels and a lower-speed D channel used for signaling. An ISDN terminal adapter (T/A) connects the data devices (router, terminal, digital phone, and so forth) to the NT1 interface (Network Termination type 1), which in turn connects to the ISDN line. The ISDN line itself is a four-wire twisted-pair line with special differential line encoding that allows it to carry over three miles without repeaters. Figure 7-3 illustrates a typical ISDN hookup.

Figure 7-3 An ISDN connection.

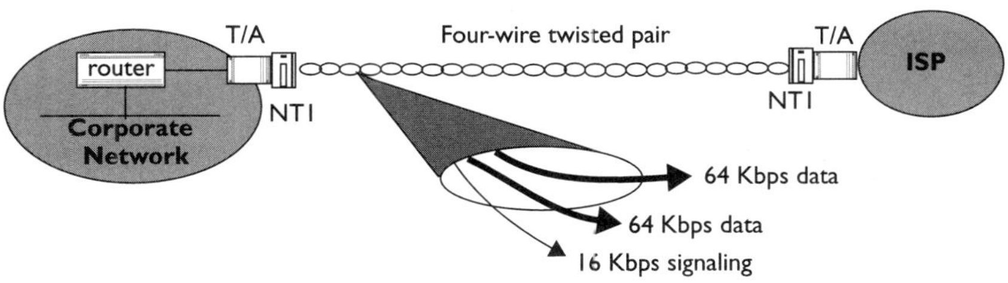

In some applications, a single connection can be made across both B channels, yielding a 128 Kbps channel. This capability is referred to as BOND (Bandwidth on Demand) and is used when traffic exceeds the single 64 Kbps capacity of one B channel. The cost of ISDN is usually based on a flat rate for the line plus additional metered charges for usage.

Many ISPs provide both dial-up ISDN, where your assigned port is shared, and dedicated ISDN, where the port is assigned to only you.

T-1 AND FRACTIONAL T-1(FT-1)

In the late 1980s T-1 became the standard for high bandwidth corporate networks. T-1 is a digital connection divided into 24 DS0s (Digital Signal 0), each 64 Kbps, which yields a total capacity of 1.544 Mbps (usable capacity is somewhat less owing to signaling bandwidth). See Figure 7-4.

Figure 7-4 T-1 channel allocation.

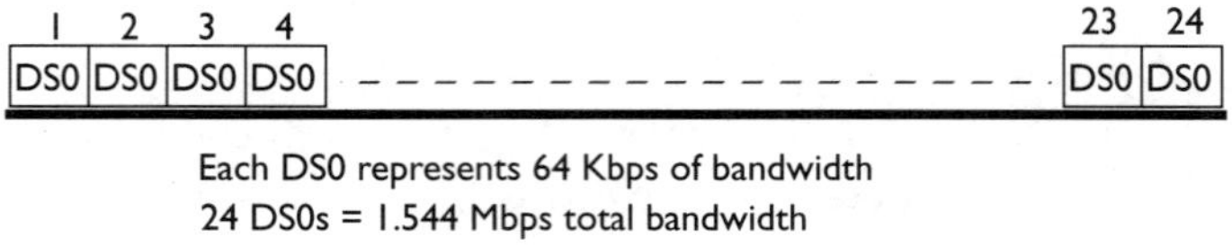

T-1 lines are now commonly used by large organizations for their Internet access. ISPs frequently utilize T-1s or multiple T-1s for their access to the major Internet backbones. T3s, a grouping of T-1 lines yielding 45 Mbps, is the choice for the large backbones and the largest providers, but is generally outside of the budget of most companies.

Many vendors offer Fractional T-1 (FT-1) connections at multiples of DS0s (64 Kbps). This is a very scalable approach, but at a certain point (approximately four DS0s) it is cheaper to go with a full T-1.

COMMUNICATION PROTOCOLS

Once the physical connection to the ISP has been established, the next choice a company or organization installing a news server has to make is which protocol to use. Often this decision is dictated by the ISP and may be a proprietary protocol requiring ISP-supplied devices at either end. Other choices include *point-to-point protocol* (*PPP*) and *frame relay.*

POINT-TO-POINT PROTOCOL (PPP)

PPP is a very common protocol in use today for data connections. PPP is a standards-based method of encapsulating data and establishing and maintaining a connection. The PPP standard also provides for some level of error detection. Most analog modems and ISDN connections employ PPP. Another standard called SLIP (Serial Line Interface Protocol) is also in use.

FRAME RELAY

Frame relay is a standard for transmitting small packets that has become an increasingly popular choice for wide area networks (WANs) owing to its high efficiency and elastic bandwidth property. Frame relay has largely replaced its predecessor X.25. A number of national frame relay networks have been set up with points of presence (POPs) in most major cities. The point of presence is the access point to the frame relay network. When a company uses a frame relay service for its WAN, it is assigned Private Virtual Circuits (PVCs) between sites and is charged by the number of PVCs employed and the packet traffic. The distance the packets travel within the network is irrelevant and hence generates no long-distance charges. Like the telephone network, frame relay is often represented as a cloud since you can't tell exactly what happens inside. Figure 7-5 illustrates a frame relay WAN. FRAD stands for Frame Relay Assembler/Disassembler and is the device that converts ordinary data into frame relay packets.

Figure 7-5 A frame relay WAN.

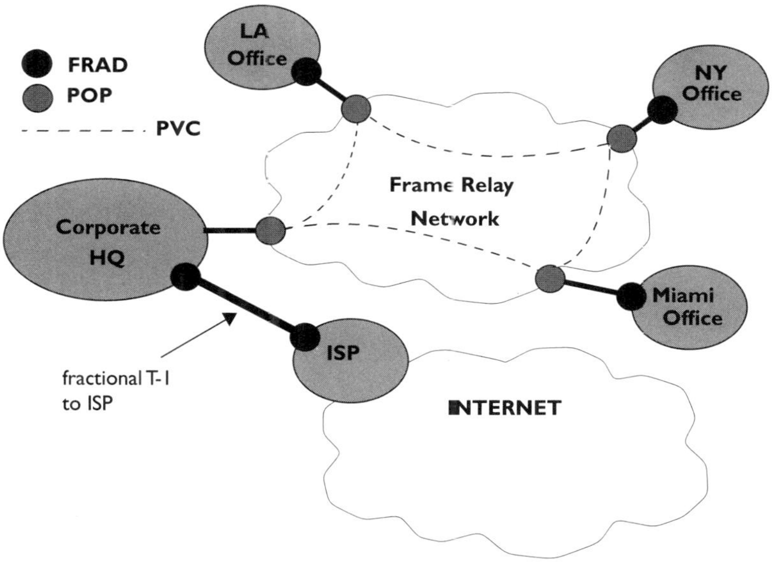

Although it is not yet widely employed on the ISP connection, frame relay is nevertheless a good choice for the corporate WAN, especially if the company has offices spread across the country or globe.

Although the access port into the cloud or the ISP may be at 384 Kbps, most vendors allow the subscriber to transmit at higher rates, hence the concept of elastic bandwidth. This can be very cost effective if the company normally requires only a 56 Kbps connection but occasionally requires higher bandwidth for graphic file transfers or remote database synchronization. Of course, the physical connection must be able to support the higher bandwidth.

Table 7-1 shows some of the more common offerings, the bandwidths they support, the pricing, and the company profiles they are most suited to.

Table 7-1 Choices for Physical Connection

Physical Connection	Typical Monthly Cost	Bandwidth	Application
28.8 Analog Modem—dial-up	$50	28.8 Kbps	Small office, telecommuter, or personal use
ISDN one B channel	$200	64 Kbps	Small office or power user
ISDN two B channels	$300	128 Kbps	Branch office
Fractional T-1 (4 DS0s)	$700	256 Kbps	Corporate office
T-1 (24 DS0s)	$2,000	1.544 Mbps	ISP or large corporation

NEWS REQUIREMENTS

A full news feed requires at least a 64 Kbps connection in order to keep up with the approximately 400MB of news traffic spawned each day by the USENET community. Therefore a single ISDN B channel is capable of handling a full news feed at today's volume, but in a year's time at least two B channels will be required.

Since most Internet access has to handle not just news (World Wide Web, e-mail, and so forth), a full ISDN using both B channels is probably the minimum connection for today's volumes in order to handle a full news feed without compromising the other Internet-related traffic. Considering the news growth factor, a 256 Kbps fractional T-1 may be required.

To make more equitable use of the access bandwidth, you can do advanced optimization of the routers in your network, such as prioritized queuing—assigning less priority to news packets and higher priority to interactive traffic such as TELNET, HTTP, and so on. But the effects of priority queuing are hard to predict, and the use of these optimizations is questionable as their effects depend too much on very low-level settings that are very hard to do correctly.

REGIONAL NEWS SERVERS

If your company is global, you will probably want your regional offices to have a connection to the Internet. For general news reading the local ISP's news server may be sufficient. Corporate Intranet newsgroups can be supported on an internal news server and accessed via the secure corporate WAN.

SECURITY CONSIDERATIONS

The Internet is not a very secure place. When a company connects its internal network to the Internet, it is well advised to put some kind of access security in place. There are a number of security options.

PACKET FILTERING

Special routers can be set up to inspect packets entering the internal network and then, based on a predefined rule set, allow or deny the packet to pass through. Although useful in aiding other security measures, by itself packet filtering is a poor defense against today's sophisticated hackers.

PROXY-BASED FIREWALL

A proxy-based firewall is a specialized host machine running firewall software.

Even though Internet services are provided, no packets go directly to the Internet. Instead, the contents of all packets on one side of the firewall are delivered to the other side via proxy agents running on the firewall. Security is achieved by allowing only certain people or computers to use these proxies.

User-based service proxies, such as TELNET and FTP, require strong user authentication. Host-based service proxies, such as NNTP and Sendmail, are permitted only from known hosts.

A Bastion host machine can also be added to further enhance security. A Bastion host runs a number of applications such as the netnews software DNS and Sendmail. Packets arriving from the Internet are routed directly to the Bastion host, which in turn relays them to the firewall. The firewall machine inspects the Ethernet address present in the packets hitting it and ensures that only traffic from the Bastion host (whose Ethernet address is known and uncompromisable) is acceptable for bringing inside the internal network.

Inside application servers receive packets from the firewall proxies as if they were coming directly from the Internet. Figure 7-6 depicts a typical proxy-based firewall setup. The Bastion host would perform the normal news handling procedure but would likely be configured to expire articles rapidly, after they have been delivered to the internal news server.

Figure 7-6 A proxy-based security firewall.

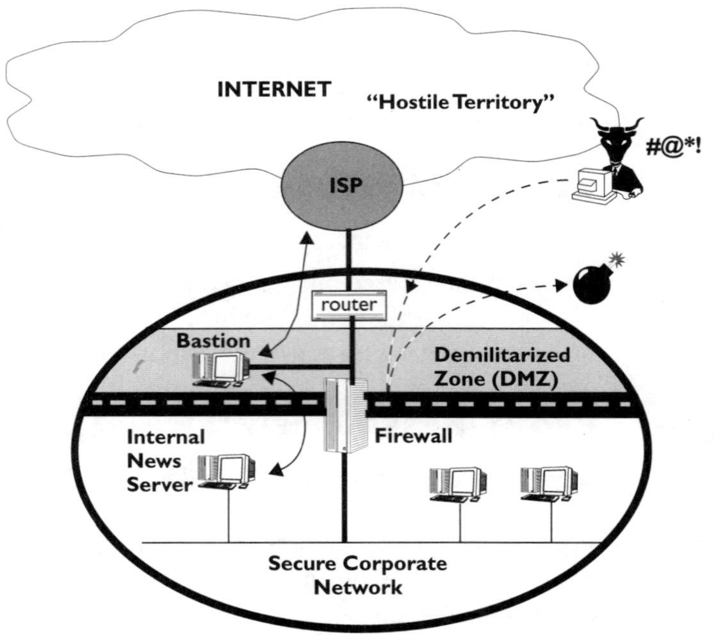

8 Netnews Software

Protocol NNTP Dominates

The foundation for USENET News is NNTP, the news transport protocol for TCP/IP. At most sites, NNTP has replaced UUCP for server-to-server news transfer. UUCP still has a legacy following, especially in areas where a leased-line connection is impractical, or where people obstinately refuse to change. But make no mistake, NNTP is the foundation upon which news propagation is currently built.

Refer to Chapter 2 for a brief synopsis of NNTP, or for more detailed information, refer to RFC 977, referenced in the bibliography.

Table 8-1 lists some of the more common NNTP-based netnews software packages in use today.

Table 8-1 Netnews Software

Software	Source	Price
INN	Downloadable from the ISC WWW page and other FTP sites. Included on CD-ROM	Free
Netscape News Server	Netscape Communications Inc., a commercial variant of INN bundled as part of their Suite Spot server software	$999 U.S.
CNEWS	Downloadable from many FTP sites	Free
DNEWS	NetWin Ltd., downloadable from the NetWin WWW site. Sample version included on CD-ROM	$485 U.S.

INTERNET NEWS (INN)

The majority of the large news servers in operation today run a version of INN software written and maintained (until recently) by Rich Salz. INN differs from CNEWS and its predecessors in that it negotiates article transfers between servers using NNTP, rather than by exchanging batched files. This avoids transferring articles the downstream server already has. INN has the following advantages:

- Scalability. INN can support numerous news feeds, both incoming and outgoing, the maximum number of feeds being restricted only by hardware. This makes INN ideal for a major feeder site.

  Since INN is native to UNIX, it can use the inherent multitasking capability of UNIX to spawn independent processes. This allows INN to handle efficiently many simultaneous tasks, such as servicing a large news reader community, supporting multiple news feeds, and so on.
- Built-in NNTP and reader support. The INN distribution comes with NNTP, avoiding the need for support of a separate piece of software over and above INN. INN also supports most popular readers directly.
- Built-in expansion capability. The capability of INN is expandable through hooks to other popular languages and applications such as PERL (Practical Extraction and Report Language) and PGP (Pretty Good Privacy). PERL can be used to create custom filters to handle such things as spams and unwanted postings. PGP allows automatic verification of control messages. Also, because the source code is readily available, in-house customization is also possible, although it requires strong UNIX expertise.
- Third-party tools and utilities. Because of the popularity of INN, there is a plethora of ready-to-use tools and utilities, most available free of charge. (Many of these are covered in Chapter 20.)

INN has recently been handed over to the Internet Software Consortium (ISC), which will maintain and advance INN from now on. According to its home page (http://www.isc.org/isc/),

> The ISC is a nonprofit organization dedicated to software engineering for the Internet. Reference implementations of Internet standards often have the weight of "de-facto standards," and to that end, we want to ensure that those reference implementations are properly supported.

The ISC also manages other popular and free software including BIND (Berkeley Internet Name Domain, an implementation of DNS) and DHCP (Dynamic Host Configuration Protocol).

At the time of this writing, version INN 1.5.1 was available for downloading (included on the CD-ROM). The Construction section, Part III of this book, covers the compilation, installation, and configuration of INN 1.5 in great depth.

CNEWS

CNEWS is an old software package that replaced an even older BNEWS. Neither of these software packages is network centric, to use a phrase, relying instead on dial-up lines and point-to-point connections, and both relied a lot on batching. A line came up for a few minutes, and compressed news was sent over a dial-up UUCP connection and then uncompressed at the other end. Such systems do not generally use Internet technology to transfer news, and they are becoming less interesting as UUCP is not used much anymore. It is, of course, also possible for CNEWS to use the Internet as a transfer medium; in this case, sites use the compressed UUCP over TCP/IP technique to transfer news in batches. This practice is not widespread.

To sum up, CNEWS is a batch-oriented legacy system that doesn't make a lot of sense in the current Internet context and is not recommended for new installations.

DNEWS

DNEWS is a newcomer to the netnews arena and is rapidly gaining in popularity. It will run under a variety of operating systems, including most versions of UNIX, Windows NT, Macintosh, and OS/2 and is considerably simple to set up and maintain. The New Zealand company NetWin Inc., the developers of DNEWS, started with the idea that a large portion of all articles downloaded to a news server are never read by anyone. These articles nevertheless spend their short life span being propagated around the world from server to server, chewing up bandwidth and disk storage space. DNEWS was designed to address this issue and to be simple to use.

DNEWS supports the traditional Ihave-style feeds but also supports a sucking feed.

Although not a serious contender to INN as of yet for use in large news servers, DNEWS is very attractive to lots of the smaller ISPs and companies that lack the resources to support an INN-based news server.

SUCKING FEED

DNEWS can use what is referred to as a *dynamic sucking feed* to download articles from the upstream server. Under this system the news server retrieves articles depending on the predilections of the news readers themselves. If no one is reading *alt.golf.gimmicks.laserputter,* then no articles from this group are retrieved from the upstream news host. Users have complete freedom to read any of the 20,000 available newsgroups, but the news server doesn't waste valuable network bandwidth or local disk space storing the groups not currently being read.

Here is how it works: DNEWS gets the full list of 20,000 newsgroups (the names only), so when a reader connects, he or she sees a listing of all the newsgroups. In each newsgroup there appears to be only one message, something like this:

> Sorry we don't have this group here yet, but try again in a few seconds and it will be here.

The reader clicks on the Reload Group button, and sure enough the newsgroup is full of articles. DNEWS then remembers that someone is interested in that newsgroup, and it keeps getting articles as long as interest is maintained.

Given a user population of 500 people, most systems end up with about 100 to 200 cached news groups out of the possible 20,000. By not taking all of the available newsgroups, the news server saves on bandwidth and disk storage space. This translates to a huge savings. According to the vendor of DNEWS, the break-even point is probably about 3,000 readers, assuming they have diverse interests. At that point, the statistics are such that it probably makes sense to get all the news groups. But if the company's readership is such that everyone is interested in the same area (say, telecommunications), the dynamic sucking feed may still make sense even for very large companies.

Self-Adjusting Expiration

DNEWS allows expiration rules to be related to the number of items in a group, allowing low-volume groups to be retained longer. Expiration requirements can be set and can be adjusted according to the available disk space, making the system much more stable under a large influx of news.

Search Capability

A full-text searching (FTS) database engine comes standard with DNEWS. The FTS system allows a user to type in a query of the form "jokes, socks, cheese" and most likely get in return a joke about socks and cheese. This can obviate the need to wade through knee-high piles of junk messages and misleading newsgroup titles. DNEWS also comes with the application DNEWSWEB, a gateway between news and a Web page that allows selected news articles to be dropped into an HTML page for viewing by a standard browser.

Support

The other benefit to consider is that DNEWS is a commercial product. So although it costs money to purchase it, user support is available to help you get the package up and running and to address bugs.

Potential Abuse

A controversy is brewing over the use of sucking feeds. Apparently accounts set up for news readers are being used to suck down a full feed from their news server. This results in the server resources and bandwidth being consumed by an unauthorized news feed. A number of newsgroups have recently been actively debating this issue. Is there a real problem, or is it just overreaction to a few abusers? The jury is still out on this, but the latest version of INN (1.5.1) has incorporated a mechanism whereby a small delay is inserted between article transfers. Sucking a full feed under this condition would take a prohibitive amount of time and would likely discourage the practice.

DNEWS is relatively new compared to INN, and marketplace feedback is just beginning. However, if your company has limited news bandwidth and server resources or uses platforms not supported by INN, you may want to give DNEWS a look. A configuration holding promise is the use of small DNEWS servers at regional offices or departments for Intranet newsgroups and the delegating of a large INN-based corporate server to handle the public news and deal with the global USENET community.

Implementation of DNEWS is covered in the Construction section, Part III, of the book.

NETSCAPE NEWS SERVER

The News Server application is part of Netscape Communications Inc., Suite Spot offering, which has modules for Mail, HTTP, as well as News.

News Server is built on the INN 1.4 engine but has some enhancements, such as

- Advanced SSL encryption between client and server. This provides security for user authorization, newsgroup subscription, and posting.
- Simplified installation and configuration through a Web-based administration interface.
- Open standards for supporting any NNTP client, USENET News feeds, and rich documents such as MIME, GIF, and JPEG.

As in the case of DNEWS, News Server is a commercial product with a price tag but also with service and support, in this case provided by Netscape Communications Inc.

9 Client Software

General

News readers software allows users to read articles, post responses, and provide control over which newsgroups they subscribe to. Because there is such a large number of newsgroups, a good reader is essential if users are to be productive in using news.

Client-Server Architecture

Most companies will employ a client-server architecture for accessing news. In this scenario, the news reader is in the role of the client and accesses news from the news server over the corporate network using NNTP.

Recommended Features

There was a time, not so long ago, when users would tolerate almost any kind of convolution to access their favorite newsgroups, much the same way that traditional Internet surfers would use FTP to find and retrieve information on the Net. Today surfers have access to easy-to-use graphical browsers to navigate the World Wide Web, and the news-reading community demands similar easy access.

Modern news readers must provide at least the features discussed in the following paragraphs.

MULTIMEDIA SUPPORT

Many news servers support the use of standard MIME (Multipurpose Internet Mail Extensions) types and image formats, including GIF and JPEG, and allow the attachment of documents in a variety of multimedia formats. If users want to view *alt.binaries* pictures, they can download the article then send it off to a special viewer. Some readers automatically launch helper applications based on the extension of the attached filename. Merely reading the article causes the helper to be launched, and the image appears directly.

THREADING

One popular and indispensable feature of a news reader is the ability to follow message threads. A thread is the sequential chain of replies to the original posting. Secondary threads can start with a reply to a reply instead of a reply to the original article. Threads can therefore become multistranded, and navigation can become quite complex. Despite this fact, many news readers, especially the GUI-based ones, handle threading very well, showing the threads and subthreads in a nested hierarchy. Ideally you'd like to be able to scan down the list of news articles, click on one, go off and follow the response thread to the very end, then automatically come back to where you left off. Figure 9-1 demonstrates threading.

Figure 9-1 News article threads.

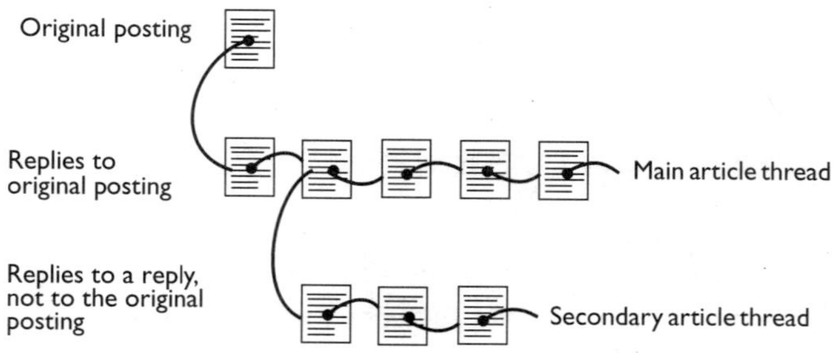

THE KILL FILE FEATURE

The Kill File feature allows the reader to be spared any article, original post or response from an individual identified by username or any item that contains certain keywords. If you find yourself in a flame war or are easily offended by provocative articles, you'll be grateful that your news reader has a Kill File feature.

VIRTUAL NEWSGROUPS

If you are a news administrator (news master), you may have to read *new.software.nntp, news.admin.technical, news.software.readers,* and many other newsgroups in order to keep current on developments and issues affecting news. Readers that support virtual newsgroups allow the user to amalgamate selected newsgroups into a single virtual newsgroup.

LOCAL LIST OF NEWSGROUPS

The first time a user logs onto the news server he or she will have to download the list of all newsgroups handled by the server. Given that there are 20,000 or so newsgroups, this process can take considerable time. The user then subscribes to selected newsgroups from this list, and these are stored locally. Some readers cache the full list locally, avoiding the lengthy download cycle every time they connect.

ROT13 SUPPORT

With ROT13 support on your news reader, articles containing potentially offensive material can be scrambled by shifting each letter in the message by 13 places in the alphabet sequence, thus turning the message into gibberish. The message can be recovered, because the scrambling process is reversible.

MULTIPART MESSAGE HANDLING

News messages, like e-mail messages, are often limited by the administrator to a maximum size. If an article contains a binary image, it may exceed the limit your administrator (or some other administrator down the line) allows. In this case, the message must be broken into parts and sent as separate messages. News readers need to offer multipart message handling so that the pieces of the image can be reconstructed into a viewable whole.

HEADER MANIPULATION

A news reader should feature the ability to modify the header information, so that users can have access to intelligent cross-posting and follow-up designations.

NOCEM

Although not widely available on news readers at the time of writing, the NoCeM feature (pronounced "no see 'em") promises to put an end to spamming once and for all. In this scheme the news reader accesses a trusted database (or moderated newsgroup) of offending articles and hides them from view. If all news readers implement NoCeM, the spams and other junk should gradually disappear.

GOOD NET-KEEPING SEAL OF APPROVAL

Ron Newman came up with the idea of the "Good Net-keeping Seal of Approval" to certify a news reader's compliance to RFC 1036 and other RFCs that define USENET News. To qualify for the seal of approval, a news reader must implement a minimum set of guidelines to ensure that it interacts properly with the rest of the USENET world. It is not a *wish list* of favorite features. The full text of the document describing the seal of approval can be found on many newsgroups, in particular *news.software.readers,* but it is summarized below:

COMPLIANCE ITEMS

1. All essential header information must be displayed.
2. Clear, separate commands for new posting, follow-up, and e-mail reply must be provided.
3. Cross-posting must be implemented.
4. Users must be able to change essential headers in new articles and follow-ups.
5. Follow-ups and e-mail replies must contain correct Subject headers.
6. Follow-ups must be directed to the correct newsgroups.
7. Follow-ups must contain a valid References header.
8. E-mail replies must be directed to the correct address.
9. Quotation and attribution must be possible.
10. Subject header is mandatory.

11. Users must provide a valid From header.
12. The system must allow users to cancel their own articles (and no others!).
13. The 80-character line-length convention must be respected.
14. Obvious user errors must be prevented.

CATEGORIZING NEWS READERS

There are two main categories of news readers: character-based and GUI-based. Character- or text-based readers were the first readers available, and they harken back to the era when a VT-100 terminal was the main form of computer access. They generally lack the features and ease of use of the more modern graphical user interface models, but they are still in widespread use, especially in the UNIX world.

GUI-based readers involve a point-and-click-style interface and employ powerful word processors for aid in creating postings. Many GUI-based readers have Help programs that allow users to immediately view MIME and Rich text formatted images.

Table 9-1 lists some of the more popular character-based news readers for the UNIX operating system.

Table 9-1 Character-based News Readers

Application	Comments
RN	One of the first. User must step through each article.
TRN	A threaded version of RN, capable of "menu-based" selection of articles.
STRN	Built on TRN but has a newsgroup browser, virtual newsgroups, and capacity for scoring/rating articles.
TIN	A threaded, easy-to-use reader based on TASS, an older news reader.
NN	A powerful improvement over RN; allows user to select threads of interest.
XRN	Features include sorting by subject, user-settable key bindings, and many of the features of RN.
XVNEWS	X11-based news reader.
GNEWS	A macro package that can be used with the GNU Emacs text editor.
PINE	A tool for reading, sending, and managing electronic messages.

Most of the GUI-based readers are commercial packages designed to run on the desktop. They all support advanced features such as threading and preselection of threads. Table 9-2 lists some of the more popular ones.

Table 9-2 Desktop GUI-based Readers for Various Operating Systems

Model	Operating System	Comment
NewsWatcher	Macintosh	Supports locally cached list of newsgroups and threading
NewsXpress	Windows	Supports threading; provides news to mail gateway
WinVN	Windows, Windows 95, Windows NT	Highly developed GUI for navigating news; allows simultaneous viewing of multiple articles
NTNews	Windows 95, Windows NT	Awarded "Good Net-keeping Seal of Approval"
Netscape Navigator Browser	Windows 95, Windows NT, Macintosh, UNIX	Supports threading; automatically launches helper applications
Microsoft Explorer Browser	Windows 95, Windows NT, Macintosh	Supports threading; automatically launches helper applications

10 Project Plan

This chapter looks at the cost and schedule issues for implementing a news server. It is assumed that your company already has acceptable Internet access, a registered domain name, and a network support infrastructure.

Tangible Costs

There is no way to give an accurate total cost for your server as it depends on too many factors. Use Table 10-1 as a checklist to ensure nothing is forgotten.

Table 10-1 Equipment List

Item	Needed Y/N	Description
UPS		
Cabling		
Racks		
Server (includes operating system)		
Disk drive		
RAM		
Tape drive		
Media (tapes, disks)		
News feed		
Client software		
Consultant (see next page)		

RESOURCES

To build a news server, a person experienced at the UNIX system level is recommended. Much of the Install and Build exercises are script-based, so the person responsible for installing your news server need not possess kernel-level knowledge. Rather he or she should know how to edit files and be familiar with the UNIX file systems, commands, and applications.

CONSULTANT

A consultant can be a cost-effective alternative when in-house expertise is either nonexistent or unavailable. Hiring a consultant can also be an expensive mistake depending on how your contract is defined, who you retain, and what monitoring system you put in place.

Here are some factors to consider when hiring a consultant:

- Issue a contract that follows a defined PERT chart schedule.
- Identify clearly on the PERT chart schedule which tasks are the direct responsibility of the consultant.
- Avoid mission creep by clearly defining the consultant's tasks.
- Avoid cost-plus contracts. If more work is required, issue another, separate contract.
- Make sure that the ownership of software developed in the course of the project is clearly spelled out in the contract.
- Have the consultant sign a nondisclosure or confidentiality agreement.
- Ask for references and check them out.
- Make the supplying of documentation a part of the contract deliverables, and include such requirements as a printout of all key files, the file layout, any special scripts or tools employed, and so forth. Remember, once the contract is finished, you may not have any further contact with the consultant.

Consultant rates range from $350 a day for someone relatively junior to well over $1,000 a day for the more experienced consultants.

NEWSMASTER

You may need to hire a part- or full-time newsmaster, depending on whether or not you plan to use Intranet newsgroups. Following are some of the duties of the newsmaster:

- Monitoring disk usage and taking appropriate action when problems arise;
- Creating/deleting newsgroups, especially Intranet ones;
- Possibly acting as moderator for Intranet newsgroups; and
- Enforcing company news policy.

SCHEDULE

Many information technology (IT) projects are managed using nothing more than a task list with some preliminary milestone dates. For this reason, most IT projects are late, don't deliver what was promised, or create a "run for the goal line" mentality. Such an approach makes seeing the true project status difficult and very often leads to an announced slippage just before expected delivery.

Here are some tenets for a more effective project management methodology:

- Use a PERT chart that includes all key tasks, task durations, and task interdependencies. This becomes the project plan. There are many project management software packages on the market that support PERT charts, including AutoPlan (UNIX) and Microsoft Project (Windows, Mac).
- Task durations should be based on elapsed calendar workdays required to complete the task, not the effort required. For example, if programming a script took a mere 30 minutes of focused work time, but the person doing the task was interrupted and didn't finish his task until later that week, the elapsed duration would be four or five days, not 30 minutes.
- Estimate future meetings, vendor visits, and so forth, initially as requiring five days since, from a distance, you can't tell which day of the week people will be free.

- Make weekly updates to the project plan by adding or deleting tasks, modifying dependencies, and inputting duration remaining information for each active task.
- Compile a weekly project status report consisting of this week's report, the last report, and baseline dates for key milestones. Also include a brief discussion of specific accomplishments, problems and suggested work-arounds.
- Schedule project meetings only as required using an agenda based on project status report issues.

TASK LIST

Table 10-2 lists the major tasks and associated information for the news server project.

Table 10-2 Task Information

Task	Duration	Comments
Select hardware	5 days	See equipment list—Table 10-1.
Procure hardware	20 days	This includes cutting purchase orders, vendor turn-around and delivery time.
Build/Install operating system	1 day	See Chapter 14.
Configure operating system	1 day	See Chapter 15.
Build/Install netnews software	2 days	See Chapters 16 or 17 depending upon which Netnews software was chosen.
Test news service	2 days	Ensure reading and posting work correctly.
Roll out news service	10 days	Includes announcement, activation of accounts, and so forth.
Hold news policy meeting	5 days	Get consensus on newsgroups, usage restrictions, coverage. See Chapter 12.
Complete site work-sheet	2 days	Gather key information. See Chapter 13.
Create news usage policy	10 days	Based on news policy meeting.
Select news feed	5 days	See Chapter 5.
Select news reader software	5 days	See Chapter 9.

Table 10-2 Task Information (Continued)

Task	Duration	Comments
Procure news reader software	15 days	This includes cutting purchase orders, vendor turn-around and delivery time, license activation.
Distribute news reader software to early adopters	5 days	Choose a small cross-section of beta testers, preferably experienced news users.
Dry run	5 days	Test using real Internet newsgroups.

THE PERT CHART

A PERT chart (often called a CPM chart) relates tasks to each other in terms of predecessors and successor dependencies. Figure 10-1 shows a typical PERT chart for implementing a news service. The circled numbers represent the duration of the task in workdays. The darkened tasks and dependencies indicate the so-called *critical path*. Slippage in tasks on a critical path result in a day-for-day slippage in the end date of the project. The critical path helps focus effort to the most important tasks. For example, shaving some time off the Procure hardware task, can in turn shave time off the overall project end date (up to a point, since another path might become critical). Shaving time off the Procure news reader software step will have no immediate effect on the end date (although it might free up someone to help on another, more critical task).

Overall, the elapsed duration for the project with the estimates given is 41 days (the length of the critical path). Consequently, the project will take slightly longer than two months at 20 working days per month.

Figure 10-1 A PERT chart for news server project.

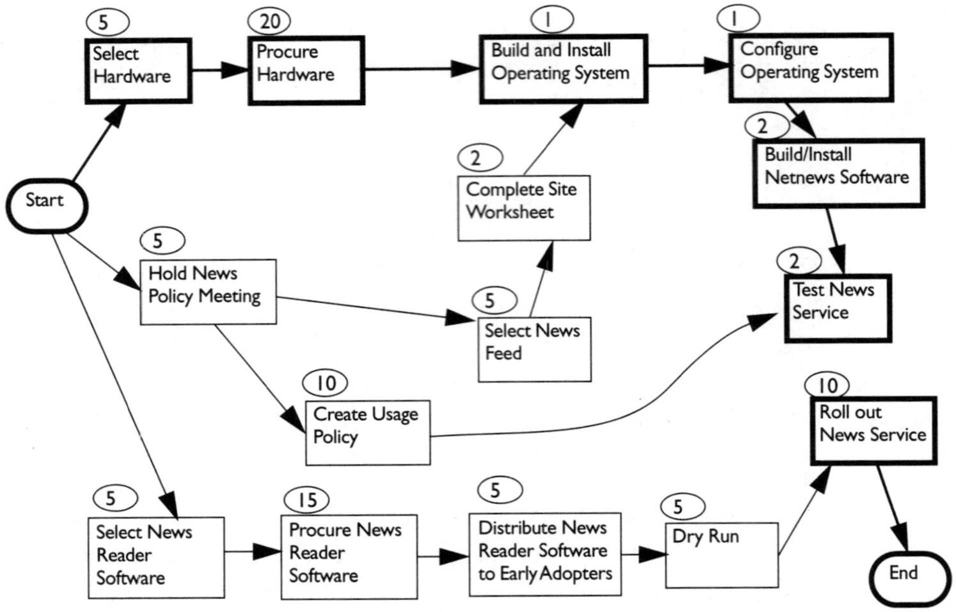

11 Setting User Expectations

When a company's news server resides at the ISP, news may be brought in on a selected basis, and its use may not be widespread. When news is brought inside the company, it will generally be readily available, and virtually everyone from the shipper with the VT-100 terminal to the designers with UNIX workstations will want news. As a result there will be a lot of beginners and naive users who will be learning about news hands-on. Also, veteran news readers may find that they do not have the features, coverage, or freedom they have through their home Internet connection. It is therefore important to establish reasonable user expectations within the company or organization ahead of time.

Newsgroup Content

The news primer (Chapter 3) touched on the type of material you can expect to find in newsgroups. On the positive side, especially in moderated newsgroups, there is a wealth of technical, business, and personal information. On the negative or dark side, offensive articles and spamming (indiscriminate, multiple posting of articles) abound in newsgroups, so users should be forewarned.

COVERAGE

Simply put, you can't bring in all the newsgroups in the world. A full feed with the so-called big eight and the *alt* groups requires at least a dedicated 64K bandwidth pipe all day and all night just to keep up. And this doesn't provide you with all the newsgroups. You can get only what your upstream provider can get, and not even UUNET (a major news source) gets all of the foreign groups. To get better coverage you may require an additional feed from another news provider.

News is growing exponentially. Therefore it may be necessary in the future to drop some newsgroups in order to handle properly ones that are more important to the company. Candidates for dropping may be the popular but frequently valueless *alt.binaries,* which account for 40–50 percent of all the news traffic. Reinforce to users that access to news, even though a free speech vehicle in the public domain, is a privilege within the company, especially on company time. Some groups, particularly in the *alt* arena, may be dropped because of their offensive nature or may be disallowed from the very beginning.

SECURITY ISSUES

News is public, and, as a result, any article posted on a public newsgroup can potentially be read by anyone. Care in posting is therefore essential, especially since your posting may carry your company's domain name. Do you really want your company associated with a newsgroup devoted to helping urban terrorists make pipe bombs? Do you want company users exposing company secrets for the world to see?

In a later section of the book, we describe the *company.posted* technique, which can be used to curb employees from posting to offensive newsgroups on company time. Users should be warned that if this mechanism is in effect, anything they post will be posted locally for everyone within the company, including supervisors, to see.

EXPECTED PERFORMANCE

News can be slow. New articles may rattle around the Internet for days before reaching your local news server. For example, it is not uncommon for a posting to take two or three days to propagate throughout the USENET community. Also, the company news feed can be erratic because of upstream problems beyond your control. Users should be aware that these factors can contribute to a latency in the propagation of articles and newly created newsgroups.

THE SHORT LIFE SPAN OF NEWS

News can take up a huge amount of disk storage space depending on how many newsgroups you access. For this reason news articles have to be expired routinely after so many days. Users should be told of this, and, if necessary, long-term archiving schemes should be set up.

COMPANY POLICIES

Getting news while at work, especially from public newsgroups is a privilege, not an inalienable right. Irresponsible use by employees can result in company liability, loss of good name, as well as network problems. Give the employees a news usage policy and train them in netiquette. Activities such as posting to offensive newsgroups, spamming, or the posting of proprietary company information material should not be tolerated. The Administration section, Part IV, goes into greater depth on this subject.

RESOURCE COMMITMENT

News, like any other network service, is going to require training, routine maintenance, and emergency repair. The Help Desk (or equivalent) should expect and be prepared to handle as many calls and complaints for news as it gets concerning mail. Also, owing to automatic expiry and the somewhat unpredictable nature of news propagation, there will be additional complexities to deal with, for which your company should be prepared to devote both resources and time.

12 Getting Help

USENET News is a community, and when you put a server on the USENET network, you are joining this global community, a fraternity that relies on cooperation and goodwill to keep things running. Owing to the nature of the flooding propagation algorithm used to support News, your site is inexorably linked to all other sites, and actions taken at your site can have profound effects not only on your upstream site but also on the entire News community. For example, if someone from your site sends a multiple posted message (spam) to all 20,000-plus newsgroups (a process that can easily be automated), each news server will have as many copies of your post as there are newsgroups. Considering that there are well over 100,000 news servers, this translates into approximately 2 billion copies of your probably useless message wasting valuable disk space as well as the bandwidth it took to propagate it. For this reason it's important to learn as much as you can about News, news servers, and the news reading community and to pass along this information to all potential users. This book covers many of the important areas, but it is by no means comprehensive in its coverage of these topics. You will need to do your own additional research and to be prepared to operate your news server responsibly.

Online Resources

There are many dedicated people involved in USENET News, and they range from the occasional helper who writes a useful little script, to totally far-out zealots who make and enforce their own policies and rules of behavior. Most people fall somewhere between these two extremes, doing their best to deal with spams, to help coordinate the creation of new groups, to write useful perspectives on USENET for newcomers, and to evolve acceptable use policies. Following are a few of the online information sources for News.

Newsgroup for Newcomers

Most of the good work and helpful references people have produced can be found or referenced in the newsgroup *news.announce.newusers.* This newsgroup contains regular posts such as "A Primer on How to Work with the USENET Community" and "Frequently Asked Questions about USENET," both of which are recommended reading.

INN Home Page et al

One of the more important Web sites for News is

http://www.isc.org/isc/inn.html.

This site is sponsored by the Internet Software Consortium (ISC), the same people who are taking care of BIND and DHCP. It is an excellent starting point that will lead you to many excellent news-related sites. One such site is "Dave Barrs' INN Page"

http://www.math.psu.edu/barr/INN.html

which contains a wealth of important information as well as some lighter trivia on News. A very eclectic site is "Michael Grubb's News Page"

http://www.duke.edu/~mg/usenet/

which has information both on News and on the Internet in general.

NEWS ARCHIVE

Newsgroups tend to have a windowing effect owing to the expiration of articles, so unless you are a regular visitor to a newsgroup, you may miss something important. The Web site

http://www.dejanews.com

maintains a database of archived news articles covering most newsgroups and allows users to search the news database with their Web browser. You can get posting statistics and history on posters (to help determine if their opinions are worth listening to), search for applicable newsgroups by topic or interest, and even post. Dejanews also has a hands-on tutorial for newbies which can serve as a good first introduction to News.

OTHER GOOD SITES

http://www.landfield.com/usenet/usenet-software.html

has just about every possible USENET-related link covering such things as netnews and news reader software, FAQs, useful tools, RFCs, and a news archive and search capability.

http://www.ifi.uio.no/~larsi/notes/notes.html

is maintained by Lars Magne Ingebrigtsen and contains a convenient reference to RFCs related to news readers as well as some useful news links.

Like all World Wide Web sites, over time news links get added or deleted, links may change, and some sites may disappear altogether, but if you use the resources we've just mentioned as starting points, you'll probably be able to find more than you need.

NEWS ADMINISTRATORS

News administrators, aka newsmasters, have a number of tasks: Not only do they keep their own news server running (managing disk capacity, archiving, reader problems), but they also coordinate with the rest of the global USENET community to address widespread problems.

There are idiots, exploiters, and rebels in every crowd, and it can be a full-time job for newsmasters just to keep up with the fallout of deliberate acts of sabotage, such as news bombing, illegal cancels, and spams. It often takes a collaborative and cooperative effort to identify and eradicate these problems, which can potentially affect service. Mix in maintenance of their own user community, and the workload of newsmasters can be overwhelming.

It's not surprising, then, that many newsmasters cast a skeptical and wary eye at a news server coming online for the first time. Yes, there is a chance that the new site might be one of the bad ones from the get go, perhaps an online spam-generating advertiser, but more likely they are concerned that the new site will inadvertently cause problems—and can this ever make their lives miserable! Here are just a few of the dangers they may be wary of:

- Leave your NNTP port unguarded and hackers can use your site as a sidedoor to USENET through which they may pump news bombs, spams, and offensive articles while all the time laying the blame on your site.
- News newbies connecting to your server may break some or all of the netiquette rules and invent a few tragic faux pas of their own.
- A few experienced users at your site might turn out to be bad eggs and create spams, post offensive material, or commit other nasty News crimes.

The Local News Community

Initially you might want to enlist the help of a fellow newsmaster. Newsmasters tend to form closely knit communities. If you screw up and spam or otherwise make your fellow news administrators' lives miserable, they may not be very friendly toward you. So try to build a good relationship with them from the very beginning. Tell them, "I'm coming on. I don't know too much. Here's what I've got." More often than not you'll get valuable advice during setup, and when the inevitable disasters happen, you'll have someone to call for help. Besides, your fellow newsmasters have all been in your shoes, and they're likely to be sympathetic, especially if they know you'll do whatever it takes to set things right.

To find news colleagues in your area, start with your upstream news feed or ask around at some of the larger companies or at nearby universities. In addition the network administrators of local companies and organizations (whose identity you can ascertain using the application Whois) will likely tell you who their newsmaster is.

A word of advice: Do your homework first. Don't look upon using other newsmasters as a substitute for learning about News on your own.

PART III

CONSTRUCTION

Many people have built news servers with nothing more than the INN FAQs, newsgroup postings, and trial-and-error learning. Although this process can work, often the implementation takes longer than expected, costs a whole lot more than budgeted, and doesn't work as well as it could.

Techies are nothing if not resourceful, and by news postings, e-mails, frantic phone calls, or with the help of consultants, the news server eventually gets stabilized, and complaints drop off to a somewhat manageable level. The hope is that this section of the book will help the person responsible for implementing the news server to avoid common pitfalls and problems and make getting the news server up and running a more pleasant and rewarding experience. This section is technical and is intended for the constructor, the network engineer, or the support person who has been given the job of building the news server. Many of the steps involved in installing and configuring the operating system and netnews application are easily followed even by a nontechnical person, but a word of caution is in order. Even though everything seems to compile and install properly, the resulting system can fall short of expected performance or even be dysfunctional. The reason lies in the vast number of possible variants on hardware, software, and environment that may be encountered. For this reason, a technical person, experienced in UNIX and TCP/IP networking, should be involved, at least in an advisory capacity

In the following pages a complete construction of a news server is presented—from the installation and configuration of the operating system to the building and installation of the news reader application. Two news servers configurations are presented here: a large site running INN and a smaller site (as might be used for a regional news server over the corporate WAN) running DNEWS. Figure III-1 shows where these two configurations might find application. Both the corporate INN server and the regional DNEWS server have at least two feeds (one to an ISP and one to the other corporate entity). The corporate WAN would normally carry only selected Intranet newsgroups, but it may also carry some public ones such as regional newsgroups of interest to the head office readers. Most other public newsgroups and almost certainly the *alt* group would likely be barred. Unless specifically programmed to do so, no Intranet newsgroups would leak out into the Internet. This type of configuration is readily obtained by adjusting entries in a few configuration files.

Figure III-1 Corporate news topology.

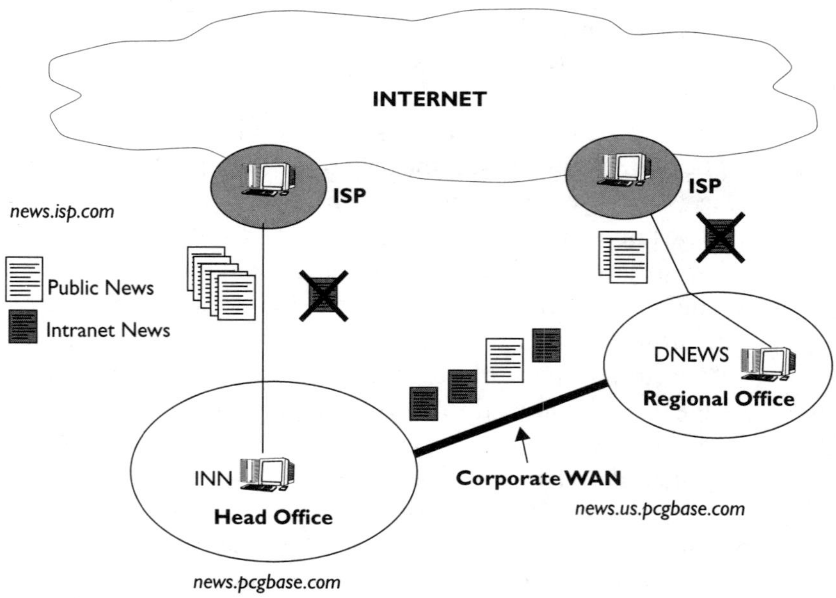

Some specifics on the hardware and software that could be used for the two configurations of news servers are presented in Table III-1.

Table III-1 Sample News Servers

Type of Server	Platform	Operating System	RAM	Netnews Software	Hard Disk
Corporate	UltraSPARC	Solaris 2.5.1	192MB	INN 1.5.1	16GB
Regional	SPARC 5	Solaris 2.5.1	32MB	DNEWS 2.7	2GB

13 Preliminaries

Before beginning construction of the server, you'll need to make many decisions, such as which netnews software, server hardware, disk configuration, host name, and so forth, to use. With luck the previous chapters have made these decisions easier.

Site Worksheet

Many of the entries you'll need to make during the operating system and the netnews software installation are standard defaults, but some, such as host name, are obviously site specific.The Site Worksheet, Table 13-1, lists some of the areas where your individual site values may be required, along with values used during the construction of the sample news server. It is recommended that you fill out column 3 of the worksheet in advance and keep the worksheet handy during the construction phase. (Note the INN server used as sample.)

Table 13-1 Site Worksheet for News Server

Information Required	Sample Values	Site Value
Platform	Sun Microsystems UltraSPARC serial # ***** ROM version ***	
RAM size, type, speed	256MB, 8 x 32MB, 70ns	

Table 13-1 Site Worksheet for News Server (Continued)

Information Required	Sample Values	Site Value
Disk subsystem	two, 8GB, SCSI	
Host name	*news.pcgbase.com*	
Network connectivity?	yes	
Primary network interface	le0	
IP address of host	205.233.33.5	
Name of service employed	DNS	
Subnet	yes	
Netmask	255.255.255.0	
Time zone information	Geographic region, Canada, eastern	
System type	Standalone	
Software group	Developer system support	
Software customization	Automated security Enhancement tools System accounting	
Domain name	*pcgbase.com*	
Name server	*NS.pcgbase.com*	
Name server IP	205.233.33.1	
Default router	205.233.33.7	
News user	news	
Newsgroup	news	
Newsmaster	newsmaster	
Upstream news host	*news.isp.com*	
Intranet newsgroup prefix	pcg	
Type of news feed	Ihave	

SOME FINAL RECOMMENDATIONS

Finally, before getting started, here are some recommendations of ways you can make things go smoothly:

- Make sure all hardware and software support contracts or plans are in place at this time, and that a copy of all licenses is on file.
- Ensure that all hardware has been received and installed. Resist the temptation to start the server implementation before you have accumulated all the necessary parts. For example, it may be tempting to start the operating system installation without the tape media (which may be in the mail), but avoid this move because you will encounter a problem when you get to the end of the day and you want to save the work in progress. Racks are often on order while servers are being programmed. This sounds okay, but most administrators will find it difficult to stop the technical team once they have achieved some momentum, because they'll want to run the service while the server sits on the floor, their desk, your desk. . . .
- Configure all SCSI devices with proper target ID and terminate the SCSI chain.
- Install a UPS (Uninterruptable Power Supply) device of sufficient capacity to power the server and all peripheral devices.
- The ideal location for the news server is in the server room, if you have one. If not, consider building one. A server room is a secure, climate-controlled area that houses servers and disk drives. Internet connection brings with it the potential for compromising electronic sabotage and damaging access. Even a power cord, inadvertently unplugged, can cause a serious disk crash or server malfunction. Locating the news server in a separate, secure room can protect you from many forms of disaster.
- Follow the manufacturer's advice for the proper power-up sequence of your system. To avoid damage, some devices may require that both termination and connection are in place before power can be applied.
- Make sure all relevant vendor documentation and reference books are on hand.
- Complete all network registration activities.
- Ensure that you have a stable network connection.
- Put an off-site storage facility in place.

14 Installing the Operating System

Information required in this chapter should already be present in the Site Worksheet (Table 13-1), which you should have already filled out. If you have not already done so, complete the worksheet now, before proceeding.

This chapter on installing the operating system is included for illustrative purposes and features SunSoft Solaris O/S 2.5.1 since this operating system was used both in the INN and DNEWS news servers. Other operating system installations will differ in minor or major ways. Although this chapter can be skipped by experienced UNIX personnel, the reader is encouraged to at least skim this chapter because there are a few areas (marked by the caution symbol) that are very important to USENET News implementation.

Conventions

Not all windows are shown. Both user input and user choices are highlighted in bold-faced text. Text the user must add to configuration files is bold-faced. Unless otherwise indicated, the Continue button is used to advance to the next installation step.

This chapter describes the complete installation process for SunSoft Solaris O/S 2.5.1. The sequence and screen captures were derived from a real-life Install operation. Although the specific syntax and steps may differ, the principles are largely the same for most UNIX setups.

Vendors of UNIX operating systems generally provide a printed version of their complete installation procedure, and the user is encouraged to have this on hand as reference material. The applicable manual for this installation, *SPARC: Installing Solaris Software on the Desktop,* has been used as a general guide, but additional information and clarification have been added.

THE BOOT PROCESS

Start the boot process by powering up the computer and peripherals. If the computer begins loading an existing operating system, you may hold down the Stop key and press **A** (Stop-A). Type **n** to go to "New command mode." The computer screen should say:

Type "go" to resume.

Type help for more information.

OK

Type one of the following boot instructions from Table 14-1 depending on the SPARC platform you're using (the most common is **boot cdrom**).

Table 14-1 Boot Instructions

PlatformBoot	Command
SPARCstation 1(4/60)	boot sd(0,6,2)
SPARCstation 1+(4/65)	boot sd(0,6,2)
SPARCstation SLC™(4/20)	boot sd(0,6,2)
SPARCstation IPC™(4/40)	boot sd(0,6,2)
SPARCengine® 1E	boot sd(0,6,5)
All other Sparc platforms	boot cdrom

The boot process will take a few minutes. Then you will see two windows. The first window, the Solaris Install Console (Figure 14-1), shows the progress as the installation proceeds.

The second window, the Solaris Installation Program window (Figure 14-2) will explain the three sections of the installation process.

Figure 14-1 Solaris Install Console.

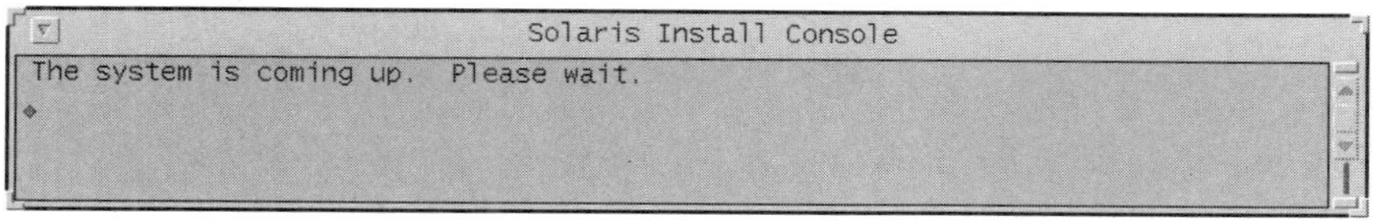

Figure 14-2 The first of the Solaris Installation Program windows.

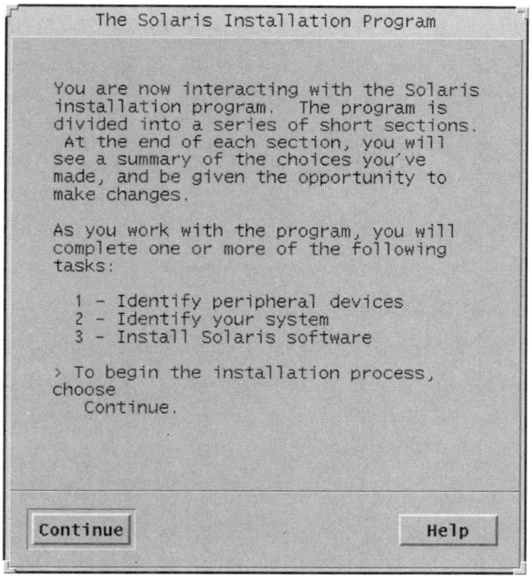

Because of a quirk in the on-screen install programming, these sections may not come up in the order indicated here, but all three will eventually come up. Click **Continue**.

SYSTEM IDENTIFICATION

The next screen presented (not shown) is an information screen—no entry is required. Click **Continue**.

The host name shown in the Host Name window (Figure 14-3) is only a sample. You'll need to enter the real information for the host you are installing from the Site Worksheet you have already prepared (Table 13-1). Enter **Host Name**. As the screen warns, make sure the name you select is unique within the network.

Figure 14-3 Host Name window.

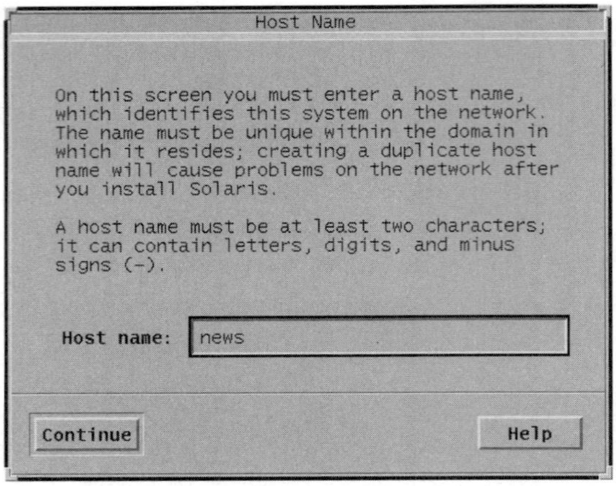

Click **Continue**.

Because this computer will be connected to a network, click **Yes** when you see the Network Connectivity window (Figure 14-4).

Figure 14-4 Network Connectivity window.

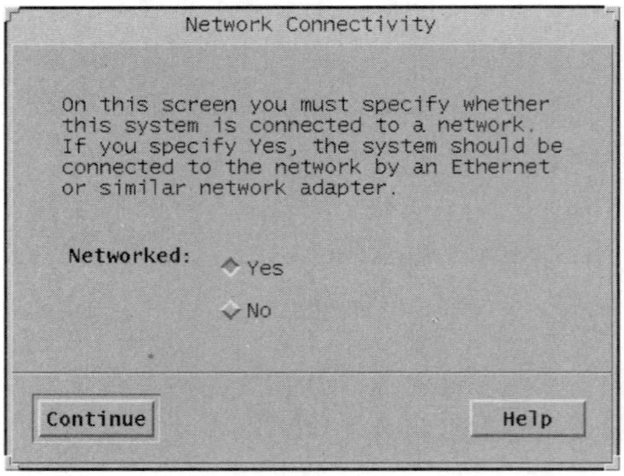

Click **Continue**.

The IP address shown in the IP Address window (Figure 14-5) is only a sample. You'll need to enter the real information for the server you are installing from yourworksheet entries. Enter **IP Number**.

Figure 14-5 IP Address window.

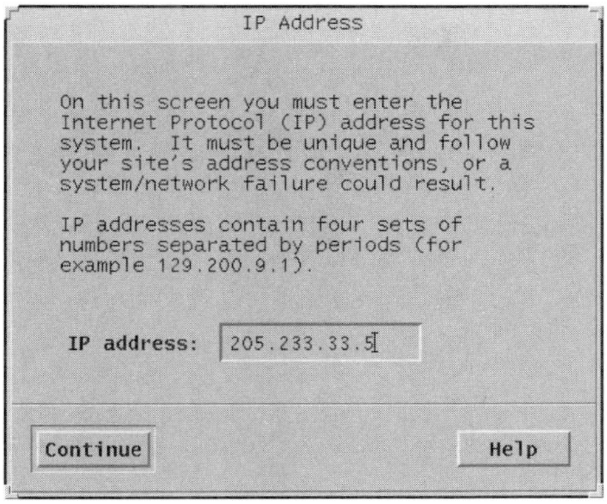

Click **Continue**.

After the IP Address window closes, a Confirm Information window (Figure 14-6) will allow you to confirm and/or change any information you've entered up to this point. Make any necessary changes now.

Figure 14-6 Confirm Information window.

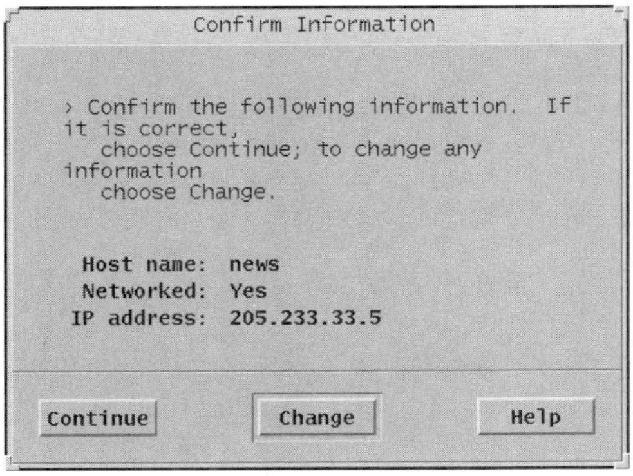

Click **Continue**.

Since the news server is connected to the Internet, it will rely on the Domain Name System or (DNS); therefore select **Other** in the Name Service window (Figure 14-7).

Figure 14-7 Name Service window.

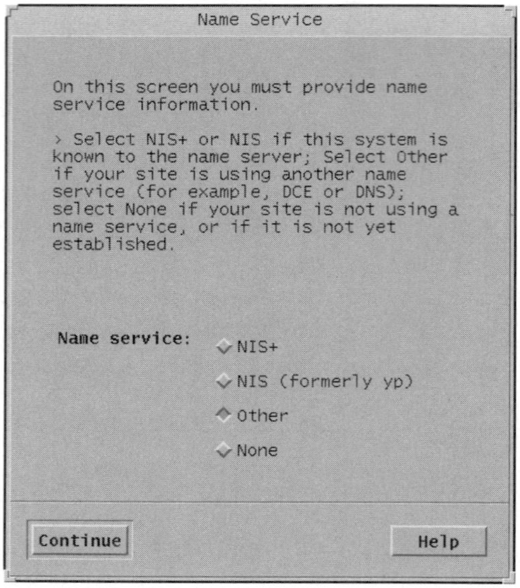

Click **Continue**.

After the Name Service window closes, a Confirm Information window (Figure 14-8) will allow you to confirm and/or change any information you've entered up to this point. Make any necessary changes.

Figure 14-8 Confirm Information window.

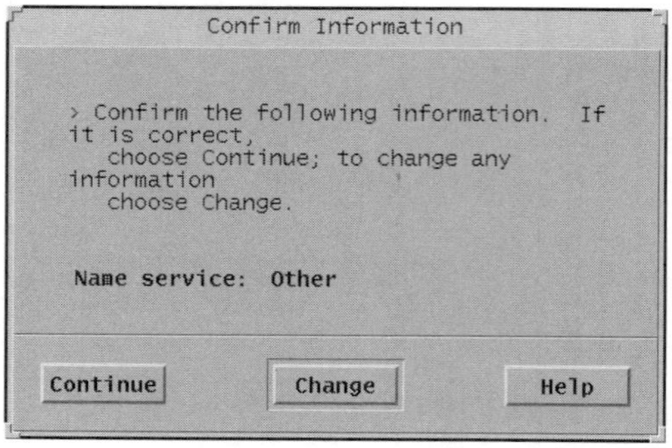

Click **Continue**.

The local address space has been divided into subnets. This makes the network more manageable. Click **Yes** in the Subnets window (Figure 14-9).

Figure 14-9 Subnets window.

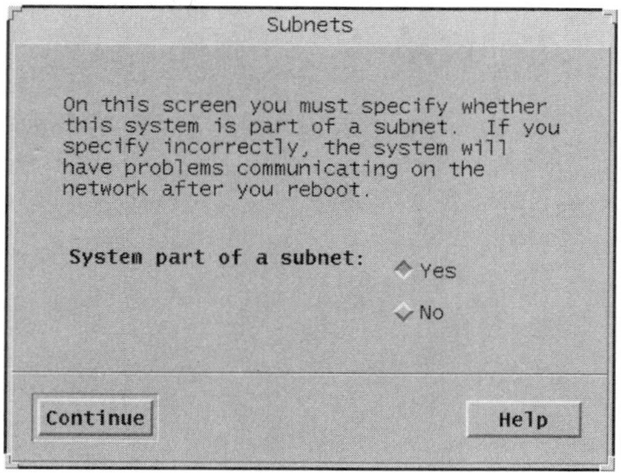

Click **Continue**.

In the Netmask window (Figure 14-10), you will mask off the portion of the network number to use for networks with the number 255.The part of the network number meant to be used for hosts is shown with zeros. Get the correct **netmask** from the Site Worksheet (Table 13-1). Then click **Continue**.

Figure 14-10 Netmask window.

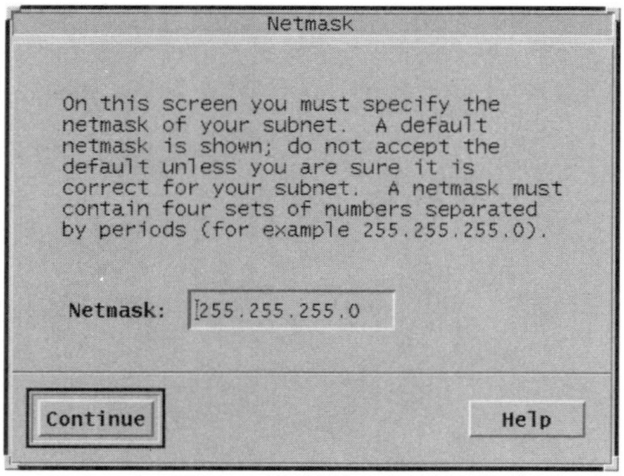

On all servers, specify the time zone according to Geographic region. In the Time Zone window (Figure 14-11), click **Geographic region**.

Figure 14-11 Time Zone window.

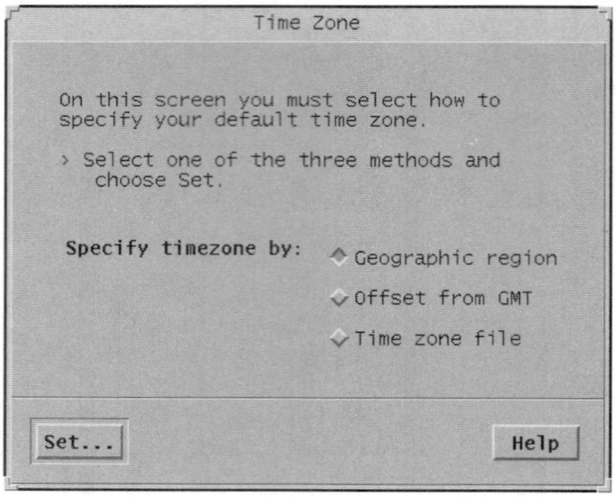

Select the appropriate **region** in the Regions section of the Geographic Region window (Figure 14-12). Then select your **time zon**e from within the Time zones section.

Click **Set.**

Figure 14-12 Geographic Region window.

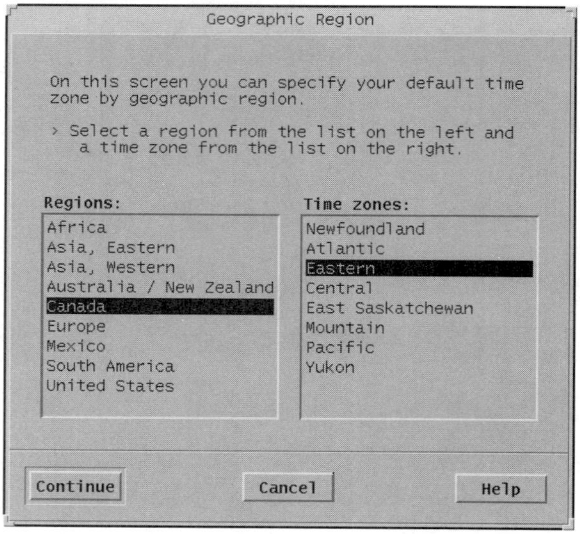

Click **Continue.**

The data shown in the Date and Time window (Figure 14-13) are for illustration only. Enter the appropriate **time** and **date**.

Figure 14-13 Date and Time window.

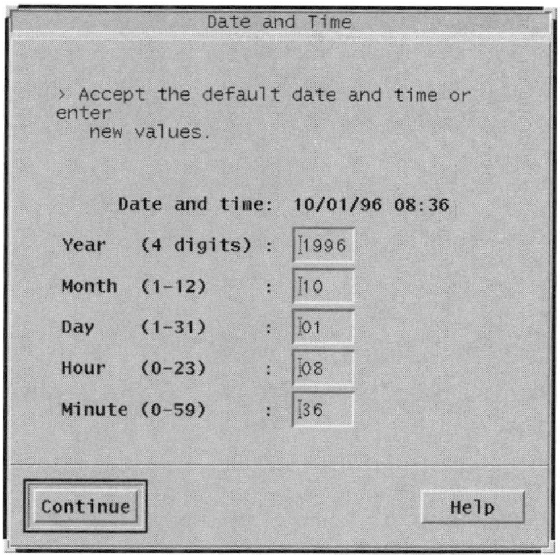

Click **Continue**.

After the Date and Time window closes, a Confirm Information window (Figure 14-14) will allow you to confirm and/or change any information entered up to this point. Make any necessary changes.

Figure 14-14 Confirm Information window.

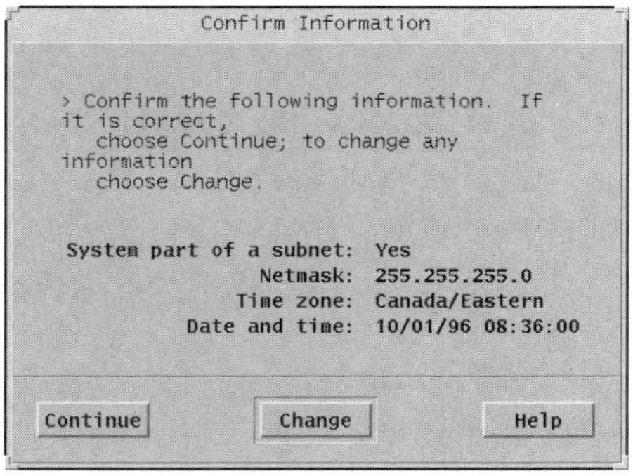

Click **Continue**.

It may seem as if the server is idle for a long time. The Solaris Install Console (Figure 14-15) will even read, "System Identification is completed." Be patient; the message "Starting Solaris installation program . . . " will eventually appear.

Figure 14-15 Solaris Install Console.

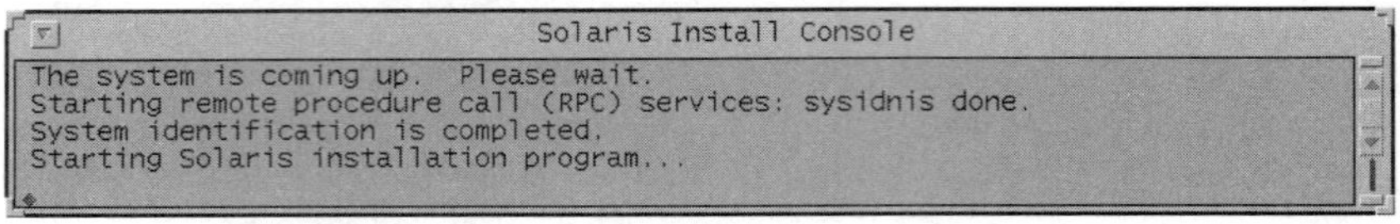

INSTALLATION

At this point the Install Solaris Software—Initial window (Figure 14-16) will come up, marking the start of the Installation routine. This window provides an overview of what is to follow. Be sure to read and understand its contents. If you do not wish to proceed, click **Exit**. The installation will abort, and you will return to the Boot level.

Figure 14-16 Install Solaris Software—Initial window.

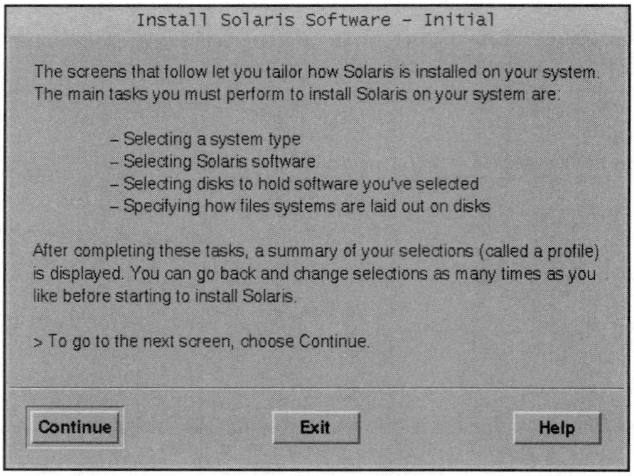

Otherwise click **Continue**.

In the Upgrade System window (Figure 14-17) that appears, click **Initial**.

It is very important to tell the system that you are embarking on an initial installation and not on an upgrade procedure.

Figure 14-17 Upgrade System window.

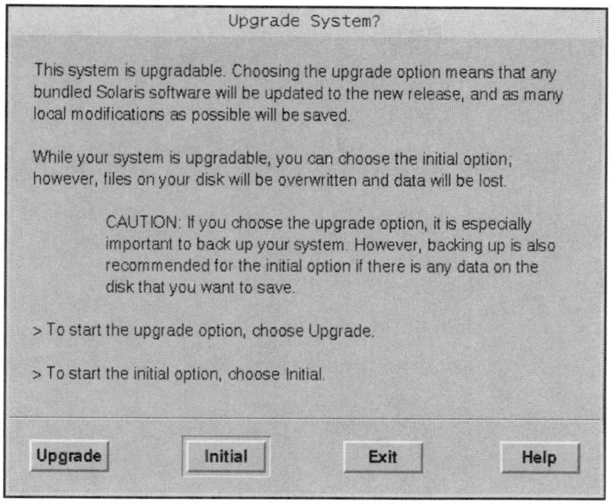

Your server will be autonomous, so click **Stand-alone** in the System Type window (Figure 14-18).

Figure 14-18 System Type window.

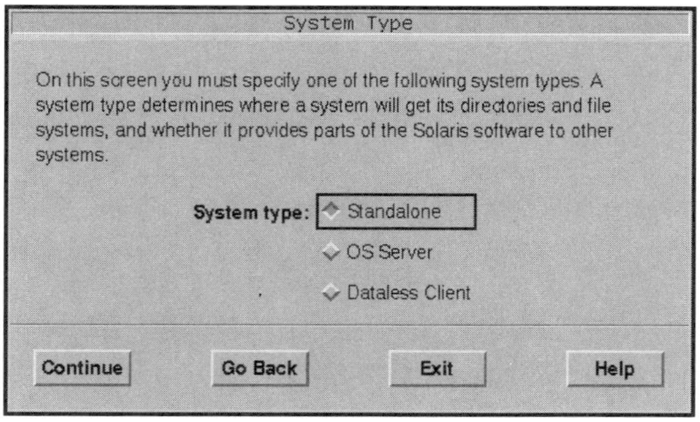

Click **Continue**

In the Software window (Figure 14-19) under the Software Group section, click **Developer System Support** to include additional software libraries required for INN compilation. Since two additional packages will be required, click **Customize** to bring up a secondary window. You will be returning to the Software window after completing the customization process.

Figure 14-19 Software window.

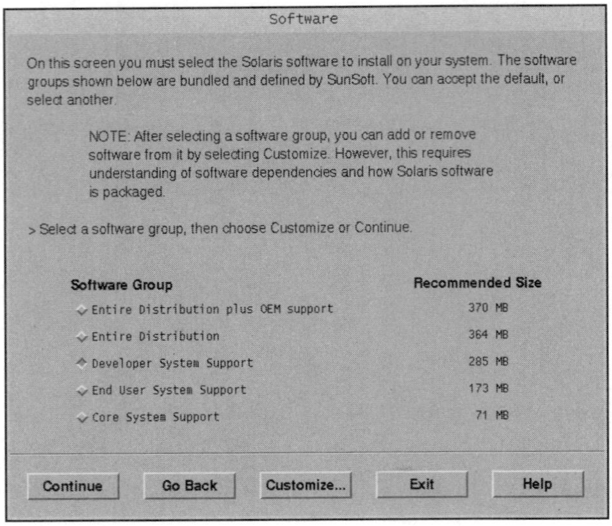

In the Customize Software window (Figure 14-20), select **Automated Security Enhancement Tools** and **System Accounting,** if you would like to create user audit trails.

Figure 14-20 Customize Software window.

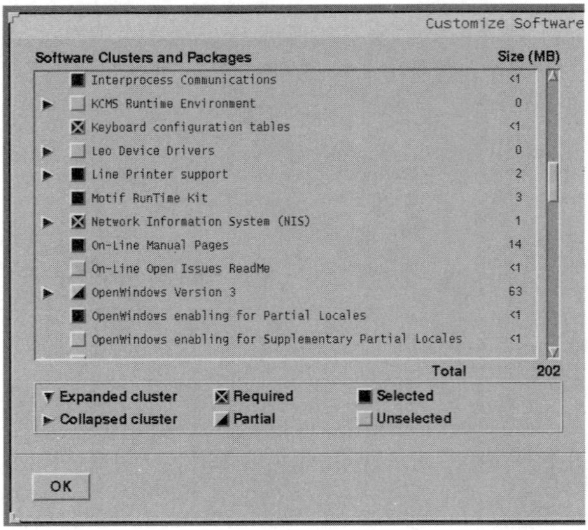

Click **OK** to return to the Software window.

Click **Continue**.

In the Disks window (Figure 14-21) in the Available Disks section, click on **disks,** then click **Add**. Repeat this process until all your listed disks are in the Selected Disks section on the right side of the window. You are selecting the disk volumes the operating system will be installed on. By selecting them all, you provide maximum flexibility for later configuration.

Click **Continue**.

Figure 14-21 Disks window.

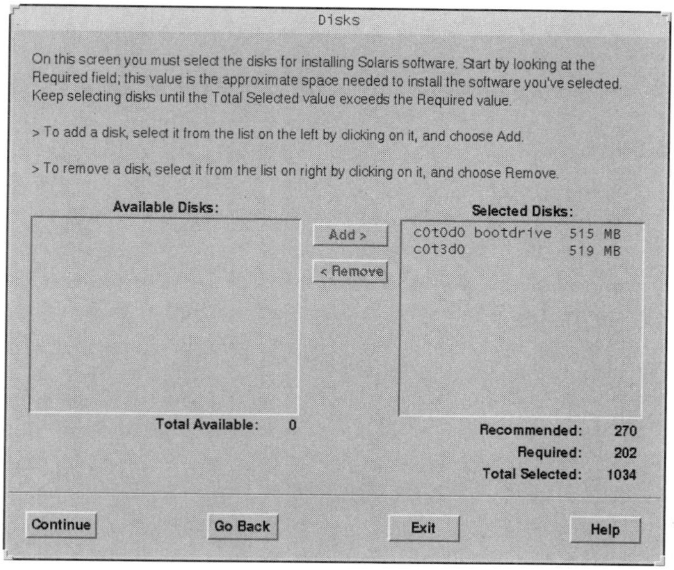

In the Preserve Data window (Figure 14-22), click **Continue** to overwrite existing data. Since this is an initial installation, there is no need to preserve any data that might be on the disks.

Figure 14-22 Preserve Data window.

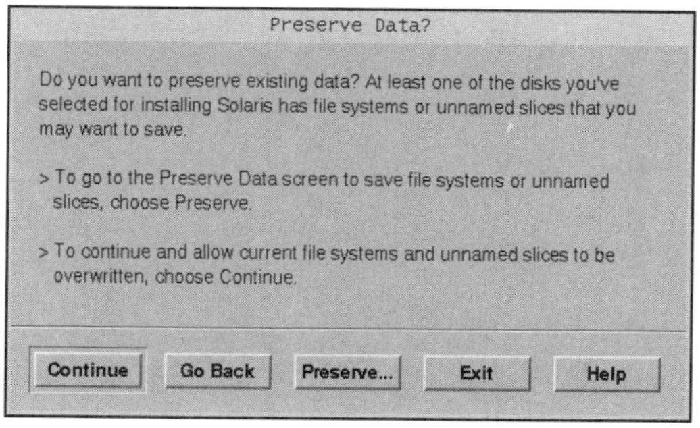

In the Automatically Layout File Systems? window (Figure 14-23), click **Auto-layout**.

Figure 14-23 Selecting Auto-layout in the Automatically Layout File Systems? window.

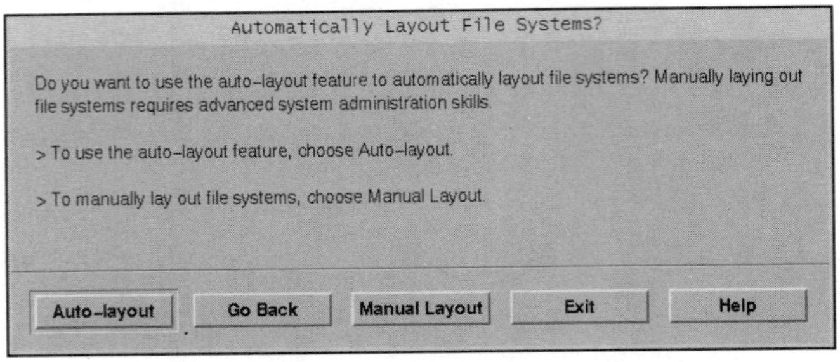

A follow-up window will appear, also labeled Automatically Layout File Systems (Figure 14-24).

Figure 14-24 Selecting File Systems in the Automatically Layout File Systems window.

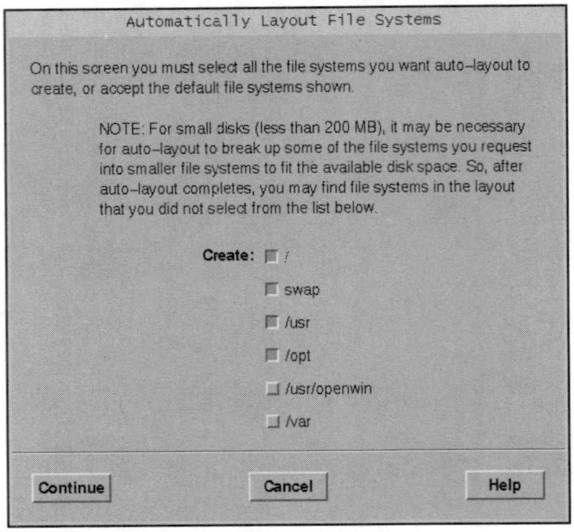

Under **Create**, select **/**(root), **swap**, **/usr**, and **/opt** as the file systems to be created.

Click **Continue**.

In the File System and Disk Layout window (Figure 14-25), click **Customize.**

Figure 14-25 File System and Disk Layout window.

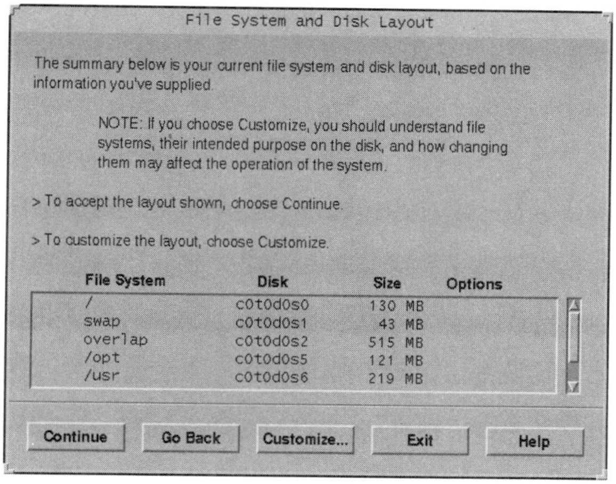

This brings up the Customize Disks window (Figure 14-26), which allows you to adjust the size of the file systems.

Figure 14-26 Customize Disks window.

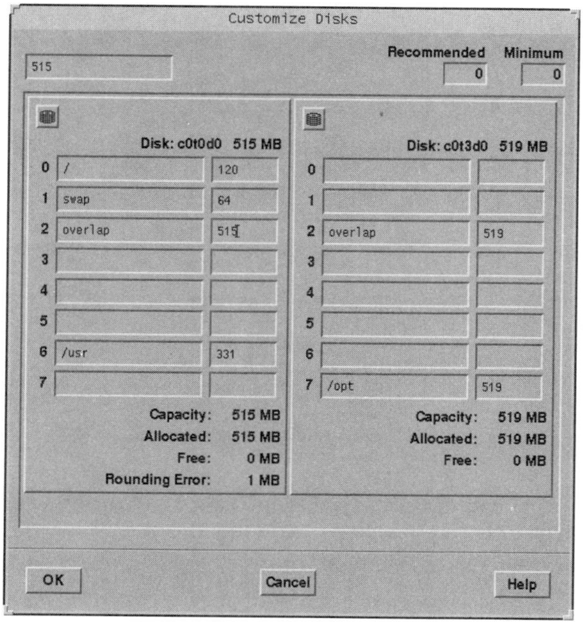

First, remove any unwanted file systems that may appear such as /export/home. You must select the size of the unwanted file system and then press the Back Space key. Repeat this process to remove the names of all unwanted file systems.

Next enter settings for the remaining file systems—at least 120 for **/**, double the physical memory for **swap**, 225 for **/usr**, and the rest of any remaining free space for **/opt**. The size of your overlap, swap, and /opt file systems may vary, depending on the size of the disk and memory installed.

If the words *Rounding Error* are displayed at the bottom of the Disk section under the word *Free*, click on the **small disk platter icon** in the top left-hand side of the Disk section. The Customize Disks by Cylinders window (Figure 14-27) will appear, giving you a chance to adjust the actual cylinders of the disk. Increase the size of the last file system by the number of cylinders displayed in the Free section. Click into another file system to update and refresh the screen. Make sure that the number displayed for free cylinders equals zero.

Figure 14-27 Customize Disks by Cylinders window.

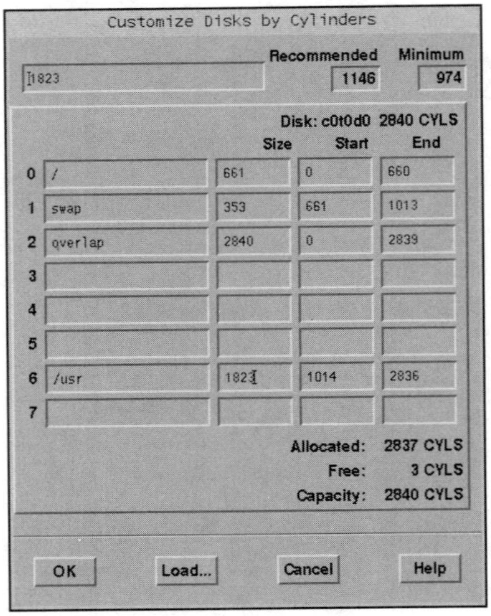

Click **OK** to return to the Customize Disks window. Click **OK** again to return to the File System and Disk Layout window (Figure 14-28) to confirm the size of the file systems.

Figure 14-28 File System and Disk Layout window.

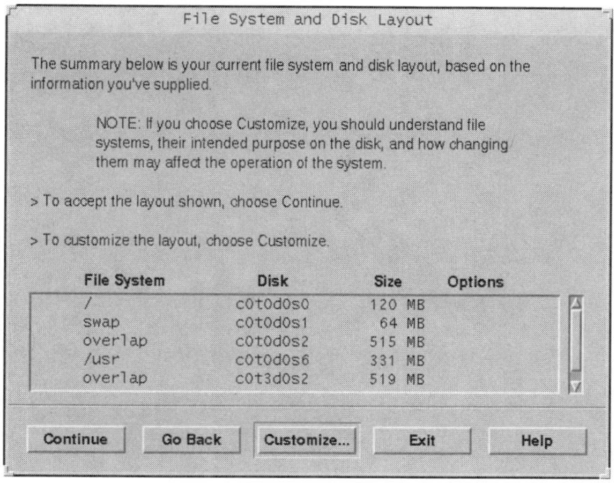

Click **Continue**

Your news server will be totally autonomous and will not mount any remote file systems from other servers. Therefore click **Continue** in the Mount Remote File Systems window (Figure 14-29).

Figure 14-29 Mount Remote File Systems window.

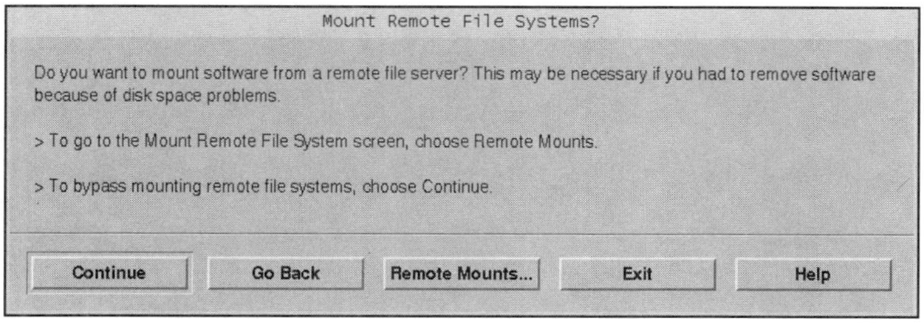

The Profile window (Figure 14-30) provides a last chance to review your choices and make necessary changes.

Figure 14-30 Profile window.

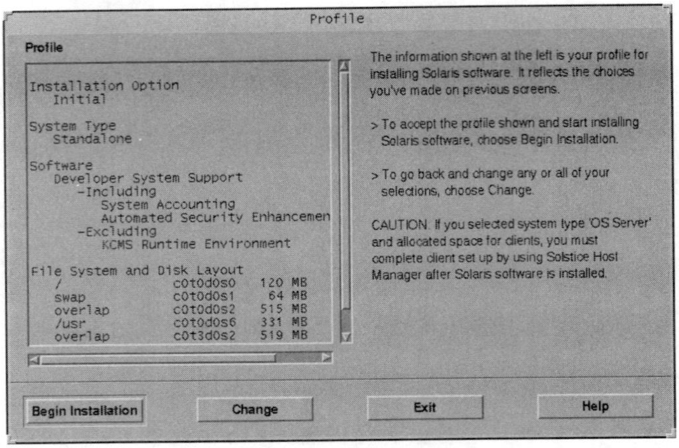

Next click **Begin Installation.**

On the untitled window (Figure 14-31) that appears, click **Reboot.**

Figure 14-31 Untitled window.

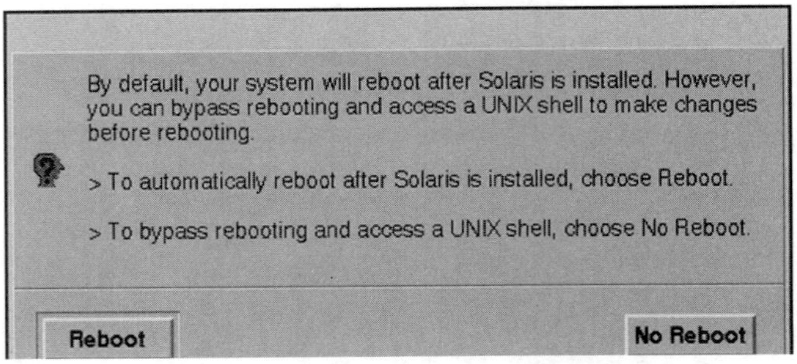

The Installing Solaris—Progress window (Figure 14-32) will appear. The slide bar will move to the right as the installation proceeds, allowing you to monitor progress.

Figure 14-32 Installing Solaris—Progress window.

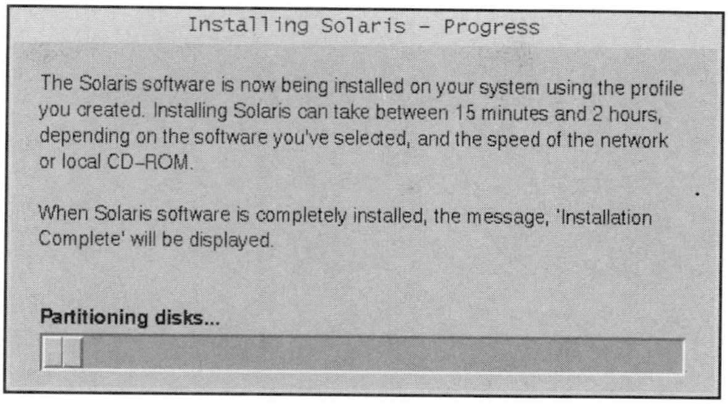

After the Solaris installation is complete, the system will reboot, and you can then begin configuring the system files.

15 Configuring the Operating System

Although SunSoft Solaris O/S 2.5.1 is featured in this chapter, the concepts presented are generic. The reader is encouraged to understand this chapter thoroughly. Information required in this chapter should already be present in the Site Worksheet (Table 13-1). If you have not already done so, please complete it now before proceeding.

Conventions

Bold is used to indicate user entries, underlines are for files or directories, and *italics* are used to highlight terms or concepts.

This chapter covers preparation of the operating system and includes editing and adding configuration files.

Prerequisites

- The SunSoft Solaris operating system should be installed.
- All network connections should be in place and working.

- The support contract should be in place with authorization to download patches.
- The Site Worksheet (Table 13-1) should already be completed.

EDITING CONFIGURATION FILES

A number of configuration files must be edited to create a workable news server environment. When changing configuration files, it is always a good policy to make backups first. Before any of the original files are changed, simply copy the original filename to the same name, adding the extension .dist

```
news# cp filename filename.DIST
```

Do not leave any backup files in an RC directory. When the computer boots, it executes all files in the RC directories, and one of these temporary files might get executed by accident.

CONFIGURING THE O/S

The best approach for configuring the operating system is to divide the work into the three areas that correspond to the three main layers of the TCP/IP model: the physical layer or device driver, the IP layer, and the application layer. See Figure 15-1.

Figure 15-1 TCP/IP stack.

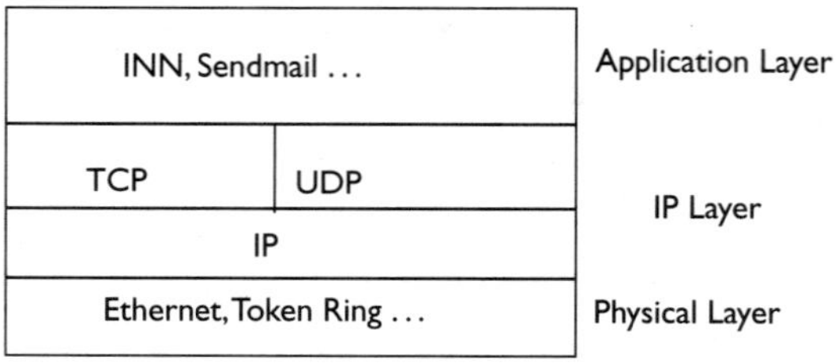

PHYSICAL LAYER

The first layer in the TCP/IP model is the *physical layer*. The built-in Ethernet interface of the SPARC motherboard uses the 48-bit Ethernet address assigned to the machine at the factory. The Ethernet driver is automatically loaded into the kernel at boot time.

IP LAYER

The next layer in the TCP/IP model is the *IP layer.* Here an IP address must be assigned so that the computer can communicate with the network. During the Boot process, the computer uses the contents of four system files for IP configuration: /etc/hosts, /etc/netmasks, /etc/defaultrouter, and /etc/hostname.le0. Two of these files—/etc/hosts and /etc/defaultrouter—need to be edited. The other files were created by the install process and probably do not need to be changed.

The first file, /etc/hosts, is really a link to a file. The actual file is in the /etc/inet directory. As the computer boots, an rc script parses a name from the file /etc/hostname.le0. Then using that name, the /etc/hosts file is parsed to find an IP number. This IP number is then assigned to the interface *le0.* To configure the file, change directories to /etc/inet, add the fully qualified name of your host and the fully qualified names of key computers it will communicate with. (Note: The host name shown here is only a sample. The real information for the host you are installing should come from your Site Worksheet (Table 13-1).) Following is the edit for the /etc/hosts file.

Note: The system prompt includes the host name "news." Your system may only show the "#" sign.

```
news console login: root
Password: XXXXX
Sep 11 19:29:59 news login ROOT LOGIN /dev/console
Last login: Wed Sep 11 12:57:24 on /dev/console
Sun Microsystems Inc. SunOS 5.5 Generic November 1995
news# cd /etc/inet
news# cp hosts hosts.DIST
news# vi hosts

#
# Internet host table
#
127.0.0.1      localhost
205.233.33.1 ns.pcgbase.com
205.233.33.5 news.pcgbase.com news loghost
```

The /etc/defaultrouter file is used to add the address of the router or gateway that will send packets from your local network to other networks. A quick way to create the file is to echo the information into the file. Remember to use the IP number of the defaultrouter listed on the Site Worksheet (Table 13-1).

```
news# cd /etc
news# echo "205.233.33.7" > defaultrouter
```

APPLICATION LAYER

The first application to configure will be the type of naming service your computer will use. As has been mentioned earlier, the Domain Name System (DNS) allows computer names that humans can read (usually using recognizable names) to be converted to numbers the computer can use. Name service selection is configured in two files. The name service switch file, /etc/nsswitch.conf, is where the use of DNS is specified.

```
news# cd /etc
news# cp nsswitch.conf nsswitch.conf.DIST
news# vi nsswitch.conf

#
# /etc/nsswitch.files:
#
# An example file that could be copied over to /etc/nsswitch.conf; it
# does not use any naming service.
#
# "hosts:" and "services:" in this file are used only if the
# /etc/netconfig file has a "-" for nametoaddr_libs of "inet" transports.

passwd:     files
group:      files
hosts:      files [NOTFOUND=continue] dns
networks:   files
protocols:  files
rpc:        files
ethers:     files
netmasks:   files
```

The second file is /etc/resolv.conf. In this file you need to specify which domain you are in and where the DNS server is located. Use the information provided on the Site Worksheet (Table 13-1) to configure your resolv.conf.

```
news# cd /etc
news# vi resolv.conf

#
#
domain    pcgbase.com

nameserver    205.233.33.1
```

CONTROLLING NETWORK SERVICES

Network services can be managed by running a master program called Inetd, which involves a master daemon that will start other programs on demand. An alternative method of providing network services involves starting all the programs at startup and letting them run continuously.

The file that controls which services the Inetd program will call is /etc/inetd.conf. The syntax of the file is one service per line, and lines that begin with a "#" are comments. Because this file is preconfigured for a full suite of the most commonly run services, most lines in this file should be commented out.

```
news# cd /etc/inet
news# cp inetd.conf inetd.conf.DIST
news# vi inetd.conf
```

Listed below are the only services you should leave uncommented.

```
ftp   stream   tcp   nowait   root   /usr/sbin/in.ftpd   in.ftpd
telnet   stream   tcp   nowait   root   /usr/sbin/in.telnetd   in.telnetd
```

LINKS

All software in this book is kept separate from the operating system files by placing everything in /opt. In order to conform to a standard commonly used on the Internet, create a link from /opt/local to /usr/local, and /local.

```
news# ln -s /opt/local /local
news# ln -s /opt/local /usr/local
```

Be warned that the Solaris operating system installation process creates a directory /var/news, and then creates a link from this directory to /usr/news. If you want to keep your news files in the /usr file system, remove this link and create a /usr/news directory.

```
news# rm /usr/news
news# mkdir /usr/news
```

16

Building and Installing INN

Some information required in this chapter should already be present in the Site Worksheet (Table 13-1). If you have not already done so, please complete the worksheet now, before proceeding.

CONVENTIONS

The user is required to make many modifications to data files in order to match the site. Where data files require editing, the file is reproduced in whole of in part, and necessary or recommended changes are highlighted with a check mark in the left-hand side of the page. **Bold** signifies user entries, an underline designates files or directories, and *italics* are used to highlight a word or term.

INN has been around for a number of years and is really the standard for large news servers. As a result many sources of information exist to help build the INN application, including

- News postings,
- The INN install guide included with the INN,

- INN FAQs, and
- Man pages (manuals electronically provided with the application).

This chapter includes information drawn from these sources, but important explanations and additional steps have been added to help the process go more smoothly and to enable the builder to better understand what's transpiring. Because INN must be compiled before installation, this chapter is very detailed. Appendix C contains additional technical information about INN.

Like any project, building INN can be broken down into steps. These steps are:

1. Setting up the Build environment,
2. Getting the source code,
3. Configuring the source code,
4. Compiling and installing the programs,
5. Configuring and installing the INN data files, and
6. Completing miscellaneous tasks.

In the sample configuration being used throughout this section, the INN-based news server is the corporate or main news server and gets its news feed from the ISP. From the point of view of the INN server, the regional DNEWS server is just a news reader. Figure 16-1 illustrates this arrangement.

Figure 16-1 Corporate news topology.

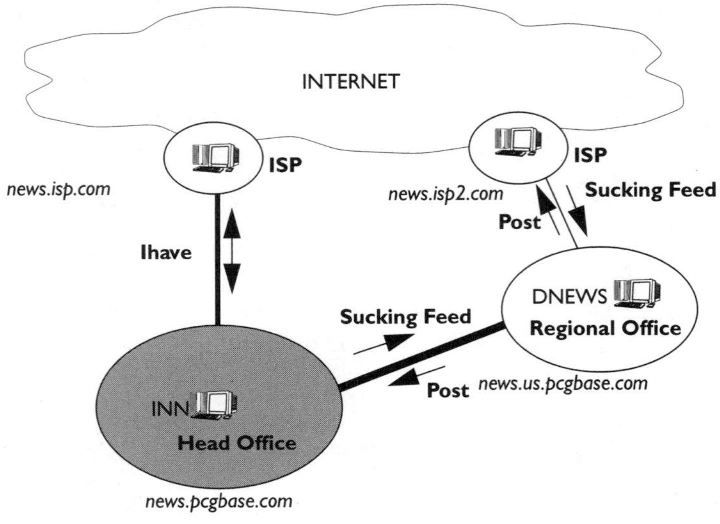

INN is a comprehensive and complex package and, at times, complicated. To fully understand all the intricacies and features of the package requires significant study and experimentation. However, you may never have to go beyond the depth covered in this chapter, which guides the reader through the build and configuration of a news server with basic capability.

The INN primer presented below attempts to compliment this process by presenting the building blocks of INN, the major files and directories involved, and the basic news process. It is by no means intended as an INN treatise.

INN PRIMER

INN is a collection of four modules that together perform and/or direct all the main functions of the news server (see Table 16-1).

Table 16-1 Main Components of INN

INN Module	Functions
INNd (daemon)	Scans port 119 for NNTP connections Handles all incoming news feeds Files and queues up articles for propagation Spawns NNRPd process for news readers
CTLINNd (daemon)	Handles all communication with INNd (such as shutdown, pauses, newsgroup, etc.) Controls the adding and deleting of newsgroups
INNXMIT	Propagates new articles to other news feeds
NNRPd (daemon)	Handles the sending and receiving of articles to and from news readers

Figure 16-2 shows the interaction of the various INN modules. The main data files and directories affected by INN are listed in Table 16-2.

Here's how the news is processed. When an article is received from your upstream news host, the article's corresponding newsgroup is checked against entries in the active file to see if that newsgroup is allowed. If the newsgroup doesn't exist, the article is sent to junk or rejected, depending on site configurations. If it does exist, the article is written into the spool directory with a filename derived from highest article number information contained in the active file entry for that newsgroup. The highest number information in the active file is then incremented by one. An entry is also added to the history file, indicating that the article has been stored in the spool and when. An entry is also made in a batch file for use when feeding other sites. Periodically, the Expire program removes dated articles from the spool directory and also updates the history file. When an article is posted from a local reader, it goes through a similar process.

Figure 16-2 INN architecture.

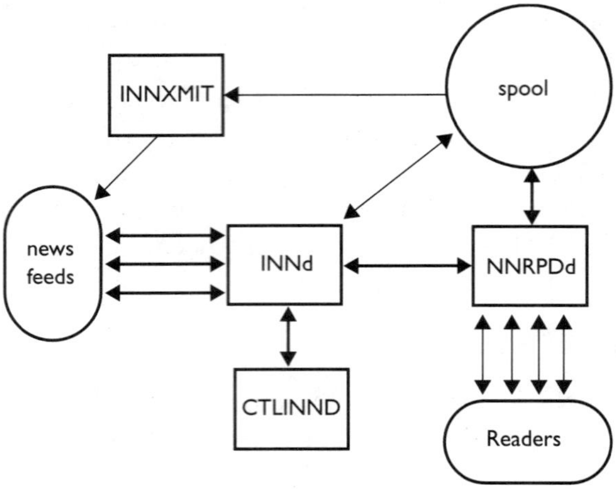

Table 16-2 Major INN Files and Directories

Data	Description
spool	A directory structure matching the newsgroup hierarchies and containing all current articles for this site. The spool directory is created by INN.
active	This file is read into memory at start-up and contains one line with four fields for each newsgroup the server receives. The fields are names of newsgroups, highest and lowest article number, and a flag to control article posting. The article numbers are assigned by the local server as a way of indexing the articles and to create their filenames.
overview	The overview database is a database of files, one for each group, containing a reference to each article, with seven or eight of the most popular headers. These headers can be used by the client news reader to perform article threading.
history	This file keeps a record of all articles currently stored in the news system, as well as those that have been received but have since expired. INNd appends a new line each time it files an article, and Expire builds a new version of the file by removing old articles and purging old entries.

SETTING UP THE BUILD ENVIRONMENT

GNU COMPILER AND UTILITIES

INN will not install or run on Sun SPARCstation under 2.5.1 unless you install some additional software packages and utilities. These utilities are included on the CD-ROM and are listed in Table 16-3.

Table 16-3 Additional Software Required to Run INN

Item	Description
bison	Compiler compiler
flex	Generate programs for lexical tasks
gawk	Pattern scanning and processing language
gcc	C compiler
grep	Global pattern searching
gzip	Compression utility
make	Utility to maintain groups of programs
patch	Utility to apply a different file to the original
PERL	Practical Extraction and Report Language
sed	Stream editor
tar	Tape archive
texinfo	Documentation system

LOADING CD-ROM FILES

It is now time to download the CD-ROM files. The CD-ROM contains many programs such as pre-compiled GNU utilities, INN netnews source, scripts, and so forth. It was created with the directory structure shown in Figure 16-3.

A word of caution: Files downloaded from the CD-ROM may require in excess of 200MB disk space, so check free disk space before proceeding.

Insert the CD-ROM. If the CD-ROM mounts, copy the CD-ROM files and directories to the disk with the following commands:

```
news# cd /cdrom/opt
news# tar cf - . | (cd /opt; tar xBpf -)
```

If the CD-ROM is not mounted, use the following command:

```
news# /usr/sbin/mount -F hsfs -r /dev/dsk/c0t6d0s0 /cdrom
```

After installing the software, you will need to execute the following commands to build *fixed* include files on your system.

```
news# cd /opt/gnu/src/gcc-2.7.2
news# make CC=gcc install
```

ENVIRONMENT VARIABLES

Variables can be set at login time through the start-up file profile.

Figure 16-3 CD-ROM directory structure.

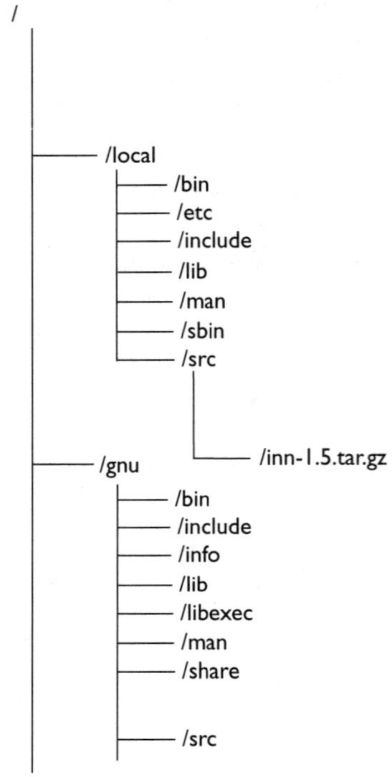

The environment variables of interest are *PATH*, *EDITOR*, *CC*, and *MANPATH*. The *PATH* variable determines which directories will be searched and what order they will be searched in each time you issue a command. If there are two versions of the same program located in separate directories, the program that is specified first in your path environment variable will be run.

The *EDITOR* variable determines which editor will be used when you issue commands such as *crontab -e* to edit the cron file.

The *CC* environment variable will overide any *CC* settings in Make files while compiling. By setting *CC* to **gcc**, you are certain to use the GNU C compiler right from the start.

The *MANPATH* variable specifies the location and search order of man pages.

Following is an example of environment variable settings:

```
PATH=/opt/gnu/bin:/opt/local/bin:/usr/sbin:/usr/openwin/bin:/usr/ccs/bin
PATH=$PATH:/usr/bin:/usr/ucb:/etc:.
export PATH

EDITOR=vi; export EDITOR
CC=gcc; export CC
MANPATH=/opt/gnu/man:/opt/local/man:/usr/news/man:/usr/man;
   export MANPATH
```

GETTING THE SOURCE CODE

The source code is provided on the enclosed CD-ROM and has already been placed on the disk.

As an alternative, if your computer is connected to the Internet and has the operating system installed and configured, you may download the software using FTP from ftp.vix.com. If you are using an HTTP browser, the URL is

```
ftp://ftp.vix.com/pub/inn
```

Example:

```
news# mkdir /opt/local/src
news# cd /opt/local/src
news# ftp ftp.vix.com
Connected to info-sys.home.vix.com.
220 gw.home.vix.com FTP server (Version 5.102 Sat Sep 7 00:50:17 PDT 1996)ready.
Name (ftp.vix.com:jep): ftp
331 Guest login ok, send ident as password.
Password: jep@pcgbase.com
230 Guest login ok, access restrictions apply.
ftp> cd pub/inn
250 CWD command successful.
ftp> bin
200 Type set to I.
ftp> get inn-1.5.1.tar.gz
```

Other programs such as PGP and PERL are required and are also available on the CD-ROM as tar files. The documentation contained in the tar directories for each program directs the user to the appropriate FTP site.

Note that the file inn-1.5.1 may need to be changed depending on what version of INN is being used.

Now uncompress and untar the file using GNU tar. You can make sure GNU tar is the version you are using with the Which command.

```
cd/opt/local/src
news# which tar
/opt/gnu/bin/tar
```

If GNU tar comes up as expected, issue the following command:

```
news# tar xvzf inn-1.5.1.tar.gz
```

This will create a subdirectory named inn-1.5.1 and place all files it it. This directory will be referred to as $inn from now on.

CONFIGURING THE SOURCE CODE

The files in the source distribution are divided into the directories listed in Table 16-4.

Table 16-4 Major INN Directories

Directory	Contents
frontends	Programs to feed articles to INNd and control it
innd	The NNTP server software
backends	Programs to transmit articles to other sites
expire	Programs to expire articles and manage history files
nnrpd	An NNTP server for news readers
lib	Library files
include	Header files
samples	Prototype scripts and configuration files
site	A directory to store scripts and configuration files after they have been customized
doc	Manual pages
config	Tools to configure the source code

Various files will be in the top of the $inn directory structure.

CONFIGURING THE CONFIG.DATA FILE

To begin the configuration, change to the $inn/config directory and copy the substitutions file config.dist to config.data.

```
news# cp config.dist config.data
```

Editing the config.data file is the most difficult task of building INN, because it can require a great deal of modification. In order to make this process easier, a diff file of the author's configuration has been provided. If this is close to your own configuration, then use this diff file to make the majority of the changes automatically, then fine-tune the config.data file to match your system. With this file you can build INN exactly as the authors have done. Here are the commands you'll need to enter:

```
news# cd $inn/config
news# cp config.dist  config.data
news# patch -i config.diff config.date
```

The Patch utility copies the file config.data to config.data.orig and then inserts changes from config.diff. Regardless of whether you choose to use the Patch utility to make the changes automatically, you will probably find it instructive to follow the detailed instructions below, especially if changes are required. But if you anticipate no changes to the config.data file and wish to skip this section altogether, go to the section "Compiling and Installing the Programs," later in this chapter.

Most of the configuration of INN has been automated by using the Subst program developed by Henry Spencer and Geoff Collyer. Subst uses information in a substitutions file (config.data) to make changes in victim files.

The syntax of the substitutions file is

```
parameter <one or more tabs> value.
```

The following text comes from the *INN Manual*:

> The *substitutions* file contains one line per substitution. A line consists of two fields separated by one or more tabs. The first field is the name of the substitution; the second is the value. Neither should contain the character "#," and use of text-editor meta characters like "&" and "\" is also unwise; the name in particular is best restricted to be alphanumeric. A line starting with "#" is a comment and is ignored.

In the *victims*, each line on which a substitution is to be made (a target line) must be preceded by a prototype line. The prototype line should be delimited in such a way that it will be taken as a comment by whatever program processes the file later. The prototype line must contain a "prototype" of the target line bracketed by "=()<" and ">()="; everything else on the prototype line is ignored. *Subst* extracts the prototype, changes all instances of substitution names bracketed by "@<" and ">@" to their values, and then replaces the target line with the result.

Substitutions are done using the *sed* editor, which must be found in either the /bin or /usr/bin directories. To specify a different executable, use the *-e* flag. (Underscores and italics have been added by authors; text is slightly modified.)

In our case, config.data is the substitutions file. The victim files are mostly Make files and header files. Each of the victim files contains target lines preceded by prototye lines.

Remember, if you want to leave a substitution blank, you must still have a name followed by one or more tabs.

A last step before embarking on the tailoring of the config.data file is to print a copy. It will help to have a hard copy you can use as a reference.

The following is the real config.data for Solaris 2.5.1 and GNU GCC. If this matches your environment, you will have to make only a small number of the suggested substitutions. The check mark in the left-hand column denotes that a substitution needs to be made. Carriage returns and additional comments have been added to the file for clarity. Those readers using a different operating system or compiler may have to make more widespread changes.

The config.data file is broken down into the following sections:

1. Make config parameters,
2. Logging levels,
3. Ownerships and file modes,
4. C library differences,
5. C library omissions,

6. Miscellaneous config data,
7. Paths to common programs,
8. Paths related to the spool directory,
9. Execution paths for INNd and Rnews,
10. Sockets created by INNd or clients,
11. Log and config files,
12. Innwatch configuration,
13. TCL configuration,
14. PGP configuration,
15. Local configuration,
16. Actsync configuration, and
17. PERL configuration.

1. MAKE CONFIG PARAMETERS

```
## $Revision: 1.1 $
##
## InterNetNews configuration file.
## Note that if you leave a field blank, you must have the trailing tab!
##

## Where the DBZ sources are, from C News. INN has a (maybe old) copy.
##### =()<DBZDIR      @<DBZDIR>@>()=
DBZDIR                ../dbz
```

Leave the substitution blank. Remember it must have one or more tabs.

```
## If you have a parallel make, set this to "&"
##### =()<P           @<P>@>()=
P
```

This build needed one preprocessor flag added to define the operating system that was being used, SUNOS5.

```
## C pre-processor flags
##### =()<DEFS        @<DEFS>@>()=
DEFS                  -I../include -DSUNOS5
```

Here the GNU C compiler is chosen. It was also set with the CC Environment variable so GCC would be used to build the Subst program before this substitutions file could be parsed.

```
## C compiler
##### =()<CC               @<CC>@>()=
CC                        gcc

## Does your compiler properly do "char const *"? Pick DO DONT or DUNNO
##### =()<USE_CHAR_CONST@<USE_CHAR_CONST>@>()=
USE_CHAR_CONST            DO

## C compiler flags
##### =()<CFLAGS           @<CFLAGS>@>()=
CFLAGS                    $(DEFS) -O2

## C compiler flags to use when compiling dbz
##### =()<DBZCFLAGS        @<DBZCFLAGS>@>()=
DBZCFLAGS                 $(CFLAGS)

## What flags to use if profiling; -p or -pg, e.g.
##### =()<PROF             @<PROF>@>()=
PROF                      -pg

## Flags for the "cc -o" line; e.g., -Bstatic on SunOS4.x while debugging.
##### =()<LDFLAGS          @<LDFLAGS>@>()=
LDFLAGS

## If you use the standard NNTP way of connecting, where is the library?
##### =()<NNTPLIB          @<NNTPLIB>@>()=
NNTPLIB

## If you need to link in other libraries, add them here
##### =()<LIBS             @<LIBS>@>()=
LIBS                      -lsocket -lnsl -lelf

## How to make a lint library; pick BSD, SYSV, or NONE.
##### =()<LINTLIBSTYLE     @<LINTLIBSTYLE>@>()=
LINTLIBSTYLE              NONE

## Flags for lint. AIX wants "-wkD"; it and others don't want "-z".
##### =()<LINTFLAGS        @<LINTFLAGS>@>()=
LINTFLAGS                 -b -h -z $(DEFS)

## Some lints insist on putting out the filename and other stuff.
## Possible values:
##                        LINTFILTER        | sed -n -f ../sedf.aix
##                        LINTFILTER        | sed -n -f ../sedf.osx
##                        LINTFILTER        | sed -n -f ../sedf.sun
##                        LINTFILTER        | sed -n -f ../sedf.sysv
##                        LINTFILTER
```

```
#### =()<LINTFILTER                    @<LINTFILTER>@>()=
LINTFILTER

## How to install manpages; pick SOURCE, NROFF-PACK, NROFF-PACK-SCO,
## BSD4.4 or NONE.
#### =()<MANPAGESTYLE       @<MANPAGESTYLE>@>()=
MANPAGESTYLE               SOURCE

## Where various manpages should go
#### =()<MAN1               @<MAN1>@>()=
MAN1                       /usr/news/man/man1

#### =()<MAN3               @<MAN3>@>()=
MAN3                       /usr/news/man/man3

#### =()<MAN5               @<MAN5>@>()=
MAN5                       /usr/news/man/man5

#### =()<MAN8               @<MAN8>@>()=
MAN8                       /usr/news/man/man8

## Ranlib command.  Use echo if you don't need ranlib.
#### =()<RANLIB             @<RANLIB>@>()=
RANLIB                     echo

## YACC (yet another config control?)
#### =()<YACC               @<YACC>@>()=
YACC                       yacc

## Ctags command.  Use echo if you don't have ctags.
#### =()<CTAGS              @<CTAGS>@>()=
CTAGS                      ctags -t -w
```

2. Logging Levels

Solaris 2.5.1 provides the modern *syslog* that separated messages into both levels and categories. A quick Grep of the syslog.H file shows it also supports news.

```
news #grep -i news /usr/include/sys/syslog.h

##
## 2. LOGGING LEVELS
## Facility innd should log under.
#### =()<LOG_INN_SERVER@<LOG_INN_SERVER>@>()=
LOG_INN_SERVER          LOG_NEWS

## Facility all other programs should log under.
```

```
##### =()<LOG_INN_PROG    @<LOG_INN_PROG>@>()=
LOG_INN_PROG             LOG_NEWS

## Flags to use in opening the logs; some programs add LOG_PID.
##### =()<L_OPENLOG_FLAGS    @<L_OPENLOG_FLAGS>@>()=
L_OPENLOG_FLAGS            (LOG_CONS | LOG_NDELAY)

## Log a fatal error; program is about to exit.
##### =()<L_FATAL       @<L_FATAL>@>()=
L_FATAL               LOG_CRIT
## Log an error that might mean one or more articles get lost.
##### =()<L_ERROR       @<L_ERROR>@>()=
L_ERROR               LOG_ERR

## Informational notice, usually not worth caring about.
##### =()<L_NOTICE      @<L_NOTICE>@>()=
L_NOTICE              LOG_WARNING

## A protocol trace.
##### =()<L_TRACE       @<L_TRACE>@>()=
L_TRACE               LOG_DEBUG

## All incoming control commands (ctlinnd, etc).
##### =()<L_CC_CMD      @<L_CC_CMD>@>()=
L_CC_CMD              LOG_INFO
```

Only INNd, the NNTP server, needs to run as the root directory. It has to open a reserved port (119), which requires root access. The other programs will run under the *user id* and *group id* placed here. You will put an alias in the /etc/aliases file to tell the system where you want mail sent to *news* or *newsmaster* to go.

3. OWNERSHIP AND FILE MODES

```
##
## 3. OWNERSHIPS AND FILE MODES
## Owner of articles and directories and _PATH_INNDDIR
##### =()<NEWSUSER      @<NEWSUSER>@>()=
NEWSUSER              news

## Group, for same purpose
##### =()<NEWSGROUP     @<NEWSGROUP>@>()=
NEWSGROUP             news

## Who gets email about control messages? (Usually same as NEWSUSER)
##### =()<NEWSMASTER          @<NEWSMASTER>@>()=
```

```
NEWSMASTER                      newsmaster

## Who gets email on the Path line?
#### =()<PATHMASTER            @<PATHMASTER>@>()=
PATHMASTER                      not-for-mail

## Umask to set.
#### =()<NEWSUMASK             @<NEWSUMASK>@>()=
NEWSUMASK                       02

## Mode that incoming articles are created under.
#### =()<ARTFILE_MODE          @<ARTFILE_MODE>@>()=
ARTFILE_MODE                    0664

## Mode that batch files are created under.
#### =()<BATCHFILE_MODE        @<BATCHFILE_MODE>@>()=
BATCHFILE_MODE                  0664

## Mode that directories are created under.
#### =()<GROUPDIR_MODE         @<GROUPDIR_MODE>@>()=
GROUPDIR_MODE                   0775
```

4. C Library Differences

Although it is beyond the scope of the book to explain the C language with its compilers and libraries of functions, a brief description of functions, including files (header files) and libraries will help explain the choices that come up in the following section.

A *function* is a self-contained piece of code with a name. The statements in the function are designed to perform a very specific task such as return an average of numbers. Once the function has been designed and tested, it can be placed in a library file and used by a program when it is compiled.

A library file of functions usually begins with a lib prefix and an .a file extension. For example, the INN library file is libinn.a. Library files either are provided with the C compiler or can be created by compiling the source code and using the Ar command to create the library file.

In order to make these functions available to your program, you need to define them first. Function definitions are usually placed in Include or Header files and incorporated into the source when it is compiled. The C language has an Include directive that lets a preprocessor incorporate the contents of a specified file when source code is compiled. These Include or header files are specified with an .h file extension and are located in the include directories.

```
(/usr/include
/opt/gnu/include
/opt/local/include)
```

The basic questions in this next section focus on discovering whether or not your system provides certain functions in its library files or whether your system has the necessary Include or header files to define the functions included with the INN distribution.

Here are two quick ways to determine whether your system has the necessary function, file, or library asked about below:

- If the question is whether you have something.*h*, look for the file with the same name in the Include directories.
- If the question is whether you have a *function*, or something about a function, Grep the man pages for the function itself or another function that uses it.

For example:

```
news# ls -l /usr/include/string.h
/usr/include/string.h
news#

news# grep -i offset_t /usr/man/*/*

If the grep returns "Arguments too long" you can feed it files one at a time
with the following command

news# find /usr/man -print | xargs grep -i offset_t

## 4. C LIBRARY DIFFERENCES
##
## Use stdargs, varargs, or neither? Pick VARARGS STDARGS or NONE.
## You need vfprintf and vfsprintf if not NONE.
#### =()<VAR_STYLE      @<VAR_STYLE>@>()=
VAR_STYLE               STDARGS

## If you don't have <string.h>, set this to "mystring.h"
```

```
##### =()<STR_HEADER                @<STR_HEADER>@>()=
STR_HEADER                          <string.h>

## If you don't have <memory.h>, set this to "mymemory.h"
##### =()<MEM_HEADER                @<MEM_HEADER>@>()=
MEM_HEADER                          <memory.h>

## What is a file offset?  Usually long or off_t.  *Must be long for now!*
##### =()<OFFSET_T                  @<OFFSET_T>@>()=
OFFSET_T                            long

## What is the type of an object size? Usually size_t or unsigned int.
##### =()<SIZE_T                    @<SIZE_T>@>()=
SIZE_T                              size_t

## What is the type of a passwd uid and gid, for use in chown(2)?
##### =()<UID_T                     @<UID_T>@>()=
UID_T                               uid_t

##### =()<GID_T                     @<GID_T>@>()=
GID_T                               gid_t

## Type of a pid, for use in kill(2).
##### =()<PID_T                     @<PID_T>@>()=
PID_T                               pid_t

## Generic pointer, used by memcpy, malloc, etc.  Usually char or void.
##### =()<POINTER                   @<POINTER>@>()=
POINTER                             void

## Worst-case alignment, in order to shut lint up
##### =()<ALIGNPTR                  @<ALIGNPTR>@>()=
ALIGNPTR                            long

## What should a signal handler return?  Usually int or void.
##### =()<SIGHANDLER                @<SIGHANDLER>@>()=
SIGHANDLER                          void

## Type of variables can be modified in a signal handler? sig_atomic_t
##### =()<SIGVAR                    @<SIGVAR>@>()=
SIGVAR                              sig_atomic_t

## Function that returns no value, and a pointer to it.  Pick int or void
##### =()<FUNCTYPE                  @<FUNCTYPE>@>()=
FUNCTYPE                            void
```

```
## Type of 32 bit unsigned integer.
##### =()<U_INT32_T        @<U_INT_T>@>()=
U_INT32_T                 unsigned int

## Type of 32 bit signed integer.
##### =()INT32_T          @<INT_T>@>()=
U_INT32_T                 int

## Use BSD4.2 or Posix directory names? Pick DIRENT or DIRECT.
##### =()<DIR_STYLE       @<DIR_STYLE>@>()=
DIR_STYLE                 DIRENT

## Use flock, lockf, or nothing to lock files?
## Pick FLOCK, LOCKF, FCNTL, or NONE
##### =()<LOCK_STYLE             @<LOCK_STYLE>@>()=
LOCK_STYLE                       FCNTL

## Do you have <unistd.h>? Pick DO or DONT
##### =()<HAVE_UNISTD @<HAVE_UNISTD>@>()=
HAVE_UNISTD                      DO

## Do you have setbuffer? Pick DO or DONT.
##### =()<HAVE_SETBUFFER         @<HAVE_SETBUFFER>@>()=
HAVE_SETBUFFER                   DO

## Do you have gettimeofday? Pick DO or DONT.
##### =()<HAVE_GETTIMEOFDAY  @<HAVE_GETTIMEOFDAY>@>()=
HAVE_GETTIMEOFDAY                DO

## Do you have setproctitle()? Pick DO or DONT.
##You may have to adjust LIBS for this.
##### =()<HAVE_SETPROCTITLE      @<HAVE_SETPROCTITLE>@>()=
HAVE_SETPROCTITLE                DONT

## Do you have fchmod? Pick DO or DONT.
##### =()<HAVE_FCHMOD            @<HAVE_FCHMOD>@>()=
HAVE_FCHMOD                      DO

## Do you have setsid()? Pick DO or DONT.
##### =()<HAVE_SETSID            @<HAVE_SETSID>@>()=
HAVE_SETSID                      DO

## Does your (struct tm) have a tm_gmtoff field? Pick DO or DONT.
##### =()<HAVE_TM_GMTOFF         @<HAVE_TM_GMTOFF>@>()=
HAVE_TM_GMTOFF                   DONT
```

```
## Does your (struct stat) have a st_blksize field?  Pick DO or DONT.
##### =()<HAVE_ST_BLKSIZE        @<HAVE_ST_BLKSIZE>@>()=
HAVE_ST_BLKSIZE                  DO

## Use waitpid instead of wait3?  Pick DO or DONT.
##### =()<HAVE_WAITPID           @<HAVE_WAITPID>@>()=
HAVE_WAITPID                     DO

## Use "union wait" instead of int?  Pick DO or DONT.
##### =()<USE_UNION_WAIT         @<USE_UNION_WAIT>@>()=
USE_UNION_WAIT                   DONT

## How to fork?  Pick fork or vfork.
##### =()<FORK                   @<FORK>@>()=
FORK                             fork

## Do you have <vfork.h>?  Pick DO or DONT.
##### =()<HAVE_VFORK             @<HAVE_VFORK>@>()=
HAVE_VFORK                       DONT

## Do you have symbolic links?  Pick DO or DONT.
##### =()<HAVE_SYMLINK           @<HAVE_SYMLINK>@>()=
HAVE_SYMLINK                     DO

## Do you have Unix-domain sockets?  Pick DO or DONT.
##### =()<HAVE_UNIX_DOMAIN       @<HAVE_UNIX_DOMAIN>@>()=
HAVE_UNIX_DOMAIN                 DO

## Does your AF_UNIX bind use sizeof for the socket size?  Pick DO or DONT.
##### =()<BIND_USE_SIZEOF        @<BIND_USE_SIZEOF>@>()=
BIND_USE_SIZEOF                  DONT

## How should close-on-exec be done?  Pick IOCTL or FCNTL.
##### =()<CLX_STYLE              @<CLX_STYLE>@>()=
CLX_STYLE                        FCNTL

## How should non-blocking I/O be done?  Pick IOCTL or FCNTL.
##### =()<NBIO_STYLE             @<NBIO_STYLE>@>()=
NBIO_STYLE                       FCNTL

## How should resource-totalling be done?  Pick RUSAGE or TIMES
##### =()<RES_STYLE              @<RES_STYLE>@>()=
RES_STYLE                        TIMES

## How to get number of available descriptors?
## Pick GETDTAB, GETRLIMIT, SYSCONF, ULIMIT, or CONSTANT.
##### =()<FDCOUNT_STYLE          @<FDCOUNT_STYLE>@>()=
FDCOUNT_STYLE                    SYSCONF
```

```
## If greater than -1, then use [gs]etrlimit to set that many descriptors.
## If -1, then no [gs]etrlimit calls are done.
##### =()<NOFILE_LIMIT              @<NOFILE_LIMIT>@>()=
NOFILE_LIMIT                        -1

## Do you need <time.h> as well as <sys/time.h>? Pick DO or DONT.
##### =()<NEED_TIME                 @<NEED_TIME>@>()=
NEED_TIME                           DONT

## What predicate, if any, the <ctype.h> macros need
##### =()<CTYPE                     @<CTYPE>@>()=
#CTYPE                              (isascii((c)) && isXXXXX((c)))
#CTYPE                              ((c) > 0 && isXXXXX((c)))
CTYPE                               isXXXXX((c))

## What's the return type of abort? Usually int or void.
##### =()<ABORTVAL                  @<ABORTVAL>@>()=
ABORTVAL                            void

## What's the return type of alarm? Usually int or unsigned int.
##### =()<ALARMVAL                  @<ALARMVAL>@>()=
ALARMVAL                            unsigned int

## What's the return type of getpid? Usually int or unsigned int.
##### =()<GETPIDVAL                 @<GETPIDVAL>@>()=
GETPIDVAL                           pid_t

## What's the return type of sleep? Usually int or unsigned int.
##### =()<SLEEPVAL                  @<SLEEPVAL>@>()=
SLEEPVAL                            unsigned

## What's the return type of  qsort? Usually int or void.
##### =()<QSORTVAL                  @<QSORTVAL>@>()=
QSORTVAL                            void

## What's the return type of lseek? Usually long or off_t.
##### =()<LSEEKVAL                  @<LSEEKVAL>@>()=
LSEEKVAL                            off_t

## What's the return type of free? Usually int or void.
##### =()<FREEVAL                   @<FREEVAL>@>()=
FREEVAL                             void

## What's the return type of exit? Usually int or void.
## (For gcc (not pedantic ANSI) use "volatile void" in EXITVAL and _EXITVAL.)
##### =()<EXITVAL                   @<EXITVAL>@>()=
EXITVAL                             void
```

```
## What's the return type of _exit? Usually int or void.
##### =()<_EXITVAL              @<_EXITVAL>@>()=
_EXITVAL                        void
```

5. C Library Omissions

There are no "missing libraries" in the Solaris 2.5.1 operating system as far as INN is concerned.

```
##
## 5. C LIBRARY OMISSIONS

## Possible values:
##          MISSING_MAN         strcasecmp.3 syslog.3
##          MISSING_SRC         strcasecmp.c syslog.c strerror.c getdtab.c
##          MISSING_OBJ         strcasecmp.o syslog.o strerror.o getdtab.c
## getdtab has a getdtablesize() routine if you need it; see the lib
## directory and Install.ms for others.
## OSx systems should add $(OSXATTOBJ) to MISSING_OBJ.
##### =()<MISSING_MAN           @<MISSING_MAN>@>()=
MISSING_MAN
##### =()<MISSING_SRC           @<MISSING_SRC>@>()=
MISSING_SRC
##### =()<MISSING_OBJ           @<MISSING_OBJ>@>()=
MISSING_OBJ
```

6. Miscellaneous Config Data

The parameters in this section become macros in the file include/configdata.h. Examine them and tailor them to your site.

One interesting new parameter is the new Like_pullers parameter. This deals with the new application Suck, which, as of this writing, was at version 3.2.1. Suck contains software for copying news from an NNTP server to your local machine, and copying replies back up to an NNTP server. This allows someone to get a news feed with only reader permissions.

Imagine a university news server set up to handle 1,000 news readers that will transfer only a few articles at a time. Now if several of those readers act like servers by sucking full news feeds, the machine will become overloaded. But if the Like_pullers parameter is set to **dont**, a small sleep (delay) will be inserted before each article command is processed, and this lag time may be enough of a disincentive for the wayward readers to cease from sucking full news feeds.

```
##
## 6. MISCELLANEOUS CONFIG DATA

##
## Use read/write to update the active file, or mmap? Pick READ or MMAP.
##### =()<ACT_STYLE                @<ACT_STYLE>@>()=
ACT_STYLE                         MMAP

## Do you want mail notifications of bad control messages. DO or DONT.
## Setting it to DO results in a lot of mail due to the numbers of spammers
## out there.
##### =()<MAIL_BADCONTROLS         @<MAIL_BADCONTROLS>@>()=
MAIL_BADCONTROLS                  DONT

## What type of pointer does mmap() manage? Normally ``caddr_t" or ``void *"
## or ``char *"
##### =()<MMAP_PTR                 @<MMAP_PTR>@>()=
MMAP_PTR                          caddr_t

## Should we msync when using mmap. DO or DONT. Useful
## with some slightly broken mmap implementations (like HPUX and BSD/ODS).
##### =()<MMAP_SYNC                @<MMAP_SYNC>@>()=
MMAP_SYNC                         DONT

## Should we call your msync() with 3 args? (addr, len, flags)
## Choose DO or DONT.
##### =()<MSYNC_3_ARG              @<MSYNC_3_ARG>@>()=
MSYNC_3_ARG                       DONT

## Do clients use our NNTP-server-open routine, or the one in NNTP?
## INND is nicer, but you must install inn.conf files everywhere; NNTP
## is better if you already have lots of /usr/lib/news/server files.
## Pick INND or NNTP.
##### =()<REM_STYLE                @<REM_STYLE>@>()=
REM_STYLE                         INND

## Should rnews save articles that the server rejects? Pick DO or DONT.
##### =()<RNEWS_SAVE_BAD           @<RNEWS_SAVE_BAD>@>()=
RNEWS_SAVE_BAD                    DONT

## Should rnews log articles innd already has? Pick SYSLOG, FILE, OR DONT.
##### =()<RNEWS_LOG_DUPS           @<RNEWS_LOG_DUPS>@>()=
RNEWS_LOG_DUPS                    DONT

## Look in _PATH_RNEWSPROGS for rnews unpackers? Pick DO or DONT.
##### =()<RNEWSPROGS               @<RNEWSPROGS>@>()=
RNEWSPROGS                        DO
```

```
## Should rnews try the local host? Pick DO or DONT.
##### =()<RNEWSLOCALCONNECT      @<RNEWSLOCALCONNECT>@>()=
RNEWSLOCALCONNECT                DO

## Environment variable that has remote hostname for rnews.
##### =()<_ENV_UUCPHOST      @<_ENV_UUCPHOST>@>()=
_ENV_UUCPHOST                UU_MACHINE

## Require posts to have under 50% inclusion (">") lines? Pick DO OR DONT.
## (This is only for inews and nnrpd.)
##### =()<CHECK_INCLUDED_TEXT    @<CHECK_INCLUDED_TEXT>@>()=
CHECK_INCLUDED_TEXT              DONT

## Put hosts in the inews Path header? Pick DO or DONT.
##### =()<INEWS_PATH             @<INEWS_PATH>@>()=
INEWS_PATH                       DONT

## Munge the gecos field of password entry? Pick DO or DONT.
##### =()<MUNGE_GECOS            @<MUNGE_GECOS>@>()=
MUNGE_GECOS                      DO

## How many times to try to fork before giving up
##### =()<MAX_FORKS              @<MAX_FORKS>@>()=
MAX_FORKS                        10

## Largest acceptable article size; 0 allows any size
##### =()<MAX_ART_SIZE           @<MAX_ART_SIZE>@>()=
MAX_ART_SIZE                     1000000

## Value of dbzincore(FLAG) call in innd. Pick 1 or 0.
##### =()<INND_DBZINCORE         @<INND_DBZINCORE>@>()=
INND_DBZINCORE                   1

## Should subprocesses get a nice(2) value? Pick DO or DONT.
##### =()<INND_NICE_KIDS         @<INND_NICE_KIDS>@>()=
INND_NICE_KIDS                   DO
## Value for nice(2) call in innd.

##### =()<INND_NICE_VALUE            @<INND_NICE_VALUE>@>()=
INND_NICE_VALUE                      4

## Null-terminated list of unknown commands to not log to syslog.
##        INND_QUIET_BADLIST          "xstream", "xfoo", NULL
##### =()<INND_QUIET_BADLIST          @<INND_QUIET_BADLIST>@>()=
INND_QUIET_BADLIST                    NULL
```

```
## Null-terminated set of illegal distribution patterns for local postings.
##### =()<BAD_DISTRIBS            @<BAD_DISTRIBS>@>()=
BAD_DISTRIBS                     "*.*",NULL

## Verify that the poster is the person doing the cancel? Pick DO or DONT.
## (Can't do this if cancel arrives before the article does, by the way.)
##### =()<VERIFY_CANCELS          @<VERIFY_CANCELS>@>()=
VERIFY_CANCELS                   DO

## Log "ctlinnd cancel" commands to syslog? Pick DO or DONT.
##### =()<LOG_CANCEL_COMMANDS
@<LOG_CANCEL_COMMANDS>@>()=
LOG_CANCEL_COMMANDS              DO

## File unknown "to.*" groups into the "to" newsgroup? Pick DO or DONT.
##### =()<MERGE_TO_GROUPS         @<MERGE_TO_GROUPS>@>()=
MERGE_TO_GROUPS                  DONT

## File articles in unknown newsgroups into junk? Pick DO or DONT.
##### =()<WANT_TRASH              @<WANT_TRASH>@>()=
WANT_TRASH                       DO

## Record rejected articles in history? Pick DO or DONT.
##### =()<REMEMBER_TRASH          @<REMEMBER_TRASH>@>()=
REMEMBER_TRASH                   DO

## Check the linecount against the Lines header? Pick DO or DONT.
##### =()<CHECK_LINECOUNT         @<CHECK_LINECOUNT>@>()=
CHECK_LINECOUNT                  DONT

## If checking, the error must be within LINECOUNT_FUZZ lines.
## Five is number of .signature lines + 1.
##### =()<LINECOUNT_FUZZ          @<LINECOUNT_FUZZ>@>()=
LINECOUNT_FUZZ                   5

## Have innd throttle itself after this many I/O errors.
##### =()<IO_ERROR_COUNT          @<IO_ERROR_COUNT>@>()=
IO_ERROR_COUNT                   50

## Default value for ctlinnd -t flag; use 0 to wait and poll.
##### =()<CTLINND_TIMEOUT         @<CTLINND_TIMEOUT>@>()=
CTLINND_TIMEOUT                  0

## Flush logs if we go this long with no I/O.
##### =()<DEFAULT_TIMEOUT         @<DEFAULT_TIMEOUT>@>()=
DEFAULT_TIMEOUT                  300
```

```
## INND closes channel if inactive this long (seconds).
##### =()<PEER_TIMEOUT        @<PEER_TIMEOUT>@>()=
PEER_TIMEOUT                  (1 * 60 * 60)

## NNRP exits if first command doesn't arrive within this time (seconds).
##### =()<INIT_CLIENT_TIMEOUT     @<INIT_CLIENT_TIMEOUT>@>()=
INIT_CLIENT_TIMEOUT               30

## NNRP exits if inactive for this long (seconds).
##### =()<CLIENT_TIMEOUT     @<CLIENT_TIMEOUT>@>()=
CLIENT_TIMEOUT               (10 * 60)

## Allow nnrpd readers when paused or throttled? Pick DO or DONT.
##### =()<ALLOW_READERS     @<ALLOW_READERS>@>()=
ALLOW_READERS               DO

## Refuse newsreader connections if load is higher then this; -1 disables.
##### =()<NNRP_LOADLIMIT     @<NNRP_LOADLIMIT>@>()=
NNRP_LOADLIMIT               16

## Don't readdir() spool dir if same group within this many secs.
##### =()<NNRP_RESCAN_DELAY     @<NNRP_RESCAN_DELAY>@>()=
NNRP_RESCAN_DELAY               60

## Do gethostbyaddr on client adresses in nnrp? Pick DO or DONT.
## (If DONT, then use only IP addresses in hosts.nnrp)
##### =()<NNRP_GETHOSTBYADDR     @<NNRP_GETHOSTBYADDR>@>()=
NNRP_GETHOSTBYADDR               DO

## How many Message-ID retrievals until nnrpd does a dbzincore? Set
## to -1 to never do incore.
##### =()<NNRP_DBZINCORE_DELAY     @<NNRP_DBZINCORE_DELAY>@>()=
NNRP_DBZINCORE_DELAY               40

## Strip Sender from posts that didn't authenticate? Pick DO or DONT.
##### =()<NNRP_AUTH_SENDER     @<NNRP_AUTH_SENDER>@>()=
NNRP_AUTH_SENDER               DONT

## Do you want to make life easy for peers to pull feeds from you (it's
## harder on your machine). Pick DO or DONT. With DONT, you get a small
## sleep inserted before each ARTICLE command is processed. (With
## apologies to the Australians in the audience.)
##### =()<LIKE_PULLERS     @<LIKE_PULLERS>@>()=
LIKE_PULLERS               DO
```

```
## Allow the NEWNEWS NNTP command?   Pick DO or DONT.
## (RFC 977 says you should; your server performance may not agree...)
##### =()<ALLOW_NEWNEWS            @<ALLOW_NEWNEWS>@>()=
ALLOW_NEWNEWS                      DONT

## How many read/write failures until channel is put to sleep or closed?
##### =()<BAD_IO_COUNT       @<BAD_IO_COUNT>@>()=
BAD_IO_COUNT                 5

## Multiplier for sleep in EWOULDBLOCK writes (seconds).
##### =()<BLOCK_BACKOFF      @<BLOCK_BACKOFF>@>()=
BLOCK_BACKOFF                (2 * 60)

## How many article-writes between active and history updates?
##### =()<ICD_SYNC_COUNT     @<ICD_SYNC_COUNT>@>()=
ICD_SYNC_COUNT               10

## Tell resolver _res.options to be fast?  Pick DO or DONT.
##### =()<FAST_RESOLV        @<FAST_RESOLV>@>()=
FAST_RESOLV                  DONT

## Drop articles that were posted this many days ago.
##### =()<DEFAULT_CUTOFF     @<DEFAULT_CUTOFF>@>()=
DEFAULT_CUTOFF               14

## Maximum number of incoming NNTP connections.
##### =()<DEFAULT_CONNECTIONS        @<DEFAULT_CONNECTIONS>@>()=
DEFAULT_CONNECTIONS                  50

## Wait this many seconds before channel restarts.
##### =()<CHANNEL_RETRY_TIME         @<CHANNEL_RETRY_TIME>@>()=
CHANNEL_RETRY_TIME                   (5 * 60)

## Wait this many seconds before seeing if pause is ended.
##### =()<PAUSE_RETRY_TIME      @<PAUSE_RETRY_TIME>@>()=
PAUSE_RETRY_TIME                (5 * 60)

## Wait this many seconds between noticing inactive channels.
##### =()<CHANNEL_INACTIVE_TIME      @<CHANNEL_INACTIVE_TIME>@>()=
CHANNEL_INACTIVE_TIME                (10 * 60)

## Put nntplink info (filename) into the log?
##### =()<NNTPLINK_LOG       @<NNTPLINK_LOG>@>()=
NNTPLINK_LOG                 DONT

## Put article size into the log?
##### =()<LOG_SIZE     @<LOG_SIZE>@>()=
LOG_SIZE               DO
```

```
## Log by host IP address, rather than from Path line?
##### =()<IPADDR_LOG          @<IPADDR_LOG>@>()=
IPADDR_LOG                    DO

## Log NNTP activity after this many articles.
##### =()<NNTP_ACTIVITY_SYNC          @<NNTP_ACTIVITY_SYNC>@>()=
NNTP_ACTIVITY_SYNC                    200

## Free buffers bigger than this when we're done with them.
##### =()<BIG_BUFFER          @<BIG_BUFFER>@>()=
BIG_BUFFER                    (2 * START_BUFF_SIZE)

## A general small buffer.
##### =()<SMBUF          @<SMBUF>@>()=
SMBUF                    256

## Buffer for a single article name.
##### =()<MAXARTFNAME          @<MAXARTFNAME>@>()=
MAXARTFNAME                    10

## Buffer for a single pathname in the spool directory.
##### =()<SPOOLNAMEBUFF          @<SPOOLNAMEBUFF>@>()=
SPOOLNAMEBUFF                    512

## Maximum size of a single header.
##### =()<MAXHEADERSIZE          @<MAXHEADERSIZE>@>()=
MAXHEADERSIZE                    1024

## Byte limit on locally-posted articles; 0 to disable the check.
##### =()<LOCAL_MAX_ARTSIZE          @<LOCAL_MAX_ARTSIZE>@>()=
LOCAL_MAX_ARTSIZE                    1000000

## Default number of bytes to hold in memory when buffered.
##### =()<SITE_BUFFER_SIZE          @<SITE_BUFFER_SIZE>@>()=
SITE_BUFFER_SIZE                    (16 * 1024)

## Do you have uustat, or just uuq?  Pick DO or DONT
##### =()<HAVE_UUSTAT          @<HAVE_UUSTAT>@>()=
HAVE_UUSTAT                    DO

## Should INN do some setsockopts on network connections. Pick DO or DONT.
## Some versions of Solaris should set to DONT (pre 2.4 it seems)
##### =()<SET_SOCKOPT          @<SET_SOCKOPT>@>()=
SET_SOCKOPT                    DO
```

7. PATHS TO COMMON PROGRAMS

If your news server has more than one disk drive, you can distribute the news application and data files across multiple spindles. This will bring an increase in performance by helping to avoid disk contention. Refer to the Site Worksheet (Table 13-1) for the value to plug in for the Path parameters.

```
##
## 7. PATHS TO COMMON PROGRAMS

## Where the raison d'etre for this distribution lives.
##### =()<_PATH_INND             @<_PATH_INND>@>()=
_PATH_INND                       /usr/news/bin/innd

## Where the optional front-end that exec's innd lives.
##### =()<_PATH_INNDSTART        @<_PATH_INNDSTART>@>()=
_PATH_INNDSTART                  /usr/news/bin/inndstart

## Where news boot-up script should be installed.
##### =()<_PATH_NEWSBOOT         @<_PATH_NEWSBOOT>@>()=
_PATH_NEWSBOOT                   /usr/news/bin/rc.news

## Where sendmail, or a look-alike, lives.
## The -t is optional and says to read message for recipients
##### =()<_PATH_SENDMAIL         @<_PATH_SENDMAIL>@>()=
_PATH_SENDMAIL                   /usr/lib/sendmail

## Where the shell is.
##### =()<_PATH_SH               @<_PATH_SH>@>()=
_PATH_SH                         /bin/sh

## Where the compress program lives.
##### =()<_PATH_COMPRESS         @<_PATH_COMPRESS>@>()=
_PATH_COMPRESS                   /opt/gnu/bin/gzip

## What extension your compress appends
##### =()<_PATH_COMPRESSEXT      @<_PATH_COMPRESSEXT>@>()=
_PATH_COMPRESSEXT                .gz

## Where egrep lives (you might need the FSF one; see scanlogs)
##### =()<_PATH_EGREP            @<_PATH_EGREP>@>()=
_PATH_EGREP                      /opt/local/bin/egrep

## Where perl lives
##### =()<_PATH_PERL             @<_PATH_PERL>@>()=
_PATH_PERL                       /opt/gnu/bin/perl
```

```
## Where awk lives
#### =()<_PATH_AWK                @<_PATH_AWK>@>()=
_PATH_AWK                         /usr/bin/awk

## Where sed lives (you might need the FSF one)
#### =()<_PATH_SED                @<_PATH_SED>@>()=
_PATH_SED                         /opt/gnu/bin/sed

## Where sort lives (you may want the FSF one).
#### =()<_PATH_SORT               @<_PATH_SORT>@>()=
_PATH_SORT                        /usr/bin/sort

## Where inews lives.
#### =()<_PATH_INEWS              @<_PATH_INEWS>@>()=
_PATH_INEWS                       /usr/news/bin/inews

## Where rnews lives.
#### =()<_PATH_RNEWS              @<_PATH_RNEWS>@>()=
_PATH_RNEWS                       /usr/news/bin/rnews

## Where generic authentication programs live.
#### =()<_PATH_AUTHDIR            @<_PATH_AUTHDIR>@>()=
_PATH_AUTHDIR                     /usr/news/bin/auth

## Where the NNRP server lives.
#### =()<_PATH_NNRPD              @<_PATH_NNRPD>@>()=
_PATH_NNRPD                       /usr/news/bin/nnrpd

## The path of the process run when an unknown host connects to innd.
## Usually the same as _PATH_NNRPD, but may be, e.g., the path to
## nntpd from the reference implementation.
#### =()<_PATH_NNTPD              @<_PATH_NNTPD>@>()=
_PATH_NNTPD                       /usr/news/bin/nnrpd

## Where the NNQR server lives. Make same as _PATH_NNRPD for now
#### =()<_PATH_NNQRD              @<_PATH_NNRPD>@>()=
_PATH_NNQRD                       /usr/news/bin/nnrpd

## Where most other programs live.
## See also _PATH_RNEWSPROGS and _PATH_CONTROLPROGS, below.
#### =()<_PATH_NEWSBIN            @<_PATH_NEWSBIN>@>()=
_PATH_NEWSBIN                     /usr/news/bin

## Where temporary files live on the server
#### =()<_PATH_TMP                @<_PATH_TMP>@>()=
_PATH_TMP                         /var/tmp
```

```
## Command to send mail (with -s "subject" allowed)
##### =()<_PATH_MAILCMD              @<_PATH_MAILCMD>@>()=
_PATH_MAILCMD                        /usr/ucb/mail
```

```
## Where scripts should have shlock create locks.
##### =()<_PATH_LOCKS                @<_PATH_LOCKS>@>()=
_PATH_LOCKS                          /usr/news/locks
```

```
## Where your GNU gzip binary is (for rnews to run on gzipped batches).
##### =()<_PATH_GZIP                 @<_PATH_GZIP>@>()=
_PATH_GZIP                           /opt/gnu/bin/gzip
```

8. PATHS RELATED TO THE SPOOL DIRECTORY

```
##
## 8. PATHS RELATED TO THE SPOOL DIRECTORY
## Spool directory, where articles live.
##### =()<_PATH_SPOOL                @<_PATH_SPOOL>@>()=
_PATH_SPOOL                          /opt/news/spool/articles
```

```
## Spool directory where overview data lives.
##### =()<_PATH_OVERVIEWDIR          @<_PATH_OVERVIEWDIR>@>()=
_PATH_OVERVIEWDIR                    /opt/news/spool/over.view
```

```
## Name of overview file within its spool directory.
##### =()<_PATH_OVERVIEW             @<_PATH_OVERVIEW>@>()=
_PATH_OVERVIEW                       .overview
```

```
## Where rnews spools its input.
##### =()<_PATH_SPOOLNEWS            @<_PATH_SPOOLNEWS>@>()=
_PATH_SPOOLNEWS                      /opt/news/spool/in.coming
```

```
## Where rnews creates temporary files until finished.
##### =()<_PATH_SPOOLTEMP            @<_PATH_SPOOLTEMP>@>()=
_PATH_SPOOLTEMP                      /opt/news/spool/in.coming/tmp
```

```
## Where rnews puts bad input.
##### =()<_PATH_BADNEWS              @<_PATH_BADNEWS>@>()=
_PATH_BADNEWS                        /opt/news/spool/in.coming/bad
```

```
## Where rnews puts bad input, relative to _PATH_SPOOLNEWS.
##### =()<_PATH_RELBAD               @<_PATH_RELBAD>@>()=
_PATH_RELBAD                         bad
```

```
## Where the XBATCH command should put the batches. Normally same as
## _PATH_SPOOLNEWS so that 'rnews -U' can find it.
#### =()<_PATH_XBATCHES          @<_PATH_XBATCHES>@>()=
_PATH_XBATCHES                   /opt/news/spool/in.coming
```

9. Execution Paths for INNd and Rnews

There are new hooks in INNd to support PERL. If you add PERL support later in this config.data file you can place PERL filter files in the path controlprogs directory.

```
##
## 9. EXECUTION PATHS FOR INND AND RNEWS

## Pathname where dups are logged if RNEWS_LOG_DUPS is FILE.
#### =()<_PATH_RNEWS_DUP_LOG     @<_PATH_RNEWS_DUP_LOG>@>()=
_PATH_RNEWS_DUP_LOG              /dev/null

## Rnews may execute any program in this directory; see RNEWSPROGS.
#### =()<_PATH_RNEWSPROGS        @<_PATH_RNEWSPROGS>@>()=
_PATH_RNEWSPROGS                 /usr/news/bin/rnews.libexec

## Path to control messages scripts.
#### =()<_PATH_CONTROLPROGS      @<_PATH_CONTROLPROGS>@>()=
_PATH_CONTROLPROGS               /usr/news/bin/control

## Default "unknown/illegal" control script, within _PATH_CONTROLPROGS.
#### =()<_PATH_BADCONTROLPROG    @<_PATH_BADCONTROLPROG>@>()=
_PATH_BADCONTROLPROG             default
```

10. Sockets Created by INNd or Clients

```
##
## 10. SOCKETS CREATED BY INND OR CLIENTS
#### =()<_PATH_INNDDIR           @<_PATH_INNDDIR>@>()=
_PATH_INNDDIR                    /usr/news/run

## Unix-domain stream socket that rnews connects to.
#### =()<_PATH_NNTPCONNECT       @<_PATH_NNTPCONNECT>@>()=
_PATH_NNTPCONNECT                /usr/news/run/nntpin

## Unix-domain datagram socket that ctlinnd to.
#### =()<_PATH_NEWSCONTROL       @<_PATH_NEWSCONTROL>@>()=
_PATH_NEWSCONTROL                /usr/news/run/control
```

```
## Temporary socket created by ctlinnd; run through mktemp.
##### =()<_PATH_TEMPSOCK          @<_PATH_TEMPSOCK>@>()=
_PATH_TEMPSOCK                    /usr/news/run/ctlinndXXXXXX
```

11. Log and Config Files

```
##
## 11. LOG AND CONFIG FILES
## Shell script that sets most of these as shell vars
##### =()<_PATH_SHELLVARS          @<_PATH_SHELLVARS>@>()=
_PATH_SHELLVARS                    /usr/news/etc/innshellvars

## Perl script that sets most of these as perl variables
##### =()<_PATH_PERL_SHELLVARS     @<_PATH_PERL_SHELLVARS>@>()=
_PATH_PERL_SHELLVARS               /usr/news/etc/innshellvars.pl

## TCL script that sets most of these as tcl variables
##### =()<_PATH_TCL_SHELLVARS      @<_PATH_TCL_SHELLVARS>@>()=
_PATH_TCL_SHELLVARS                /usr/news/etc/innshellvars.tcl

## csh script that sets most of these as csh variables
##### =()<_PATH_CSH_SHELLVARS      @<_PATH_CSH_SHELLVARS>@>()=
_PATH_CSH_SHELLVARS                /usr/news/etc/innshellvars.csh

## Where most config and data files are usually stored; not required
## to the home directory of NEWSUSER.
##### =()<_PATH_NEWSLIB            @<_PATH_NEWSLIB>@>()=
_PATH_NEWSLIB                      /usr/news/etc

##The group owner of the rnews program. Usually uucp.
##### =()<RNEWS_GROUP              @<RNEWS_GROUP>@>()=
RNEWS_GROUP                        uucp

## The server's log file.
##### =()<_PATH_LOGFILE            @<_PATH_LOGFILE>@>()=
_PATH_LOGFILE                      /var/log/news/news

## The server's error log file.
##### =()<_PATH_ERRLOG             @<_PATH_ERRLOG>@>()=
_PATH_ERRLOG                       /var/log/news/errlog

## Where most sylog log files go; see also scanlogs, innstat, etc.
##### =()<_PATH_MOST_LOGS          @<_PATH_MOST_LOGS>@>()=
_PATH_MOST_LOGS                    /var/log/news
```

```
## How many generates of log files to keep.
##### =()<LOG_CYCLES              @<LOG_CYCLES>@>()=
LOG_CYCLES                        3

## Text value of the server's pid.
##### =()<_PATH_SERVERPID         @<_PATH_SERVERPID>@>()=
_PATH_SERVERPID                   /usr/news/run/innd.pid

## The newsfeeds file, on the server host.
##### =()<_PATH_NEWSFEEDS         @<_PATH_NEWSFEEDS>@>()=
_PATH_NEWSFEEDS                   /usr/news/etc/newsfeeds

## The article history database, on the server host.
##### =()<_PATH_HISTORY           @<_PATH_HISTORY>@>()=
_PATH_HISTORY                     /usr/news/etc/history

## File listing the sites that feed us news.
##### =()<_PATH_INNDHOSTS         @<_PATH_INNDHOSTS>@>()=
_PATH_INNDHOSTS                   /usr/news/etc/hosts.nntp

## The active file, on the server host.
##### =()<_PATH_ACTIVE            @<_PATH_ACTIVE>@>()=
_PATH_ACTIVE                      /usr/news/etc/active

## A temporary active file, for writing on the server host.
##### =()<_PATH_NEWACTIVE         @<_PATH_NEWACTIVE>@>()=
_PATH_NEWACTIVE                   /usr/news/etc/active.tmp

## An old active file on the server host.
##### =()<_PATH_OLDACTIVE         @<_PATH_OLDACTIVE>@>()=
_PATH_OLDACTIVE                   /usr/news/etc/active.old

## The log of when groups are created.
##### =()<_PATH_ACTIVETIMES       @<_PATH_ACTIVETIMES>@>()=
_PATH_ACTIVETIMES                 /usr/news/etc/active.times

## Where batch files are located.
##### =()<_PATH_BATCHDIR          @<_PATH_BATCHDIR>@>()=
_PATH_BATCHDIR                    /opt/news/spool/out.going

## Where archives are kept.
##### =()<_PATH_ARCHIVEDIR        @<_PATH_ARCHIVEDIR>@>()=
_PATH_ARCHIVEDIR                  /opt/news/spool/archive

## Where NNRP distributions file is
##### =()<_PATH_NNRPDIST          @<_PATH_NNRPDIST>@>()=
_PATH_NNRPDIST                    /usr/news/etc/distributions
```

```
## Where the NNRP automatic subscriptions file is
##### =()<_PATH_NNRPSUBS          @<_PATH_NNRPSUBS>@>()=
_PATH_NNRPSUBS                    /usr/news/etc/subscriptions

## Where the default Distribution assignments file is
##### =()<_PATH_DISTPATS          @<_PATH_DISTPATS>@>()=
_PATH_DISTPATS                    /usr/news/etc/distrib.pats

##### =()<_PATH_NEWSGROUPS        @<_PATH_NEWSGROUPS>@>()=
_PATH_NEWSGROUPS                  /usr/news/etc/newsgroups

## File where client configuration parameters can be read.
##### =()<_PATH_CONFIG            @<_PATH_CONFIG>@>()=
_PATH_CONFIG                      /usr/news/etc/inn.conf

## The possible active file, on clients (NFS-mounted, e.g.).
##### =()<_PATH_CLIENTACTIVE      @<_PATH_CLIENTACTIVE>@>()=
_PATH_CLIENTACTIVE                /usr/news/etc/active

## A temporary file, for client inews to use.
##### =()<_PATH_TEMPACTIVE        @<_PATH_TEMPACTIVE>@>()=
_PATH_TEMPACTIVE                  /var/tmp/activeXXXXXX

## Where to mail to the moderators.
##### =()<_PATH_MODERATORS        @<_PATH_MODERATORS>@>()=
_PATH_MODERATORS                  /usr/news/etc/moderators

## A temporary file, for client inews to use.
##### =()<_PATH_TEMPMODERATORS  @<_PATH_TEMPMODERATORS>@>()=
_PATH_TEMPMODERATORS              /var/tmp/moderatorsXXXXXX

## Where NNTP puts the name of the server.
##### =()<_PATH_SERVER            @<_PATH_SERVER>@>()=
_PATH_SERVER                      /usr/news/etc/server

## File with name/password for all remote connections.
##### =()<_PATH_NNTPPASS          @<_PATH_NNTPPASS>@>()=
_PATH_NNTPPASS                    /usr/news/etc/passwd.nntp

## NNRP access file.
##### =()<_PATH_NNRPACCESS        @<_PATH_NNRPACCESS>@>()=
_PATH_NNRPACCESS                  /usr/news/etc/nnrp.access

## Default expire control file.
##### =()<_PATH_EXPIRECTL         @<_PATH_EXPIRECTL>@>()=
_PATH_EXPIRECTL                   /usr/news/etc/expire.ctl
```

```
## Prolog to parse control scripts
#### =()<_PATH_PARSECTL            @<_PATH_PARSECTL>@>()=
_PATH_PARSECTL                     /usr/news/etc/parsecontrol

## Access control file for control scripts.
#### =()<_PATH_CONTROLCTL          @<_PATH_CONTROLCTL>@>()=
_PATH_CONTROLCTL                   /usr/news/etc/control.ctl

## Innwatch control file.
#### =()<_PATH_CTLWATCH            @<_PATH_CTLWATCH>@>()=
_PATH_CTLWATCH                     /usr/news/etc/innwatch.ctl

## Where innwatch writes its own pid.
#### =()<_PATH_WATCHPID            @<_PATH_WATCHPID>@>()=
_PATH_WATCHPID                     /usr/news/run/innwatch.pid

## Where innwatch writes status when it gets an interrupt
#### =()<_PATH_INNWSTATUS          @<_PATH_INNWSTATUS>@>()=
_PATH_INNWSTATUS                   /usr/news/run/innwatch.status

## Format of news overview database
#### =()<_PATH_SCHEMA              @<_PATH_SCHEMA>@>()=
_PATH_SCHEMA                       /usr/news/etc/overview.fmt
```

12. INNWATCH CONFIGURATION

This section covers with how your system will check its disk space and load average to make a decision about accepting additional news articles. After the build, you may have to edit the $inn/site/innwatch.ctl file to match the values for *innwatch_inodes* and *innwatch_blocks.* Look at lines such as

```
!!! /usr/ucb/df -i . | awk 'NR == 2 { print $3 }' ! lt ! 200 ! throttle ! No spa
ce (spool inodes)
```

This line prints the second line, third field of the /usr/udb/df *-i* output. Therefore, *innwatch_inodes* should be set to 3.

```
##
## 12. INNWATCH CONFIGURATION

## Load average (* 100) at which innd should be paused.
#### =()<INNWATCH_PAUSELOAD        @<INNWATCH_PAUSELOAD>@>()=
INNWATCH_PAUSELOAD                 1500

## Load average (* 100) at which innd should be throttled.
#### =()<INNWATCH_HILOAD           @<INNWATCH_HILOAD>@>()=
INNWATCH_HILOAD                    2000
```

```
## Load average (* 100) at which to restart innd (pause/throttle undone).
##### =()<INNWATCH_LOLOAD          @<INNWATCH_LOLOAD>@>()=
INNWATCH_LOLOAD                    1000

## Space, in df output units, at which to throttle innd on _PATH_SPOOL.
##### =()<INNWATCH_SPOOLSPACE      @<INNWATCH_SPOOLSPACE>@>()=
INNWATCH_SPOOLSPACE                8000

## Space, in df output units, at which to throttle innd on _PATH_BATCHDIR.

##### =()<INNWATCH_BATCHSPACE      @<INNWATCH_BATCHSPACE>@>()=
INNWATCH_BATCHSPACE                800

## Space, in df output units, at which to throttle innd on _PATH_NEWSLIB.
##### =()<INNWATCH_LIBSPACE        @<INNWATCH_LIBSPACE>@>()=
INNWATCH_LIBSPACE                  25000

## Number of inodes at which to throttle innd on _PATH_SPOOL.
##### =()<INNWATCH_SPOOLNODES      @<INNWATCH_SPOOLNODES>@>()=
INNWATCH_SPOOLNODES                200

## How long to sleep between innwatch iterations.
##### =()<INNWATCH_SLEEPTIME       @<INNWATCH_SLEEPTIME>@>()=
INNWATCH_SLEEPTIME                 600

## How innwatch gets disk space usage (SVR4 would use /usr/ucb/df)
##### =()<INNWATCH_DF              @<INNWATCH_DF>@>()=
INNWATCH_DF                        /usr/ucb/df

## Field number of INNWATCH_DF (with -i) output that gives free
## inodes (starting at 1).
##### =()<INNWATCH_INODES          @<INNWATCH_INODES>@>()=
INNWATCH_INODES                    3

## Field number of INNWATCH_DF output that gives the free block count.
###### =()<INNWATCH_BLOCKS         @<INNWATCH_BLOCKS>@>()=
INNWATCH_BLOCKS                    4
```

13. TCL Configuration

```
##
## 13. TCL Configuration
## Do you want TCL support?  Pick DO or DONT
##### =()<TCL_SUPPORT              @<TCL_SUPPORT>@>()=
TCL_SUPPORT                        DONT
```

```
## Where your tcl header file lives. Blank if no TCL
##### =()<TCL_INC                    @<TCL_INC>@>()=
TCL_INC
#TCL_INC                             -I/usr/local/include

## How do you get the TCL library?  Probably -ltcl -lm, blank if no TCL
##### =()<TCL_LIB                    @<TCL_LIB>@>()=
TCL_LIB

## TCL Startup File
##### =()<_PATH_TCL_STARTUP          @<_PATH_TCL_STARTUP>@>()=
_PATH_TCL_STARTUP                    /usr/news/bin/control/startup.tcl

## TCL Filter File
##### =()<_PATH_TCL_FILTER           @<_PATH_TCL_FILTER>@>()=
_PATH_TCL_FILTER                     /usr/news/bin/control/filter.tcl
```

14. PGP Configuration

In the very early days of USENET News you could let a control message add a new newsgroup automatically, because it is trivial to forge a control message that didn't last long. Now with the PGP hooks built into INN, it is possible to verify the author of a control message and let it execute automatically.

```
##
## 14. PGP Configuration

##
## Do you want PGP verification of control messages? Pick DO or DONT
##### =()<WANT_PGPVERIFY             @<WANT_PGPVERIFY>@>()=
WANT_PGPVERIFY                       DO

## PGP binary.
##### =()<_PATH_PGP                  @<_PATH_PGP>@>()=
_PATH_PGP                            /opt/local/bin/pgp
```

15. Local Configuration

```
##
## 15. Local Configuration
##
## Home of the NEWSUSER
##### =()<_PATH_NEWSHOME             @<_PATH_NEWSHOME>@>()=
_PATH_NEWSHOME                       /usr/news/bin
```

16. ACTSYNC CONFIGURATION

```
##
## 16.Actsync Configuration.
##

## Host to synchoronize active file with (see actsync and actsyncd manpages).
##### =()<ACTSYNC_HOST                    @<ACTSYNC_HOST>@>()=
ACTSYNC_HOST                              news.isp.com

## Flags actsyncd is to pass to actsync.
##### =()<ACTSYNC_FLAGS                   @<ACTSYNC_FLAGS>@>()=
ACTSYNC_FLAGS                             -v 2 -q 2 -b 0 -d 0 -g 7 -s 79 -t 2

## Actsyncd config file.
##### =()<_PATH_ACTSYNC_CFG               @<_PATH_ACTSYNC_CFG>@()=
_PATH_ACTSYNC_CFG                         /usr/news/etc/actsync.cfg

## Actsyncd ignore file.
##### =()<_PATH_ACTSYNC_IGN               @<_PATH_ACTSYNC_IGN>@()=
_PATH_ACTSYNC_IGN                         /usr/news/etc/actsync.ign
```

17. PERL CONFIGURATION

If you add PERL support, you can place PERL filter files in the control directory. Even if you don't use PERL filters at first, if you select PERL support, a startup innd.pl file must exist in the control directory specified earlier.

Two sample filters are provided with the distribution to filter incoming "make money" articles from peers, or "make money" postings. This is a useful way to help fight spam.

```
## 17. Perl Configuration

## Do you want Perl support? Pick DO or DONT
##### =()<PERL_SUPPORT       @<PERL_SUPPORT>@>()=
PERL_SUPPORT                 DO

## How do you get the PERL libraries? Probably -lperl -lm, blank if no PERL
##### =()<PERL_LIB   @<PERL_LIB>@>()=
#PERL_LIB
PERL_LIB      -L     /opt/gnu/lib/perl5/sun4-solaris/5.003/CORE -lperl -lm

## Core directory (includes, libs). See perlembed(1)
##### =()<PERL_INC       @<PERL_INC>@()=
#PERL_INC
PERL_INC                    -I/opt/gnu/lib/perl5/sun4-solaris/5.003/CORE
```

```
## Perl Filter Files
#### =()<_PATH_PERL_STARTUP_INND   @<_PATH_PERL_STARTUP_INND>@>()=
_PATH_PERL_STARTUP_INND           /usr/news/bin/control/startup_innd.pl

#### =()<_PATH_PERL_FILTER_INND    @<_PATH_PERL_FILTER_INND>@>()=
_PATH_PERL_FILTER_INND            /usr/news/bin/control/filter_innd.pl

#### =()<_PATH_PERL_FILTER_NNRPD   @<_PATH_PERL_FILTER_NNRPD>@>()=
_PATH_PERL_FILTER_NNRPD           /usr/news/bin/control/filter_nnrpd.pl
```

The config.data file has now been modified.

COMPILING AND INSTALLING THE PROGRAMS

Most of the build and install has been automated with the Build script provided with the INN software, which will automatically build and install the application. Yet at certain points in the build, the user will be asked to interact and answer questions. These are the only areas shown in the following text. You will, however, note a great deal of screen activity and disk thrashing going on between these points.

Before running the Build script, become Superuser (SU) and create a link to /bin/echo for Lint using the following command:

```
SU
password: XXXXX

ln -s /bin/echo /opt/gnu/bin/lint
```

This fakes out the Lint .

As *root*, create the directories opt/news and /opt/news/spool to be the parent of whatever you define _PATH_SPOOL to be. You must also create the user and group that you defined with *NEWSUSER* and *NEWSGROUP* in the config.data file. These are needed by the Build script in order to create subdirectories and set proper ownerships.

The user ID (UID) for *NEWSUSER* should be **6,** and the Group ID (GID) for *NEWSGROUP* should be **13.** The home directory should be whatever you defined *_PATH_NEWSBIN* to be. The shell should be /bin/sh.

Now run the script:

```
news# ./BUILD

NOTE: If you just type [RETURN] to any question, this script will
      assume you are being cautious and default to whatever answer
      is "safer." This usually means recompiling.

      You cannot install over a running system; this script will
      remind you about this later.

Use the /bin/sh version of subst, or the C version?
Type sh, c, or x if you don't care: c
Building subst...
gcc -o subst subst.c

Have you already built the executables [y or n]? n
```

At this point, the system goes off and builds the executables. This may take a few minutes. When the system returns, the substitutions are complete .

```
Continue with the build [y or n]? y
Run lint after each compile [y or n]? n
```

The actual build of the INN application now begins. This can take a long while, upwards of ten minutes, depending on the platform and operating system used.

```
Do the spool, etc., directories exist [y or n]? n
Please su to root and run the "makedirs.sh" script

news# sh makedirs.sh
```

The screen will show the directories as they are created and should end with *exit 0.* At this time, type in *exit* to return to the Build script.

```
+ [ ! -d /usr/news/bin ]
+ [ ! -d /usr/news/bin/control ]
+ [ ! -d /usr/news/bin/rnews.libexec ]
+ [ ! -d /usr/news/bin/auth ]
+ exit 0
#

news# exit
```

Back to the Build script.

```
Building the data files.
make: Nothing to be done for `all'.
Start a subshell to edit the config files [y or n]? y
```

Change to the /usr/news/etc directory and *pull* an active file and a newsgroups file from your news feed.

```
news# cd /usr/news/etc
news# ../bin/getlist -h news.isp.com > active
news# ../bin/getlist -h news.isp.com newsgroups > newsgroups
news# chown news: news*
news# chmod 644*
news# exit
```

Your server now has an active and a newsgroups file.

```
Start another shell to edit the config files [y or n]? n

Checking other data files.
Rebuilding history. This may take some time, so it is the last thing
in the installation.
news#
```

The Build script has now compiled and installed the INN software.

CONFIGURING THE INN DATA FILES

Although there are other configuration files associated with INN, only the basic files are covered in this section (see Table 16-5). By closely following the example files below, you will start to understand how these files work and be able to tailor them to match your site. Refer to Appendix C, "INN Technical Information," to find additional reference material.

Table 16-5 Basic Level Configuration Files

Expire.ctl	Control file for USENET article expiration
Hosts.nntp	List of hosts that feed NNTP news
Inn.conf	Configuration data for INN programs
Newsfeeds	Determines where USENET articles get sent
Nnrp.access	Access file for on-campus NNTP sites
Nntpsend.ctl	List of sites to feed via NNTP send

It is best to use some form of revision control, and *RCS* has been provided on the CD-ROM for this purpose. The INN data files to follow are very well documented both in the man pages that were installed by the Build script and within the files themselves.

The entire header for each file is included, as it makes the file self-explanatory. Make the entries as indicated in bold.

```
news# cd site
```

EXPIRE.CTL

The file expire.ctl is the default control file for the Expire program. It is read at start-up. Blank lines and lines beginning with a number sign "#" are ignored. All other lines should be in one of two formats.

The first format specifies how long to keep a record of expired articles. Example:

```
/remember/:days
```

The second format will consist of five colon-separated fields. Example:

```
pattern:modflag:keep:default:purge
```

There must be exactly one line with a pattern of *:A. The "A" is a modflag and indicates a match of all groups, and it is used to set the default expire for all groups. It should be the first line after the "remember" line.

Edit the expire.ctl file to set your expiry rules based on available disk capacity, expected news volume, and policy.

```
/remember/:14

## Keep for 1-10 days, allow Expires headers to work.
#*:A:1:10:never
*:A:1:10:15

pcg*:A:never:never:never
pcg.lists.*:A:1:14:30
```

```
pcg.posted :A1:15:30
alt.binaries*:A:1:3:4

## Some particular groups such as those useful to new users
## stay forever.
news.announce*,news.answers,news.list*:A:1:35:never
```

HOSTS.NNTP

INNd reads the file hosts.nntp to get the list of hosts that feed news to the local site. The server reads this file at start-up or when directed by CTLINNd. When a host connects to the NNTP port of the system on which INNd is running, the server will do a check to see if the host's Internet address is the same as that of one of the hosts named in this file. If the host is not mentioned, then INNd will spawn an NNRPd to process the connection.

Wild cards are not permitted in the host names. All lines, except comment lines, should consist of two or three fields separated by a colon.

The first field should be either an Internet address in dotted-quad format or an address that can be parsed by the utility Gethostbyname. If a host's entry has multiple addresses, all of them will be added to the access list. The second field, which may be blank, is the password the foreign host is required to use when first connecting. The third field, which may be omitted, is a list of newsgroups to which the host may send articles. This list is parsed as a news feeds subscription list; groups not in the list are ignored.

The file hosts.nntp.nolimit, if it exists, is read whenever the hosts.nntp file is read. It has the same format, although only the first field is used. Any host mentioned in this file is not subject to the incoming connections limit specified by the INNd *-i* flag. This can be used to allow local hosts or time-sensitive peers, to connect, regardless of the local conditions.

Make the following entry in the host NNTP file:

```
news.isp.com:
```

INN.CONF

The file inn.conf is used to determine various parameters used as defaults in article headers. All lines specify parameters that may be read, and should be of the following form:

name : [optional whitespace] value

Some parameters specified in the file may be overridden by environment variables, and some file parameters may be used to mask real data, such as when hiding a cluster of hosts behind a single electronic mail host name. The current set of parameters appears in Table 16-6.

Table 16-6 Inn.conf Parameters

domain	Local domain, without leading period
fromhost	What to put in the From line; default is FQDN of the local host
moderatormailer	Where to mail moderated postings, if not found in the moderator's file
pathhost	What to put in the Path and Xref headers; default is FQDN of the local host
organization	If the environment variable *ORGANIZATION* doesn't exist; what to put in the Organization header if blank
server	If the environment variable *NNTPSERVER* doesn't exist; local NNTP server host to connect to

Everything after the white space and up to the end of the line is taken as the value; multiword values should not be put in quotes. The case of names is significant. For example, "server" is not the same as "Server" or "SERVER."

Make the following entry in the inn.conf file:

```
domain:            Pcgbase.com
fromhost:          news.pcgbase.com
moderatormailer:   *:newsmaster@pcgbase.com
pathhost:          news.pcgbase.com
organization:      Phillips Consulting Group, Inc.
server:            news.pcgbase.com
```

NEWSFEEDS

This file is extremely complicated, and readers are urged to read the associated man pages thoroughly before experimenting with the more advanced settings and capabilities of this file. Included below is the complete file for the sample INN news server.

```
NEWSFEEDS
## $Revision: 1.2 $
## newsfeeds - determine where Usenet articles get sent
## Format:
##     site[/exclude,exclude...]\
##          :pattern,pattern...[/distrib,distrib...]\
##          :flag,flag...\
##          :param
## Summary of flags:
##     <size        Article must be less then size bytes.
##     Aitems       Article checks -- d (must have Distribution header)
##                  p (don't check for site in Path header).
##     Bhigh/low    Internal buffer size before writing to output.
##     H[count]     Article must have less then count hops; default is 1.
##     Isize        Internal buffer size (if a file feed)
##     Nm           Only moderated groups that match the patterns.
##     Nu           Only unmoderated groups that match the patterns.
##     Ssize        Start spooling if more than size bytes get queued.
##     Ttype        Feed types -- f (file) m (funnel; param names the
##                  real entry) p (pipe to program) c (send to stdin
##                  channel of param's sub-process); x (like c, but
##                  handles commands on stdin).
##    Witems        What to write -- b (article bytesize) f (full path)
##                  g (first newsgroup) m (Message-ID) n (relative
##                  path) s (site that fed article) t (time received)
##                  * (names of funnel feed-in's or all sites that get
##                  the article) N (Newsgroups header) D (Distribution
##                  header) H (all headers) O (overview data) R
##                  (replication data).
##    Param field depends on T flag.  For Tf, relative paths are from the
##    out.going directory.  For Tp and Tc, it is a shell command to execute.
##    If a Tm refers to this entry (which will have its own T param) then "*"
##    is expanded to all the funnel sites that triggered this one.  Useful
##    for spawning one mail process, e.g.
##
##    This file is complicated -- see newsfeeds.5!

##    This is the local site.
##    The "pattern" field gives the intial subscription list for
##    all other sites. You might want to put "!control,!junk,!<local>.*"
##    there. The "distrib" subfield limits incoming articles.
##
##    You can also have ME/bad.site: to refuse articles from a particular
##    site (by matching the Path: entry).  Other pseudo-sites may be put
```

```
## in here, to REFUSE certain types of 3rd-party cancel messages
## (See the "Cancel FAQ" news.admin.net-abuse.misc):
##     cyberspam      Spam cancels, munged articles, binary postings
##     spewcancel     just munged articles from runaway gateways
##     bincancel      just binary postings to non-binaries groups
##
## Note that refusing articles means you won't offer them to sites you
## feed
```

Make the following entries in the newsfeeds file:

ME:*,!control,!junk,!pcg.*::

news.isp.com::Tf,Wnm:

```
## News overview
```
overview!:*:Tc,WO:/usr/news/bin/overchan

INN is very powerful and flexible in its ability to feed news to other sites. The newsfeed file controls how the news is fed and which groups are involved. The sample implemented uses the NNTP Ihave stype (log).

NNRP.ACCESS

Edit this file to grant access to IP numbers in your domain. Names can be used instead of IP numbers, but this will work only if your reverse name translation is set up correctly. Some discretion should be employed in giving access to anyone but testers or early adopters who will help shake bugs out of the service. Giving broader access at this time before the company policies are laid down (covered in Chapter 18, "Acceptable Usage Policy") may cause problems not only for the company but for the larger USENET community.

The file nnrp.access specifies the default list of sites to be fed by nnrp.access. The comments within the file make it self-explanatory. For this reason the entire file is included here with changes made for the sample configuration in bold.

```
NNRP.ACCESS
## $Revision: 1.1 $
## nnrp.access - access file for on-campus NNTP sites
## Format:
##     <host>:<perm>:<user>:<pass>:<groups>
## Connecting host must be found in this file; the last match found is
## used, so put defaults first.
```

```
##     <host>        Wildcard name or IP address
##     <perm>         R to read; P to post
##     <user>        Username for authentication before posting
##     <pass>        Password, for same reason
##     <groups>       Newsgroup patterns that can be read or not read
## To disable posting put a space in the <user> and <pass> fields,
## since
##  there is no way for client to enter one.
##
## Default is no access, no way to authentication, and no groups.
*:: -no- : -no- :!*
##  Foo, Incorporated, hosts have no password, can read anything.
```

Make the following entries in the nnrp.access file:

```
*pcgbase.com:Read Post:::*
*.us.pcgbase.com:Read Post:::!*,pcg.*
news.us.pcgbase.com:Read Post:::*
#*.foo.com:Read Post:::*
#stdin:Read Post:::*
#localhost:Read Post:::*
#127.0.0.1:Read Post:::*
```

NNTPSEND.CTL

The file nntpsend.ctl specifies the default list of sites to be fed by nntpsend. The comments within the file make it self-explanatory. For this reason the entire file is included here with changes made for the sample configuration in bold.

```
NNTPSEND.CTL
## $Revision: 1.1 $
## Control file for nntpsend.
## Format:
##     site:fqdn:max_size:[<args...>]
##     <site>        The name used in the newsfeeds file for this site;
##                   this determines the name of the batchfile, etc.
##     <fqdn>          The fully-qualified domain name of the site,
##                   passed as the parameter to innxmit.
##     <size>         Size to truncate batchfile if it gets too big;
##                   see shrinkfile(1).
##     <args>         Other args to pass to innxmit
## Everything after the pound sign is ignored.
```

Make the following entries in the nntpsend.ctl:

```
news:news.isp.com:-t60

#nsavax:erehwon.nsavax.gov::-S -t60
#walldrug:walldrug.com:4m-1m:-T1800 -t300
#kremvax:kremvax.cis:2m:
```

Now install the INN data files.

```
news# make install
```

MISCELLANEOUS

There are just a few additional actions that need to take place before the INN application will run properly.

MAIL ALIASES

Add mail aliases for *news* and *newsmaster*. Root is used as a default. Choose aliases to match your local newsmaster.

```
news# vi /etc/aliases

############################
# Local aliases below #
############################
news:   root
newsmaster:     root
```

After modifying the aliases file, execute the *newaliases* to rebuild the Aliases database.

```
news# newaliases
/etc/mail/aliases: 5 aliases, longest 15 bytes, 96 bytes total

news#
```

EDITING THE /ETC/SYSLOG.CONF FILE

To set up complete logging of the server activities and have them ready for a report by the News.daily script, you have to edit your /etc/syslog.conf file.

First create the necessary log files:

```
news# touch /var/log/news/news.crit
news# touch /var/log/news/news.err
news# touch /var/log/news/news.notice
```

Now edit the /etc/syslog.conf file. Be sure to use tabs.

```
## Send critical messages to everyone who is logged in and to the console.
news.crit		*
news.crit		/dev/console

## Log news messages to separate files.
## Note that each level includes all levels above it: notice includes crit.
## =()<news.crit		@<_PATH_MOST_LOGS>@/news.crit>()=
news.crit		/var/log/news/news.crit
## =()<news.err		@<_PATH_MOST_LOGS>@/news.err>()=
news.err		/var/log/news/news.err
## =()<news.notice	@<_PATH_MOST_LOGS>@/news.notice>()=
news.notice		/var/log/news/news.notice
```

In order to make the Syslog daemon reread it's configuration file, you must send it an *HUP* signal. Use the Ps command to locate the process *id* of the Syslog daemon and then send it a *HUP* signal.

```
news# ps -ef | grep syslog
	root  129    1 0  Oct 11 ?      0:06 /usr/sbin/syslogd
	root 7857 2388 1 22:08:10 pts/2 0:00 grep syslog
news# kill -HUP 129
news#
```

ADDING THE CRON ENTRIES

Now add the cron entries for news.

To get daily reports on the news server activity from the News.daily script, to enable the Expire utility, to send articles on a regular basis, and to send all spool messages, type:

```
news# /bin/crontab -e news
```

Insert the following lines:

```
40 23 * * * /usr/news/bin/news.daily delayrm expireover
0,5,10,15,20,25,30,35,40,45,50,55 * * * * /usr/news/bin/nntpsend
01,21,41,* * * * /usr/news/bin/rnews-u
```

There is one last step before starting the news server. Change to the directory /usr/news/bin and run the utility Inncheck. Inncheck examines various configuration files and databases and verifies things about them. Things verified are permissions, ownership, syntax errors in configuration files, and so on.

```
news# cd /usr/news/bin
news# ./inncheck

/usr/news/etc/newsfeeds:0: warning you accept all incoming article distributions
```

Disregard this warning message that resulted from a deliberate choice to take all newsgroups made in the newsfeed file. If no other messages appear, the news server is now ready to run. If any other error messages appear, they should be detailed enough to aid in debugging the system. If a problem with a configuration file is detected, fix the problem in the $inn/site directory, then type:

```
news# make install-config
```

STARTING NEWS

To start the news server for the first time, make sure that you are the *root* user and that you are in the directory /usr/news/bin. Then type the following two commands. The first command will start the news server, and the second command will build the Overview databases.

```
news# ./rc.news
news# ./expireover -a -s
```

You will get a message like this when you start the news:

```
Message 1/7  From Super-User          Oct 9, 96 07:32:25 pm -0400

Date:Wed, 9 Oct 1996 19:32:25 -0400 (EDT)
To: newsmaster@news.pcgbase.com
Subject: Boot-time Usenet warning on news

No .news.daily file; need to run news.daily?
```

Not to worry, the news.daily file will be created by the cron job.

A run control script can be created to execute rc.news at startup.

VERIFICATION AND TESTING

Use a news reader to try out the news server, but make sure the reader is in the nnrp.access file and not the host.nntp. Remember to adjust the options in your news reader to point to the news host. Ask for *news.newusers.questions.* If everything is working correctly, you should see a number of articles in this group.

If this process is unsuccessful, check the nnrp.access file to ensure that the reader is allowed. You may have to TELNET to your news server on port 119—the NNTP port—and run a manual NNTP session. Again, do so from a machine that is in the nnrp.access file, but not in the hosts.nntp file. Here is a sample session:

```
telnet news.pcgbase.com 119
group news.newusers.questions    (Select a group currently in the active file.)
head                             (display the header)
body                             (display the body)
next                             (next item please)
help                             (show valid commands)
quit                             (exit the connection)
$
```

If INN is not running, you will get the following message:

```
telnet: Unable to connect to remote host: Connection refused.
```

Clues to any other problems such as *being denied access* may be discovered in the log files. Part 4 of the INN FAQ, the debugging tutorial, may be helpful here.

If read capability is functional, try posting to the *alt.test* newsgroup. This will trigger autoresponder robots located at news sites around the world who receive the post to respond with an e-mail. Using *alt.test* rather than a regular newsgroup is a courtesy, expected of you by the news community.

Here is an e-mail response received by *news.postech.ac.kr*, a news server of the Pohang University of Science and Technology in Pohang, South Korea, on 19 Nov 1996 02:19:06 KST (18 Nov 1996 17:19:06 GMT).

```
Forwarded message:
>From autoreply@news.postech.ac.kr Mon Nov 18 12:19 EST 1996
Date: Tue, 19 Nov 1996 02:19:06 +0900
Message-Id: <199611181719.CAA03686@news.postech.ac.kr>
To: "John E. Phillips" <jep@pcgbase.com>
From: autoreply@news.postech.ac.kr (POSTECH Autoresponder)
Subject: Re: FIXED AND TESTED
Reply-To: nobody@news.postech.ac.kr
References: <329087BF.2F10@pcgbase.com>
Newsgroups: alt.test
```

```
Precedence: junk
Content-Type: text
Content-Length: 1621

This is an automated reply to a test posting in the alt.test newsgroup.

This serves to confirm for you that your test post was sucessfully distributed to this
machine via the Usenet path shown in the header of your article, included below. To
avoid receiving this automated reply, place the word "ignore" anywhere in the subject
line of your posts to *.test newsgroups.

According to your article's header, it was posted on:
   18 Nov 1996 15:58:55 GMT

The posting was received by news.postech.ac.kr, a news server of the Pohang
University of Science and Technology in Pohang, South Korea on 19 Nov 1996 02:19:06
KST (18 Nov 1996 17:19:06 GMT). The transit time of the message was 1 hour, 20
minutes and 11 seconds.

This autoresponder will not reply to any message which includes the word "ignore" in
the Subject line of an article. To reach the administrator of news.postech.ac.kr, send
mail to usenet@news.postech.ac.kr.

The header and first 10 lines of your message were:

Path:
news.postech.ac.kr!usenet.kornet.nm.kr!howland.erols.net!newsfeed.internetmci.com!
zeke.ebtech.net!loki.tor.hookup.net!nic.ott.hookup.net!news.pcgbase.com
From: "John E. Phillips" <jep@pcgbase.com>
Newsgroups: alt.test
Subject: FIXED AND TESTED
Date: Mon, 18 Nov 1996 10:58:55 -0500
Organization: Phillips Consulting Group, Inc.
Lines: 4
Message-ID: <329087BF.2F10@pcgbase.com>
NNTP-Posting-Host: news.pcgbase.com
Mime-Version: 1.0
Content-Type: text/plain; charset=us-ascii
Content-Transfer-Encoding: 7bit
X-Mailer: Mozilla 3.01 (X11; I; SunOS 5.5.1 sun4c)

This is a test of a INN server
--
John Phillips

jep@pcgbase.com
```

To avoid receiving this automated reply, place the word "ignore" anywhere in the subject line of your posts to *.test newsgroups. The autoresponders will not reply to any message which includes the word "ignore" in the Subject line of an article.

17 DNEWS

Some information required in this chapter should already be present in the Site Worksheet (Table 13-1). If you have not already done so, please complete the worksheet now before proceeding.

Conventions

The user is required to make some modifications to data files. **Bold** is used to indicate user entries, <u>underline</u> designates files or directories, and *italics* are used to highlight words or terms.

DNEWS is a relatively new software package and is going through rapid change as improvements are added and bugs fixed. The manual and install guides currently shipping with the software are somewhat limited, but as the code stabilizes and more attention is placed on documentation, this situation should improve. Today, the best source of help comes from the online FAQ (also on CD-ROM), which will answer many of the questions and concerns users may face when installing this package. This chapter includes information drawn from these sources, but important explanations and additional steps have been added to help the process to go more smoothly. Since DNEWS is precompiled, this chapter is somewhat less complex than the equivalent INN chapter. Appendix B contains additional technical information.

Sucking or Ihave Feed?

With DNEWS you have two choices: You can bring news into your system using a conventional NNTP Ihave exchange with your upstream news server, or you can use the dynamic *sucking* feed. Ihave is the standard way of sending news but it has two disadvantages:

- An NNTP Ihave feed provides a random selection of items from various newsgroups. As a result you cannot optimize the arrangement when creating indexes and storing items.
- An NNTP Ihave feed must be set up from the other end. This prevents autoconfiguration of what is fed; it also makes configuration difficult since you may have limited or virtually no access to the feeder site configuration.

If you use Ihave, you must take a full feed, or at least a fixed subset, and you cannot use the DNEWS dynamic sucking feed system. The sucking feed can be more efficient, and under this system DNEWS essentially pretends to be a news reader. In the case of the sample corporate/regional configuration (see Figure 17-1), the DNEWS server looks like a news reader to both the ISP and the corporate INN server, and uses the sucking feed. The use of the sucking feed in both cases optimizes bandwidth.

Figure 17-1 Corporate news topology.

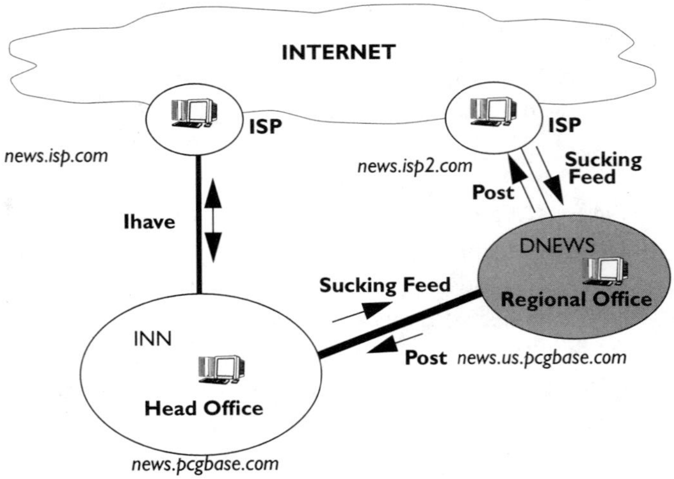

GETTING THE APPLICATION

DNEWS provides a time-limited evaluation copy that is downloadable over the Internet. Getting DNEWS up and running is a relatively easy process, and since DNEWS is a commercial package, it comes fully precompiled for most platforms. All that is required is to download, configure, and install it. DNEWS is available from

```
ftp://ftp.netwinsite.com/dnews
```

This site contains versions for many platforms as well as many older versions for each. Choose the most recent version for your platform then download.

Set directory to opt/local/src using the following command:

```
news# cd /opt/local/src
```

An example of a DNEWS FTP download follows.

```
news# ftp ftp.netwinsite.com
Connected to falcon.webpros.com.
220 falcon FTP server (Version wu-2.4(3) Thu Nov 9 16:36:15 PST 1995) ready.
Name (ftp.netwinsite.com:jep): ftp
331 Guest login ok, send your complete e-mail address as password.
Password:
230 Guest login ok, access restrictions apply.
ftp> bin
200 Type set to I.
ftp> cd dnews
250 CWD command successful.
ftp> get dnews27q_solaris.tar.Z
200 PORT command successful.
150 Opening BINARY mode data connection for dnews27p_solaris.tar.Z
(640903 bytes).
226 Transfer complete.
local: dnews27q_solaris.tar.Z remote: dnews27q_solaris.tar.Z
640903 bytes received in 1.1e+02 seconds (5.9 Kbytes/s)
ftp> bye
```

Now untar the file using the following command:

```
news# tar
xvzf dnews→dnews27q_solaris.tar.Z
```

Configuring DNEWS

This section covers setting up DNEWS for a dynamic sucking feed. Although DNEWS is virtually ready to go, you must still enter your site-specific information. There are three files you must modify (dnews.conf, newsfeeds.conf, and access.conf), and each has some resident text (not shown) to further explain the parameters used in the file in case you need more information. Five other configuration files make up DNEWS, but discussion of these files is deferred to Chapter 20, "Maintenance."

Dnews.conf

Edit dnews.conf to configure a basic set of parameters, such as the system identity, who the upstream news feed is, the mail address for messages, the expiry cycle, and so on. Table 17-1 provides explanations and hints for the various parameters in this file.

Table 17-1 Main Parameters for Dnews.conf

Parameter (Keyword)	Explanation
Nntp_feeder	Host name for the main upstream server that DNEWS should get newsgroups from. This is generally the site where you have news reader access.
Nntp_suck2	Second feed using sucking. If a third sucking feed were required, it would require the use of Nntp_suck3, and so on.
Myname	The IP name of your own machine. Yes, it should be possible to get this from the system, but there is no reliable-portable call for doing this, so put it in by hand.
Diskspace	Total disk space available, in megabytes. The vendor recommends 10–100MB for dynamic, 500–2000MB for full feed.
Manager Timezone	Person to e-mail log files and control messages, and so forth. (Example: EST, PST... [VMS only].)
Mail	Internet mail transport name for VMS; for example, in, MX, SMTP.
DF	This parameter defines the path to the DF (display filesystem).
Sendmail	Path to sendmail on your system (or equivalent mailer).
Confirm	The system can be set up to send a confirming e-mail to a designated host (typically your news server) following a successful post to the upstream news server. If no confirmation is desired, then comment the command line out with a "#" symbol.
Too_old	Refuse news articles with a date more than this old. This is just to avoid accepting news from a restored news disk.
Report	Send daily reports. Default is yes if you leave the line commented out.
Loglvl	Logging and debug settings: error, warn, info, debug.

Table 17-1 Main Parameters for Dnews.conf (Continued)

Parameter (Keyword)	Explanation
Life	Number of days to keep each newsgroup after it's uploaded.
Update_at m h	Defines the update cycle for updating the news feed. The fields are separated by spaces. The last two are integer patterns that specify minutes (0–59) and hours (0–23). Each of these patterns can be either an asterisk or a list of elements separated by commas. For example, Update_at *5 *, would cause the system to do an update on all times ending in a 5; that is at 05, 15, 25 ... every 10 minutes.
Expire_at m h	This parameter defines the expire cycle. For example, Expire_at 5 2,19 would cause expire to run at 2:05 A.M. and 7P.M.
config, logdir	These two parameters define where the config and log files are stored (all except the dnews.conf file, which will probably be stored in the /etc/ directory). *WARNING: if you mess with these definitions, then don't forget to fix the Setprot.sh and Install.sh scripts correctly. Also, if logdir is moved, it must be a directory that the user news can create files in.*
Workarea	Defines the directory for work files such as active.dat, *.feed ...
History	Defines the directory where the history files history.dat and history.idx, which comprise the history database, are stored. This database contains all pertinent information on all articles currently in the spool directory.
Spool	Defines the directory where the articles' hierarchies will be served.
Workarea_min n History_min n Spool_min n	These parameters define the minimum megabytes of free space for workarea, history, and spool. If less than *n* megabytes are free in any of these three areas, DNEWS will stop sucking and accepting feeds. Posts will still be allowed.

To avoid changing the scripts provided with the source code, it is better to leave the following default directories in the configuration file and create symbolic links to your real directories, if they are different from these. For example, here are the two commands to create a DNEWS directory on the /opt file system and create a link to it.

news# **mkdir /opt/dnews**
news# **ln -s /opt/dnews /var/spool/dnews**

The modified dnews.conf file looks like this:

config	**/usr/local/dnews**
logdir	**/usr/local/dnews**
workarea	**/var/spool/dnews**
history	**/var/spool/dnews**
spool	**/var/spool/dnews**

workarea_min	**5**
history_min	**20**
spool_min	**10**

NEWSFEEDS.CONF

Edit newsfeeds.conf to define and set parameters for your site, to exclude certain news sites, and to define which groups your server will receive and which it will propagate. There are three reserved site names—*me*, *$nntp_feeder*, and *$nntp_suck2*—used in this file. *Me* refers to your site, and the associated parameters define which groups you will accept; *$nntp_feeder* and *$nntp_suck2* refer to your ISP news feed and the INN server sucking feed respectively; and the associated parameters define which groups each will send. The site names *$nntp_feeder* and *$nntp_suck2* are defined in the dnews.conf file.

In the sample, the DNEWS server is acting as the regional news server and gets a feed from an ISP. It is also able to get a sucking feed over the corporate WAN for private groups. Selected regional newsgroups not available to the corporate news server could also be acquired from the regional news server.

Table 17-2 provides explanations and hints for the various commands used in newsfeeds.conf.

Table 17-2 Commands to Define News Feeds

Command	Explanation
Groups	All the newsgroups you will allow and/or disallow. A comma can be used as a list delimiter. The character "*" can be used as a wild card entry. The "!" character is used to denote NOT these groups. For example, the default setting does not allow any binary groups by using *!alt.binary.**.
Builtin	The command Builtin tells DNEWS to use its own internal NNTP link to send any articles to this feed.
Posting	Posting means to use Post instead of Ihave to send messages upstream. Posting is best for leaf sites (where you don't feed to any sites other than your upstream news feed). A posting site can have leaf sites, but it can't accept Ihave messages from them, only Post messages.
Exclude	If your news feeder stamps news items with a name other than specified by *$Nntp_feeder,* then you will need to use Exclude to prevent your system from trying to send every item that comes in back to the feeder. To check this, use a reader or telnet to get a message from the site you feed from and inspect the Path header record. This has to be repeated for each news feed—entries separated by a comma.

The modified newsfeeds.conf file will look like this:

```
site me
            groups *,!alt.binaries.* [accept all groups except alt.binaries]
site $nntp_feeder
            groups *,!pcg.* [send all groups except internal ones]
            builtin
            posting
            exclude news.isp2.com
site $nntp_suck2
            groups pcg.*, !*.binaries   [send only internal groups to the
INN server and specifically guard against sending alt.binaries]
            builtin
            posting
```

Note that in order to suck a feed from the corporate server (in this case *news.pcgbase.com*) the regional news server must appear in the nnrp.access file in the INN server as a news reader.

ACCESS.CONF

Edit access.conf to grant access to IP numbers in your domain. Names can be used instead of IP numbers, but this will work only if your reverse name translation is set up correctly. Some discretion should be used in giving access to anyone but testers or early-adopters who will help shake out the service. Giving broader access at this time, before the company policies are laid down (covered in Chapter 18, "Acceptable Usage Policy"), may cause problems not only for the company but for the larger USENET community as well.

The format for entries is as follows:

```
<host>:<perm>:<user>:<pass>:<groups>
    host        Wildcard name or IP address
    perm        R to read; P to post; I to allow Ihave xfer's
    user        Username for authentication before posting
    pass        Password, for same reason
    groups      Newsgroup patterns that can be read or not read
```

Default is *no access, no opportunity to authenticate,* and *no groups,* which translates into the following entry:

```
*::::!*
```

Example:

```
161.29.23.*:Read:::*
161.29.23.*:Read, Post:jep:cos67:pcg.*
```

The first line allows any reader in the subnet 161.29.23.0 to read but not post. The second line gives user *jep* post privileges only to the private newsgroups.

Connecting hosts must be found in this file. Also the last match found is used, so put the defaults first.

The modified access.conf file will look like this:

```
*::::!*
205.233.33.*:Read,Post:::*
*.pcgbase.com:Read,Post:::*
```

Installing and Starting DNEWS

Once the DNEWS *.conf files have been modified and you are satisfied with the access being granted in the access.conf file, it's time to turn on the DNEWS daemon by running a provided script. At this time it's also a good idea to edit your system startup script to turn on the DNEWS daemon on power up. The location and file name varies from UNIX to UNIX, but in general you will need to add to your startup script a line something like this:

```
news# /usr/local/dnews/dnews_start.sh
```

If you have changed any of the default directories, then edit all the .sh scripts to reflect the changes.

```
news# ./install.sh
news# ./dnews_start.sh
```

The system will now try to get a list of newsgroups from your feeder site. While this is happening it will not respond to any commands, but you can check its progress by using the following command:

```
news# more dnews.log
```

When it has finished (give it 10–20 minutes), you can then try this command:

```
news# tellnews status
```

The Tellnews command is used to communicate with the server, similar to how the CTLINNd communicates with the INN daemon INNd. It is used to determine the status of the server, to modify internal settings, to reload configuration files, and to shut down the server cleanly. It will be explored in more detail in Chapter 20, "Maintenance," but here are a few examples of its use:

tellnews status—gets the server status

tellnews exit—tells the DNEWS application to shut down

VERIFICATION AND TESTING

Use a news reader to try out the news server. Remember to adjust the options in your news reader to point to the news host (in this case *news.us.pcgbase.com*). Ask for the newsgroup *news.newusers.questions.* The system should come back with a default message stating that the group is currently empty but that the group will be requested from the upstream news server, and to please try again in a few minutes.

If this routine proves unsuccessful, check the access.conf file to ensure that the reader's domain is allowed.

You may also TELNET to the server at port 119—the NNTP port—and run a manual NNTP session. Here is a sample session:

```
news# telnet news.us.pcgbase.com 119
group        news.newsusers.questions (select a group)
head         (display the header)
body         (display the body)
next         (next item please)
help         (show valid commands)
quit         (exit the connection)
news#
```

If DNEWS is not running, you will get the following message:

```
telnet: Unable to connect to remote host: Connection refused.
```

Clues to any other problems such as *being denied access* may be discovered in the dnews.log file, and the DNEWS FAQ.

If the read capability is functional, try posting to the *alt.test* newsgroup. This will trigger autoresponder robots located at news sites around the world, who receive the post, to respond with an e-mail. Using *alt.test* rather than a regular newsgroup is a courtesy, expected of you by the news community.

Here is an e-mail response received by *news.postech.ac.kr*, a news server of the Pohang University of Science and Technology in Pohang, South Korea, on 19 Nov 1996 02:19:06 KST (18 Nov 1996 17:19:06 GMT):

```
Forwarded message:
>From autoreply@news.postech.ac.kr Mon Nov 18 12:19 EST 1996
Date: Tue, 19 Nov 1996 02:19:06 +0900
Message-Id: <199611181719.CAA03686@news.postech.ac.kr>
To: "John E. Phillips" <jep@pcgbase.com>
From: autoreply@news.postech.ac.kr (POSTECH Autoresponder)
Subject: Re: FIXED AND TESTED
Reply-To: nobody@news.postech.ac.kr
References: <329087BF.2F10@pcgbase.com>
Newsgroups: alt.test
Precedence: junk
Content-Type: text
Content-Length: 1621

This is an automated reply to a test posting in the alt.test newsgroup.

This serves to confirm for you that your test post was sucessfully
distributed to this machine via the Usenet path shown in the header
of your article, included below. To avoid receiving this automated
reply, place the word "ignore" anywhere in the subject line of your
posts to *.test newsgroups.

According to your article's header, it was posted on:
    18 Nov 1996 15:58:55 GMT

The posting was received by news.postech.ac.kr, a news server of the
Pohang University of Science and Technology in Pohang, South Korea
on 19 Nov 1996 02:19:06 KST (18 Nov 1996 17:19:06 GMT). The transit
time of the message was 1 hour, 20 minutes and 11 seconds.

This autoresponder will not reply to any message which includes the word
"ignore" in the Subject line of an article. To reach the administrator
of news.postech.ac.kr, send mail to usenet@news.postech.ac.kr.
```

The header and first 10 lines of your message were:

Path:
news.postech.ac.kr!usenet.kornet.nm.kr!howland.erols.net!newsfeed.internetmci.com!zeke.ebtech.net!loki.tor.hookup.net!nic.ott.hookup.net!news.pcgbase.us.com
From: "John E. Phillips" <jep@pcgbase.com>
Newsgroups: alt.test
Subject: FIXED AND TESTED
Date: Mon, 18 Nov 1996 10:58:55 -0500
Organization: Phillips Consulting Group, Inc.
Lines: 4
Message-ID: <329087BF.2F10@pcgbase.com>
NNTP-Posting-Host: news.pcgbase.com
Mime-Version: 1.0
Content-Type: text/plain; charset=us-ascii
Content-Transfer-Encoding: 7bit
X-Mailer: Mozilla 3.01 (X11; I; SunOS 5.5.1 sun4c)

This is a test of a DNEWS server
--
John Phillips
jep@pcgbase.com

To avoid receiving this automated reply, place the word *ignore* anywhere in the Subject line of your posts to **.test* newsgroups. The autoresponders will not reply to any message that includes the word *ignore* in the Subject line of an article.

REGISTRATION

With most commercial software packages, there is the dreaded registration process. DNEWS is no exception, although the company does provide a free trial period during which you can assess the software. It also builds in an interactive registration application that makes the registration process relatively painless: Tellnews register.

The program will ask you a few questions and create a file register.txt, which you then e-mail to this address:

netwin@world.std.com.

You will receive an e-mail reply confirming your registration or license or support contract, depending on which options you selected. The confirmation e-mail will also include your registration key, which will disable the registration reminder notices. If your key is *ax343acd3*, then to enter it you would type:

```
$tellnews key ax343acd3
```

Then your registration is complete.

Installing a Normal NNTP Ihave Feed

DNEWS can also be set up as a normal news server; that is, it can perform Ihave-type exchanges with its upstream host in a peer–peer arrangement. To do this DNEWS has to be configured slightly differently from the above sucking feed implementation.

First Ihave permission must be granted in the access.conf file.

```
my.feeder.site.com:ihave:::*
```

Next in the dnews.conf file, comment out the Nntp_feeder definition and add the following:

```
nntp_feeder    news.isp2.com
cachedall true
```

In newsfeeds.conf, replace

```
site $NNTP_FEEDER
          groups *
          builtin
          posting
```

with:

```
     site my.feeder.site
          groups *
          builtin
```

You MUST get a copy of active.dat from your provider; the file is simply called the active file on INN. You need to FTP the file and copy it to /var/spool/dnews/active.dat while the server is NOT running.

If you wish to send a full feed on to another site other than your upstream news host, you will also have to activate the Xmit utility.

First add your other news hosts to your newsfeed.conf file. Then set up a timed job to send news to the other sites using Xmit. An example of this appears below.

Add lines to your Rc.local procedure, for example,

```
cd /usr/local/dnews
./xmit send.to.site.name -at "*2" "*"
./xmit send.other.site.name -at "*7" "*"
```

PART IV

ADMINISTRATION

Upon leaving the Construction section you have a news server up and running. The actual news service was deliberately left in limbo. In the following chapters you'll learn how to craft a decent Acceptable Usage Policy, the steps involved in releasing your news service to the community, and how to handle day-to-day maintenance issues and issues related to Intranet News. In the final chapter is a prognostication on the trends in news and where they might lead and a discussion on news routers.

18 Acceptable Usage Policy

An effective and enforced acceptable usage policy (AUP) is more important today than ever before. Unfortunately many organizations don't have an effective AUP, or, if they have one, they don't consistently enforce it. Policies will differ from company to company, and these, in turn, will be different from university or ISP policies. Academic institutions may put a high value on freedom of expression and may allow every newsgroup under the sun, including the notorious *alt.binaries.**. On the other hand, because of the political correctness trend many universities exhibit, their usage policies may be very restrictive, at least on paper. Most ISPs and academic institutions have existing policies, but most corporations don't, so this chapter focuses on corporate AUPs.

In some cases generic network usage policies can suffice, but USENET News is a unique mechanism and probably deserves a separate policy.

Why You Need a Policy

The absence of a policy implies that everything is allowed. A good AUP makes it much easier to define the ground rules since everything is disallowed unless specifically allowed. News users especially need to follow accepted practices because inappropriate actions can have far-reaching effects, not only on the company but on the News community itself. Some things to consider follow.

LEGAL LIABILITY

No one knows with any certainty what liability a corporation will incur if one of its employees, or someone successfully pretending to be a corporate employee, commits an illegal act via News. There are existing statutes for mail fraud that almost certainly will apply to the pyramid-style get-rich-quick schemes over the Net. Just as certain, laws on the books or in the works prohibit the distribution and possession of child pornography or harassment. The offenders, when caught, will be prosecuted under applicable laws. An example of a recent court ruling:

> *Rindos v. Hardwick*
> (No. 1994 of 1993, judgment delivered March 31, 1994)
> Western Australian case where Rindos, an anthropologist, was defamed by Hardwick on a USENET newsgroup called sci.anthropology. Rindos was awarded $40,000 by Ipp, J.

But what about the company whose news server was used to carry this contraband traffic? Are they considered guiltless common carriers, or are they considered broadcasters responsible for the content they transmit? If ruled common carriers, then they are nothing more than bit haulers, like a telephone company carrying a felony phone call—not responsible, not guilty. If ruled broadcasters, then participants in the USENET scheme *could* be held responsible, much like a television station, radio station, or newspaper. The latter scenario may sound unreasonable when it involves a rogue employee who decides to get even with the company by implicating them in his illegal scheme. But it's not so unreasonable when the company is set up as a spamming service (or online advertiser, as they prefer to be called) and pleads ignorance of supposed unsolicited acts by some of its employees. A number of cases concerning such spamming services are pending in the United States today.

It's more likely than not that the news server propagating news will be considered a bit hauler, but an organization may still be held accountable for its employee posts. By following AUP, the employee can avoid putting the company in jeopardy.

Having your employees put a disclaimer in the signature of their post is a simple way to differentiate a poster's views from those of the company, and this policy may also have some legal value. An example follows:

> This post represents the views of *employee name* and not those of ACME Tools Inc.

or

> This post is not an official publication of ACME Tools Inc.

PEACE WITHIN THE COMMUNITY

As alluded to earlier, News is a communal effort, and it takes the actions of only an ignorant or maladjusted few to upset the community. Inexperienced users, called *newbies,* are often to blame for violating netiquette as they hack and crash through newsgroups. Like it or not, many regular participants of newsgroups have evolved an informal but largely adhered to netiquette, and they get very upset when people break them. Breaking the rules can result in something as minor as an ignorant post to something as serious as a full-fledged mail bomb that can severely impair corporate resources.

Netiquette is defined in the Internet Jargon File as follows:

> netiquette: net'ee–ket\ or \net'i–ket\ [portmanteau from network etiquette] n. Conventions of politeness recognized on {USENET}, such as avoidance of cross–posting to inappropriate groups or refraining from commercial pluggery on the net.

You can find an alternate view of the rules of engagement for USENET in a satirical posting in *news.announce*: "Emily Postnews Answers Your Questions on Netiquette" written by Sally Hambridge. Here is an excerpt:

> Emily Postnews, foremost authority on proper net behavior, gives her advice on how to act on the net.
>
> Q: Dear Miss Postnews: How long should my signature be?—verbose@noisy
>
> A: Dear Verbose: Please try and make your signature as long as you can. It's much more important than your article, of course, so try to have more lines of signature than actual text. Try to include a large graphic made of ASCII characters, plus lots of cute quotes and slogans. People will never tire of reading these pearls of wisdom again and again, and you will soon become personally associated with the joy each reader feels at seeing yet another delightful repeat of your signature.

> **NOTE: this is intended to be satirical. If you do not recognize it as such, consult a doctor or professional comedian. The recommendations in this article should recognized for what they are—admonitions about what NOT to do.**

Luckily the posting comes with the above disclaimer, but it's probably not a good idea to include Emily's views in your policy because not everyone will read the disclaimer.

RFC 1855 Netiquette is a more serious paper. Here are excerpts regarding signatures:

> Again, be sure to have a signature which you attach to your message. This will guarantee that any peculiarities of mailers or newsreaders which strip header information will not delete the only reference in the message of how people may reach you.

BUDGETING COMPANY RESOURCES

Corporate bandwidth is a precious commodity in any organization. This applies to both Internet access bandwidth and internal LANs and WANs. Improper use of the news service can severerly congest bandwidth and can result in denial of service, not only for news but also for other mission critical services such as e-mail and corporate server access. For example, posters who attach files to a news article may not give much thought to the bandwidth they are chewing up. Also, they often don't realize that file size could increase significantly owing to encoding.

Employees' time is a very real corporate resource. Productivity can decrease because employees are spending time on frivolous newsgroups rather than doing their jobs. Left unchecked, a news addict can spend as much time on News as surfing the World Wide Web.

SECURITY CONSIDERATIONS

It is very easy for an employee to post confidential information to a public newsgroup. The best security firewalls on the market can't fully analyze article content to protect against company secrets making their way outside the company. Employees posting to an Intranet newsgroup may post sensitive company information to the world by improper or deliberate misuse of the Newgroups or Followup to fields in the header. Weak encryption methods (such as ROT13) may also provide employees with a false sense of security when it comes to posting company-sensitive information in public newsgroups.

COMPANY OPTICS

Many news readers hide the details of the article header, and it's easy to forget that listed in the header is the name of every machine involved in the propagation of the post, including the one that originated the post. Ask yourself the question Do you really want a post to *terrorism.pipe-bomb* carrying your organization's name? Also, if someone in your company is wreaking havoc on the News community, there is a good chance that the news administrator at one of your customer companies is being adversely affected. If the problem is habitual, this can be very bad PR!

CONTENTS OF A GOOD AUP

AUPs can vary greatly from organization to organization, both in content and in tone, and your AUP will depend to a great extent on your company's culture, legal requirements, and so forth. In some organizations you will have to blare out stern warnings and explicit punishments in the AUP. In others it may be more appropriate to phrase the policy as a series of guidelines to be followed as good, professional practices.

Following are some suggestions for content. (Note: Many companies will want to adjust the use of *must* and *should* in order to properly differentiate between a rule and a suggestion.)

CORE POLICY

- News should be used for business purposes during working hours.
- Confidential information must not be posted to public newsgroups.
- All posts to public newsgroups must carry a disclaimer in the signature to the effect that the opinions expressed are not the company's.
- Employees should adhere to generally accepted netiquette when participating in internal and public newsgroups.
- News users must not use News for illegal purposes or to participate in practices that adversely affect others, the corporate network, or the USENET community.
- The article header must not be modified in order to conceal a user's identity or to impersonate someone else.
- Employees should not let others use their machine for posting. Sharing of usernames and passwords is strongly discouraged, and all responsibilities must be borne by the person to whom a username is initially issued.

- Public News should not be used for advertising purposes unless a particular newsgroup was specifically set up for this purpose.
- News must not be used to contravene company policies already in effect.

OPTIONAL POLICIES

- News accounts may be monitored in order to collect such things as usage stats, reading habits, and so forth.
- The company uses *company.posted* (discussed in Chapter 21), which makes any outside post public within the company.
- The company does not subscribe to any of the *alt.binary* newsgroups.
- Encryption techniques for messages leaving the corporate network must be approved.

TRAINING

Education is better than enforcement.

The best policy is useless without enforcement, but enforcement by itself is not a very efficient or pleasant way to create change. Ignorance of the effects of certain actions is often more the problem than outright sabotage. Your company should provide education and training as well as enforcement of its News policies. A beneficial side-effect of training is that it permits you to encourage feedback.

Make sure your employees understand the basics, such as

- How News works,
- Netiquette,
- The content they might encounter,
- The public nature of news,
- The audit trail in the header,
- Bandwidth required when transmitting images,
- The damage that can result from improper use of News, and
- The consequences of breaking the rules.

Money invested in training will help you avoid having to deal with incidents and offenders whose only crime was ignorance.

Above all, reinforce that access to News—especially to public newsgroups—is a privilege, not an inalienable right.

19 Service Rollout

At this point the news server has been tested, but the *news service* has not been released companywide. It's time to make a formal announcement probably using e-mail or a similar vehicle.

The announcement should include the Acceptable Usage Policy (AUP), a listing of news coverage, a description of the nature of news, and so forth (as covered in Chapter 11, "Setting User Expectations"), as well as news readers being supported, USENET News reference material, and rollout schedules.

Client Issues

Users should be given a configuration guide containing basic information about what will be required by their news reader software. This information should include:

- Company,
- Name,
- Mail address,
- Organization,
- Content of signature file,

- Name of SMTP server,
- POP3 server if used (a mail server and which protocol it runs under),
- Name of news server to read from and post to (use name not IP number), and
- News directory (where saved news articles are stored).

If character-based readers such as NN are used in a multi-user environment, it is possible to set these variables in a global configuration file such as /etc/profile.

TURNING ON ACCESS TO THE SERVICE

You can control reader access to the news server by making entries in the nnrp.access file (for INN) and the access.conf file (for DNEWS). The same syntax and parameter definitions are used in both systems and both provide an option for user/password authentication. The format of the entries is as follows:

```
<host>:<perm>:<user>:<pass>:<groups>
```

Both manuals are a bit vague in describing the parameters, but Table 19-1 gives more information.

Table 19-1 Read Access Control

Parameter	Description
Host	This is the portion of your network that can connect. You may want to release the service one subnet at a time or along geographic or department boundaries. Individual users can also be added.
Perm	This parameter defines the permissions the user or users defined above have read, posted, or both. Using "I" as an entry allows for Ihave instead of Posting for transferring upstream.
User	Optional user ID, used in conjunction with password just for posting.
Pass	See *user* above.
Groups	Which groups are allowed to be read.

Here is a reader access example:

```
205.233.33.*:Read,Post:jep:cube657:*
```

In this example, the user *jep* can read and post news from any host on the 205.233.33.0 subnet. These read and post privileges are extended to each and every newsgroup on the news server.

If a company wants to control access privileges on a user-by-user basis, this would require an entry in the access file for each user. This makes management a tedious task since people move around within the company, get added and dropped from committees, and so on. Managing access to Intranet newsgroups further adds to this complexity. Of course, an employee leaving a department may also lose privileges, and this will require tweaking the file as well. A software tool called Grouper, written by James Mathiesen when he was at Brown University, provides an elegant solution to this problem.

Every group has three important components: an expression defining the group's initial membership, a list of people added to the group, and a list of people who are removed from the group. These three components are evaluated to compute the effective membership of the group; that is, expression + inclusion set – exclusion set (see Figure 19-1). A newsmaster can use Grouper to define groups and their membership along many different lines to match organizational and committee structure in the Grouper database. When an employee tries to access News, INN defers to Grouper to determine to which groups the person is allowed access.

Figure 19-1 Determining a newsgroup's membership.

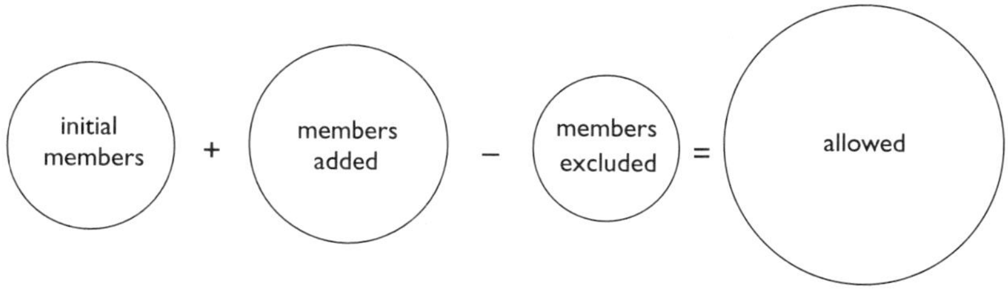

Grouper and full documentation are included on the CD-ROM, and if you followed the CD-ROM loading instructions in Chapter 16, Grouper will already be loaded on your hard disk in the directory /local/src. Grouper is also available at the following FTP site:

ftp.brown.edu/pub/netnews.

Grouper comes with a Web graphical user interface called Webgroupie, which provides administrators with an easy-to-use interface. Figures 19-2 and 19-3 depict a few sample screens.

Figure 19-2 Changing group membership.

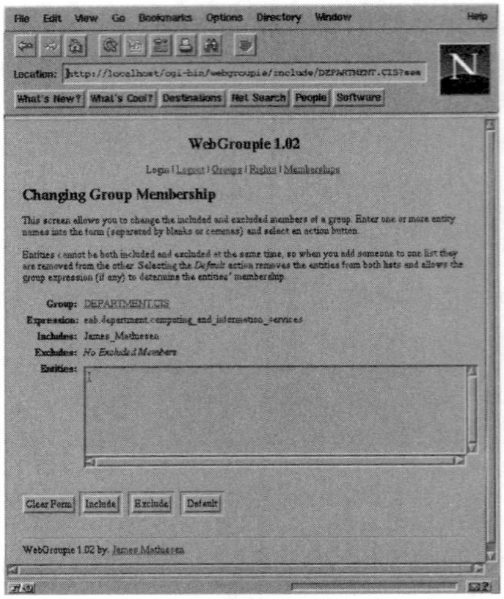

Figure 19-3 Summary of groups.

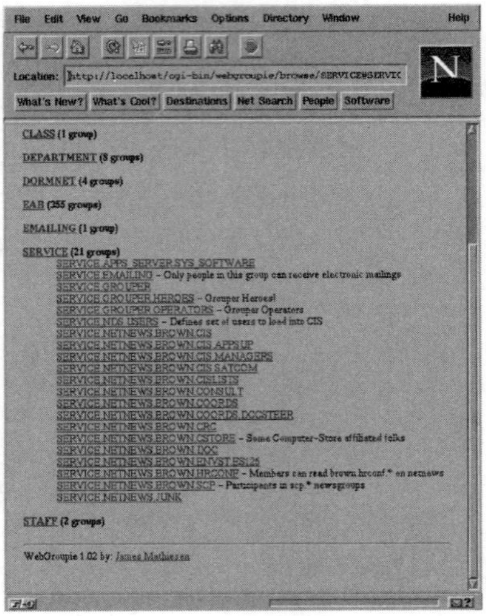

PROBLEMS TO EXPECT

The release of any new Internet service often triggers a flood of interest, at least initially. Everyone wants the new toy, whether it be e-mail, World Wide Web, or USENET News. With News, some might be attracted by the prospect of access to the *alt.binaries*, others by the ability to participate in technical discussions, still others by the *for_sale* groups. Yet, like most new toys, interest may be short-lived.

Following are some specific problems rollout of News can cause within your organization. The problems should be viewed in light of an understanding of this novelty effect. An important axiom is DON'T Overreact. Try to determine if the problems experienced today are liable to remain with you tomorrow.

INCREASED NETWORK TRAFFIC

To accommodate a full news feed you'll need at least 64K all day every day in order to keep up. If you've followed the advice given in the Planning section, Part II, of the book, storage capacity shouldn't be a problem, just an observation. The capacity of your internal network is another matter. Here the bandwidth hit depends on user habits, readers employed, number of subscribers, as well as the use of MIME attachments. As each segment of the corporate network is turned on for News, check the load using a traffic analyzer and ensure that no part is being congested. Usage statistics generated by news servers can also help you assess the cause of congestion—whether is is attributable to News or something else, such as a failing router, e-mail, World Wide Web abuse, and so forth.

INCREASED SUPPORT CALLS

Most calls to the Help Desk regarding News will be attributable to misconfigured readers. Have the user check the client configuration information; in particular ensure that he or she is pointing to the correct news host. The other category of callers will be asking the "How do I . . ." types of questions. Training should have taken place prior to releasing the news service, so users should use the training material to educate themselves. If not, there are many good references listed in the bibliography of this book which could provide some assistance. Also, Chapter 12 provides helpful starting points for useful online information about USENET News.

CORPORATE PRODUCTIVITY

News can be fun and addictive, so much so that productivity can be affected. But remember the novelty effect. Give abusers a bit of time to come to their senses or get cloyed with News. If problems persist, enforcement of the AUP is the best cure.

20 Maintenance

This chapter provides the basic tool set for maintaining a news server along with some useful tips and hints. It covers such mandatory items as logs and metrics, adding and deleting groups, and handling control messages.

> All the tools presented here have been built and tested from instruction obtained either in the associated tar file (man pages, install guides, and so forth) or from readme files. In some cases the instructions had to be modified to accommodate the sample system, and such changes are indicated. It is always a good idea to check the most recent documentation on these tools since newer versions may make the documentation in this book obsolete.

Log Files

Log files contain the current status and history of the news server and are updated by the system based on a predefined schedule or when special events occur. Both INN and DNEWS maintain log files, and, although the log files differ in the specifics, they are similar in intent. Both are designed to provide the newsmaster with detailed system information so problems can be resolved or averted in the first place. A word of caution is in order, however. Although these tools can be a tremendous help, you will still have to spend time manually reviewing the reports and log files.

INN Logs

Most log files created by INN programs reside in the /var/log/news directory and have a .log extension. Several copies are generally kept with an additional extension such as .1, .2, and so forth—the higher the number, the older the log. The older versions are compressed to save space. The Scanlogs script and related utilities are responsible for rotating and compressing these files. Some log files always have data, others are written to only if there is a problem, and still others are created only if a particular program is used or a configuration parameter is set.

Table 20-1 provides summary information on the INN log files. Consult the INN man pages and Install Guide for more information. The control.ctl file is covered in more depth later in this chapter.

Table 20-1 INN Log Files

Log File	Contents	Control Point
control.log	A count of the number of Newgroup and Rmgroup control messages seen for each newsgroup.	Controlled by the action parameter in the control.ctl file.*
errlog	Standard output and standard error of any program spawned by INNd.	Controlled by the action parameter in the control.ctl file.
expire.log	Information on expired articles.	This file is written to by news.daily.
miscctl.log	All control messages except Newgroup and Rmgroup.	Controlled by the action parameter in the control.ctl file.
newgroup.log	All Newgroup control messages.	Controlled by the action parameter in the control.ctl file.
news	Articles received by INNd.	Scanlogs summarizes the rejected articles reported in this file.
news.crit	All critical error messages issued by INNd are appended to this file via syslog.	Written to by the Scanlogs program.
news.err	All major error messages issued by INNd.	Written to by the Scanlogs program.
news.notice	All standard error messages and status messages issued by INNd.	Written to by the Scanlogs program.
nntpsend.log	All status messages.	Written to by the Nntpsend program.

Table 20-1 INN Log Files (Continued)

Log File	Contents	Control Point
rmgroup.log	All Rmgroup control messages.	Controlled by the action parameter in the control.ctl file.
unwanted.log	A count of the number of articles that were rejected because they were posted to newsgroups that do not exist at the local site.	Controlled by the action parameter in the control.ctl file.

DNEWS Log

DNEWS keeps all log information in one file, dnews.log. The location and content of this file are controlled by dnews.conf in the /etc directory.

The command Loglv1 provides a way for the newsmaster to customize the log file. Table 20-2 depicts the four levels of logging.

Table 20-2 DNEWS Log Options

Parameter	Description
Error	Serious errors.
Warn	Possible problems.
Info	General information messages.
Debug	Used for tracing bugs.
Flush	Same as debug, but the log file is flushed with every single line written; this is useful if the system is crashing but not providing a stack dump.

See also Chapter 17, "DNEWS."

Using the command Tellnews log causes the last 50 lines of the log to be displayed. A status report, containing the entire log file, can also be mailed daily to a specified address. This topic is covered in greater depth later in this chapter.

Metrics

In order to maintain an effective and reliable news service you must establish metrics to monitor the server and network resources. It's very much a case of what you *don't* know *can* hurt you. For example, if the server's free disk space is steadily decreasing, you have to act on this trend—expire articles faster, block certain newsgroups, and so forth—or risk having the disk crash. If the server normally receives 100MB of news per day, and the amount suddenly jumps to 400MB one day, what changed? Your upstream news feed could have increased its news coverage, but another possibility is that someone has penetrated your security and is using your news server for his or her own purposes. Without metrics you won't be aware of significant changes or trends.

Metrics can also assist you in planning and budgeting for your news service. It is much easier to protect your budget, or even justify a request for an increase, if you have statistical evidence of the need. If the newsmaster can't explain and justify circumstances, a "disk full" message may be interpreted by higher-ups as the newsmaster not doing his or her job properly.

For many years, newsmasters collected metrics manually or with homebrew programs. Today, there are some powerful software tools available on the Internet that significantly ease the burden of maintaining, collecting, and interpreting metrics.

INN—INNREPORT

Included in the contrib directory of the INN distribution is Innreport, a PERL script used for summarizing INN log files, with optional HTML output. This script was written by Fabien Tassin, and it's extremely useful and easy to implement.

1. Get PERL and GD.pm.

   To install Innreport you'll need Perl 5.002 or higher (version 5.003 is included on the CD-ROM). You can also download the latest version from

   ```
   ftp.prep.ai.mit.edu
   ```

   in the pub/gnu directory.

   You'll need the PERL graphic library GD.pm. This library is available at

   ```
   http://www-genome.wi.mit.edu/pub/software/WWW/GD.html
   ```

   To install the library, execute these commands:

   ```
   news# cd /opt/local/src
   news# tar xvzf GDGD.pm.tar.gz
   news# cd GD-1.14
   news# perl Makefile.pl
   ```

```
news# make
news# make install
```

Now that the interface to the GD graphics library is installed, you can install Innreport.

2. Install the application.

   Move to the $INN/contrib directory and edit Innreport. Use RCS or a similar revision control method when editing this file.

```
news# cd $INN/contrib
news# vi innreport
```

   You will probably have to change only the *HTML_dir* line, which tells the script where to install the reports and charts. Make sure the ownership and permissions on this directory are correct for your system.

```
## Directory for the Web pages (used only if the previous line is active)
$HTML_dir = "/opt/www/server_root/docs/News/stats";
## Directory for the GIF pictures (need HTML support) in the file
## space
$IMG_dir = "$HTML_dir/pics";
news# cp innreport /usr/news/etc/innreport.pl
news# chown news:news /usr/news/etc/innreport.pl
news# chmod 700 /usr/news/etc/innreport.pl
```

   Move to the site directory of your INN source code and edit the Scanlogs.

```
news# cd $INN/site
```

   In scanlogs, comment the line containing Innlog and replace it with this:

```
${NEWSLIB}/innreport.pl < ${OLD_SYSLOG}

news# make reload-install
```

   Now when the news.daily program is executed from cron, a USENET report will be generated in HTML format. Figures 20-1 and 20-2 show two examples.

Figure 20-1 Innreport chart showing hierarchy traffic.

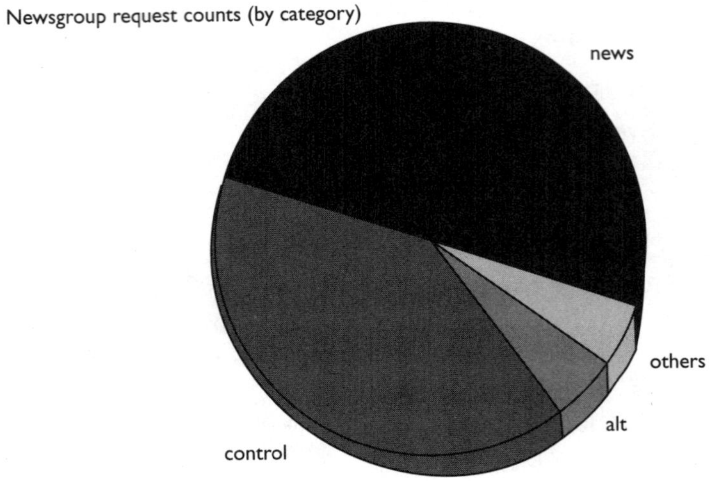

Figure 20-2 Innreport chart showing articles received by the news server.

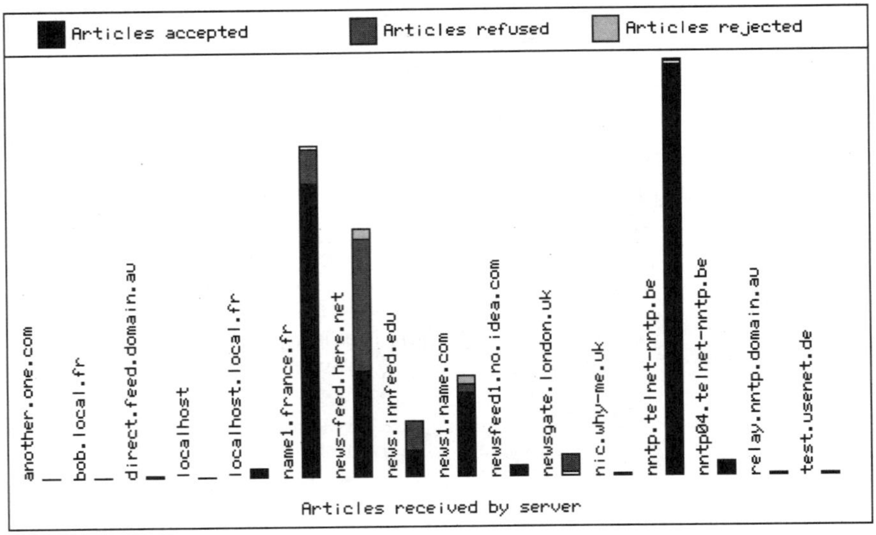

DNEWS—STATUS REPORT

As of this writing DNEWS does not have any graphical tools similar to Innreport, but DNEWS does send a comprehensive daily status report via e-mail. The following shows a typical status report with explanations (#) for each entry.

200 161.29.2.10 DNEWS Version 3.0f, posting OK
This line shows the name and version number of the server, it also tells you if posting from your ip address is possible.

Feed[0]: me *,!to.*,!*.binaries.*
Feed[1]: 161.29.2.5 Posting Builtin Posts=0 Rej=0 Req=0 Dup=0 file=100k Del=10MB *
This is a list of the feeds in newsfeeds.conf file. The number of Posts, Rejects, Reque'd and Duplicate messages sent out that feed since startup are shown. Also, if there is a queue of waiting articles then the size of the queued file is also shown. The 'del' figure is how many queued articles have been deleted because they couldn't be sent (This is automatic if the queue grows past 10MB)

Chan[0:5] B o=130 in=1/s out=6/s 161.29.2.10 test.netwin.co.nz C_CMD
Chan[1:5] o=0 in=13000/s out=600/s 161.29.2.3 test.netwin.co.nz C_IHAVE
This is the list of currently connected sessions, their IP number and name s. In this case reverse translation is disabled so it shows the IP number twice.
B - channel busy, it is still processing a command and producing output.
o=130 - output buffer has 130 bytes.
in=13000/s - input speed has been 13K /s for the last 30 seconds
out=600/s - input speed has been 600 bytes/s for the last 30 seconds
C_CMD - the channel is waiting for a normal NNTP command
C_IHAVE - the channel is part way thru an IHAVE transaction.

Expire started at Fri Feb 16 13:31:05 1996 Done, start 1% end 1%
Processed 920 removed 0 deleting 200/-1/150 speed 170.429
Expire finished at: Fri Feb 16 13:31:12 1996, Elapsed 0 hours, 0 minutes
This shows the start and finish time and%'s of the last expire run.
Processed - number of history lines in your history file.
removed - number of history lines removed
deleting - the number of items being deleted, total and actual (of 200 items deleted 50 were cross posts so don't count as real deletes)
Speed - history articles processed/second

Contents of DNEWS group fetching queue, 2 entries:
Group rec.humor.funny fetching, got 20 items
Group comp.os.vms pending (low priority)
Group comp.lang.java pending (low priority)
End of queue.

This is the list of groups DNEWS is currently trying to fetch. Reverse lookup took 80 seconds, disable lookups if possible (see nodns). This error means your name server is faulty (or can't be contacted), you should disable name translation, set NODNS TRUE in dnews.conf

History: disk 76k memory 7k/80k, Str 2k/5k/500k Malloc 1097k/1097k/2128k
Current history file is 76K (40mb would be more normal) and the in memory amount for this file is 7k (5mb would be more normal). The Str and Malloc's are for debugging, they show the total memory allocated and also what is being used at present.

Used 1MB=1%, Free work 34Mb, hist 34Mb, spool 34Mb, log 34Mb
Disk space used as a percent and how much is actually free.

Groups Cached 3 of 4624, Uptime 0 day(s) 0 hour(s)
Shows how many groups are cached, and how long the system has been running.

EXPIRING ARTICLES

As your logs will reveal, news volumes can fluctuate wildly. Without sufficient disk space to handle these spikes, the disk can be overrun. One solution is a very aggressive expire schedule to make sure there's room on the disk to take on peak traffic. This policy is certainly effective but may not allow users enough time to read articles, especially if they are busy, traveling, or on vacation.

A more equitable solution is to monitor the disk space and adapt the expire schedule to target the least desirable news when predefined disk limits are exceeded.

INN—INNWATCH

Included with the INN distribution is Innwatch. This program is normally started by Rc.news and periodically (every 600 seconds) examines the load average, free blocks, and the number of inodes on the spool partition, as described by its control file, innwatch.ctl. If the defined thresholds are crossed, Innwatch will pause the news system. In addition, on each pass through the loop it will check the logfile /var/log/news/news.crit to see if it has been modified. If so, mail will be sent to the news administrator.

The point to note here is that while Innwatch will keep the disk crunch problem from getting worse, it takes no corrective action to fix the problem. If the problem is load average, chances are that the load will decrease and things will go back to normal. If the problem is disk space or inode count, Innwatch will have to wait until the problem is resolved before it can unblock the server. Unfortunately, as soon as the server starts again, all the news that has been queued upstream will flood in causing the problem to recur.

A dynamic, adaptive expiration scheme is a much more practical solution. In this scheme, low priority news is targeted for early expiration. One program that does this is Reap.

INN—REAP

Reap is a small utility, written by David Thomas, that automatically intervenes when disk space becomes critically low. Reap is called by cron. If free space is low, Reap deletes articles according to a user-specified scheme until a minimum free space becomes available. For example, if the *alt.binaries* newsgroups were set to expire the quickest, Reap would inspect articles in this hierarchy and trash any article older than a time specified on its own expire list. If this action does not clear the problem, Reap goes to the hierarchy with the next shortest expiry, and so on. Reap can be looked at as a way of managing a second list of shorter expiry times that is only invoked when free space limits are exceeded.

Reap affects only the article spool directory. The history file and active file are adjusted by the news.daily program. The overview file is cleaned up by cron updates.

Reap is available on the CD-ROM or can be downloaded from

```
ftp://ftp.uu..net/networking/news/misc/reap
```

To install Reap perform the following steps:

1. Edit the tops of Makefile and main.c to fit your system.

   First do the Makefile changes:

   ```
   # directories where manual and executable are to be installed
   BINDIR = /usr/news/bin
   MANDIR = /usr/news/man/man8

   # your favorite C compiler
   CC = gcc

   # directory access functions library, if not in standard C library.
   LIB = [remove any value present here]
   ```

Then do the main.c file changes:

```
#define NEWSDIR          "/opt/news/spool/articles"
*scriptfile = "/usr/news/etc/reaplist"
```

2. Build the application.

```
news# make
```

3. Test Reap before installing it using the following command line:

```
news# reap [-v] [-n] [-f funcfile] freeblocks
```

Table 20-3 explains the various options.

Table 20-3 Reap Parameters

Parameter	Description
-V	With the -V option, Reap prints a verbose commentary on its progress to the standard output.
-N	Using the -N causes a dry run. When this option is specified, Reap merely reports which files it would delete if the option were left off. This is useful for debugging function scripts.
-F funcfile	By default, Reap looks in the file /usr/lib/news/reaplist for its list of functions. The -F option is used to specify an alternate function script file.
Freeblocks	Defines the desired free blocks. Be sure to use the correct version of DF. Executing the command Usr/bin/df will display the number of free blocks.

Compose a sample Function script file or use the sample provided to test Reap. A Function script file consists of a series of expire functions, one per line. Each expire function contains an age (in days; decimals are okay), followed by a list of newsgroups to be expired. Blank lines and lines beginning with a "#" are ignored. Here is a sample Function script file:

```
# function script file
0.5  talk,junk,alt.sex.pictures
2    rec,!rec.games,!rec.humor
3    misc
```

4. Do a dry run (use the -N option to avoid actually removing files).

```
news# reap -n -f sample.file
```

Reap will tell you what it would do if you let it really expire articles. The screen will display a list of affected newsgroups.

```
would unlink talk
would unlink talk.nothing
would unlink talk.politics
•
•
```

5. Install the application.

```
news# su
news# make install
```

6. Arrange to run Reap from cron.

```
0 0,6,12,18 * * * /usr/news/bin/reap
```

In the above example, if space is needed, Reap expires articles in the *talk* and *junk*, and *alt.sex.pictures* hierarchies, older than 0.5 days. If still more space is needed, the *rec* hierarchy articles (excepting *rec.games.** and *rec.humor.**) are expired to two days. If free space is still short, Reap then expires articles in the *misc* hierarchy that are older than two days. Although it would be possible to consolidate the second and third lines, leaving them separate makes it possible for Reap to stop in between them if sufficient space is cleared.

It's important to remember that cross-posts are stored as links, and all links to an article have to be deleted before the data in the article are removed from the disk. Choose the entries in your function script carefully.

DNEWS—EXPIRE.CONF

DNEWS already has a very flexible expiry capability controlled by the expire.conf file.

Table 20-4 explains the expire.conf parameters.

Table 20-4 Expire.conf Parameters

Symbol	Example	Description
upto	20%	This rule applies if less than 20 percent of the disk space is full.
groups	*alt.*,comp.binaries.**	This rule applies if the group matches this list.
keep	2	Keep items for this many days even if they have already expired (based on the expire date in the article header).
default	10	Keep items this long and then delete, unless the expiration date says to keep it longer.
purge	35	Delete after this many days even if the expire header says to keep it longer. This should be set long enough to keep FAQs and no longer, in order to prevent abuse.
maxitems	1000	Delete old items if the group has more than this many items in it. Good for controlling high-volume groups.
minitems	10	Don't apply any other rules if the group has less than this many items in it. This is good for making low-volume groups usable.

Following is an example of an expire.conf file:

```
# Default rule
upto 10000% groups * keep 0 default 1 purge 10 maxitems 0 minitems 0
# Start to panic a little
upto 90% groups * keep 0 default 2 purge 33 maxitems 100 minitems 0
# Normal operation, put your meaningful settings here.
upto 60% groups * keep 2 default 5 purge 33 maxitems 1000 minitems 10
upto 60% groups comp.* keep 2 default 10 purge 33 maxitems 2000 minitems 10
# Lots of space, just stop things getting silly (e.g. 10000 items in...)
upto 30% groups * keep 2 default 17 purge 33 maxitems 3000 minitems 100
upto 20% groups * maxitems 2000
# Keep any local groups forever (this line must be last to work)
upto 1000% groups pcg.* keep 99999 minitems 10000
```

Here is an explanation of the 10,000% value for the Default rule, which can cause some confusion. Some default rule must be in effect, and since the *diskspace* value may have been lowered since construction, there would be no guarantee that any expiry would take place if you used 100%. By using a ridiculously large number, you can always guarantee expiry (in this case after no longer than ten days).

Archiving News in INN Using Archive

Most articles don't have a long-term relevancy and can be readily expired. However, some newsgroups contain information, such as minutes from meetings, the importance of which requires that they be kept for long periods of time. You could always choose to leave them on the server by never expiring them, but a better strategy is to have them automatically archived.

Archive is a program written by Rich Salz to automate the archiving process. Archive makes copies of files specified on its standard input, copies them to a separate directory, and keeps an ASCII index file to track them. The program is normally run either as a channel feed under INNd or by a script before Expire is run. Archive reads the named input file or standard input, if no file is given. The input is taken as a set of text lines. Blank lines and lines starting with a number sign "#" are ignored. All other lines should specify the name of a file to be archived. If a filename is not an absolute pathname, it is taken to be relative to /opt/news/spool/archive.

Files are copied to a directory within the archive directory, /opt/news/spool/archive. The default directory is a hierarchy that mimics the input files; intermediate directories are created as needed. For example, the input file comp/sources/unix/2211 (article 2211 in the newsgroup *comp.sources.unix*) will be copied to directory

/opt/news/spool/archive/comp/sources/unix/2211.

Table 20-5 describes the options for Archive.

Table 20-5 Archive Options

Option	Description
-a archive	If the -a flag is used, then it tells the archive directory to use it instead of the default.
-f	If the -f flag is used, then all directory names will be flattened out, replacing the slashes with periods. In this case, the file would be copied to /opt/news/spool/archive/comp.sources.unix/2211.
-i	If the -i flag is used, then Archive will append one line to the specified index file for each article that it copies. This line will contain the destination name and the Message-ID and Subject headers.
-m	Files are copied by making a link. If that fails, a new file is created. If the -m flag is used, then the file will be copied to the destination, and the input file will be replaced with a symbolic link pointing to the new file.
-r	By default, Archive sets its standard error to /var/log/news/errlog. To suppress this redirection, use the -r flag.

A typical newsfeeds entry to archive private newsgroups is as follows:

```
company-archive\
        :!*,*pcg*,!*wanted*,!*.d\
        :Tc,Wn\
        :/usr/news/bin/archive -f -i \
          /opt/news/spool/archive/INDEX
```

CREATING AND DELETING NEWSGROUPS

In the early days of USENET News, creating a new group was a formal process. Someone proposing a new group would have to post a Call for Discussion(CFD) to *news.announce.newgroups*, and basically drum up support for the group's creation. After a specified period of time, a Call for Votes (CFV) was requested, and if enough yes votes were tallied, the new group was allowed. A designated news administrator would post a *newgroup* control message that caused the group to be created everywhere the post was received. Without the sanction of a successful vote, a Newgroup control message would be discarded by news administrators. The *alt* hierarchy was excluded from this formality. In *alt* the group's sponsor needs to convince only his or her news administrator to send the appropriate control message.

The process for creating new groups in the public USENET domain is covered in detail in an article by David C. Lawrence entitled "How to Create a New Usenet Group," which can be found in *news.announce.newusers.* The remainder of this section deals specifically with the creation and/or deletion of Intranet newsgroups.

NAMING CONVENTION FOR INTRANET NEWSGROUPS

You can choose any naming convention for your Intranet newsgroups as long as the groups stay within the internal network. If a group is to have public range, however, the choice of group name prefix is crucial. *Local* is a very common name for Intranet groups, so if a user cross-posts to *local.test,* the article will show up in all *local.test* newsgroups all over the world. To ensure uniqueness, use some form or abbreviation of your company or organization name as a prefix in each Intranet newsgroup name. Department or geographic information can also be a useful delineator. For example, the name, *pcg.uk.forsale* for employee classifieds in the overseas division would be a good choice, rather than *local.forsale* or *company.forsale.*

INN—ADDING AND DELETING NEWSGROUPS

Here are the steps required to create an Intranet newsgroup:

- Select an appropriate name for the newsgroup.
- Make sure your INNd is running.
- Add the group with

  ```
  ctlinnd newgroup local.group
  ```

- Add entries to the <u>newsfeeds</u> file to restrict the local groups to your organization.
- Modify the file <u>nnrp.access</u> to ensure that only those authorized can read/post.
- Add a descriptive entry to the newsgroups file.

For example let's assume you wish to create a finance newsgroup named *pcg.finance.*

To check that INN is running, type

```
ps -ef | grep inn
```

The system should respond with something like:

```
root  236    1  0 12:53:38 ?      0:41 /bin/sh/usr/news/bin/innwatch
news  234    1  0 12:53:37 ?      0:16 /usr/news/bin/innd -p4 -i0
```

As the superuser, use CTLINNd to add the new group. The directory structure in the spool directory will be created automatically. CTLINNd is used to send messages to the control channel of INN. Excerpts from the man pages having to do with adding and deleting newsgroups appear below. For a full description of CTLINNd refer to the CTLINNd man pages and Appendix C.

•
•

"newgroup group rest creator
Create the specified newsgroup. The rest parameter should be the fourth field as described in active(5); if it is not an equal sign, only the first letter is used. The creator should be the name of the person creating the group. If the newsgroup already exists, this is equivalent to the "changegroup'"command. This is the only command that has defaults. The creator can be omitted and will default to the empty string, and the rest parameter can be omitted and will default to "y". This command can be done while the server is paused or throttled; it will update its internal state when a "go" command is sent. This command updates the active.times (see active(5)) file.

•
•

rmgroup group
Remove the specified newsgroup. This is done by editing the active file. The spool directory is not touched, and any articles in the group will be expired using the default expiration parameters. Unlike the "newgroup" command, this command does not update the active.times file."

•
•

Therefore to add our local newsgroup *pcg.finance,* enter the following:

```
su [or you could also log in as news]
   password: XXXXXX
# cd /usr/news/bin
# ctlinnd newgroup pcg.finance m newsmaster
# exit [exit to leave super user mode]
```

Since this is a very important newsgroup, it will be moderated, hence the use of the *m* switch.

It is critical that company financials do not find their way onto public newsgroups. To ensure that this does not happen, edit the newsfeeds file. If you followed Chapter 16 carefully, this should already be taken care of. But it's worth checking just the same. To edit the newsfeed file, change to the $INN/site directory. Edit the file and then install it.

```
news# cd $INN/site
news# vi newsfeeds
ME:!pcg.*::
news.isp.com.:*,!pcg.*:Tf,Wnm:
```

Also check the nnrp.access file to ensure that no unauthorized persons can read your finance newsgroup and make necessary changes to restrict readership.

Now install the modified files using the following commands:

```
news# make reload-install
/bin/sh ../installit.sh -O news -G news -m 0444 -b .OLD newsfeeds /usr/news/etc/
newsfeeds
```

Add a descriptive entry to the /usr/news/etc/newsgroups file.

```
news# cd /usr/news/etc
news# vi newsgroups

pcg.finance   Phillips Consulting Group Finance discussions

news# exit  [return to normal mode]
```

Here are the steps you need to take to remove an Intranet newsgroup:

- Remove the group from the newsgroups file.
- Modify the nnrp.access file.
- Modify the newsfeeds file.
- Remove the group with the CTLINNd Rmgroup command:

```
ctlinnd rmgroup pcg.finance
```

DNEWS—ADDING AND DELETING NEWSGROUPS

Adding and deleting newsgroups under DNEWS is very similar to doing so under INN, the main difference being the use of the Tellnews command instead of CTLINNd.

With DNEWS you add groups with the Tellnews newgroup command; for example,

```
news# tellnews newgroup here.chat y myname Local group

here.chat = name of group
y = Normal group (m = moderated)
myname = A record of who created the group (one word)
Local group = description for active.names file.
```

To create a private Intranet newsgroup with the name *finance,* you would type the following:

```
news# tellnews newgroup pcg.finance y newsmaster finance group
```

To stop your finance newsgroup from being sent upstream, you would modify your newsfeeds.conf file to ensure that the newsgroup does not get propagated outside the company using this command:

```
groups *,!pcg.*
```

Also check the access.conf file to ensure that no unauthorized persons can read your finance newsgroup and make necessary changes to restrict readership.

To remove a newsgroup, you basically reverse the process, and use the Tellnews command with the Rmgroup option:

```
news# tellnews rmgroup pcg.finance
```

CONTROL MESSAGES

As defined in RFC 1036, a control message is an article that contains control information. Control messages are used to request that other news servers perform certain actions, such as creating or deleting newsgroups, canceling a particular article, and so forth. Generally they are not placed in the news spool for readers. An article is formally designated as having control information by the presence of a *control line* in the header, followed by a control message argument.

A listing of control messages appears in Table 20-6

Table 20-6 Control Messages

Argument	Description of Action
Cancel	This mechanism allows a user to cancel a message after the message has been distributed over the network.
Ihave	Part of NNTP; a message is sent from a remote news server announcing a new article.
Sendme	A response to an Ihave message, indicating it's okay to send the article.
Newgroup	Create a new newsgroup on the local new server.
Rmgroup	Delete a newsgroup on the local new server.
Sendsys	E-mail the issuer a list of all news feeds and corresponding coverage. This information is used to keep the map of USENET up-to-date and to determine where netnews is sent.
Version	E-mail the issuer the name and version number of the netnews software being employed on the news server.
Checkgroups	Check the server's local active list of newsgroups against the official list of newsgroups contained in the message body.

The execution of the action requested is subject to local administrative restrictions and may or may not be performed.

INN—CONTROL-MESSAGE HANDLING

When a control message is received by INN, the action that will be taken is controlled by the file control.ctl.

The format of the control.ctl file is four fields separated by a colon:

```
<message>:<from>:<newsgroups>:<action>
```

Table 20-7 gives more details on the parameters of control.ctl.

Table 20-7 Control.ctl Parameters

Parameter	Explanation
message	Which control message to respond to. Use "all" if it applies to all control messages.
from	Pattern that must match the From line.
newgroups	Pattern that must match the newsgroup being Newgroup'd or Rmgroup'd (ignored for other messages).
action (doit)	Perform action (usually sends mail too).
action (doifarg)	Do if command has an arg (see sendsys).
	Ignore message.
action (log)	Write one line to error log.
action (log=xxx)	Log to file xxx (see below).
action (mail)	Send mail to newsmaster.
action (verify-pgp_userid)	Perform PGP verification on user.
action (verify pgp_userid=logfile)	Perform PGP verification on user and log results.
action (xxx=mail)	Send log information to mail.
action (xxx=empty)	Discard log information.
action (xxx=/full/path)	Write log to file defined by full path name.
action (xxx=foo)	Write log to log file defined by ${LOG}/foo.log.

DNEWS—Control Message Handling

The handling of control messages in DNEWS is controlled by the control.conf file. The DNEWS format is identical to the INN format except for the PGP verification. Another subtle difference is the fact that all control messages are logged.

Other Tools

A lot of other tools exist today to help automate news server maintenance, and more are being created all the time, especially for INN. Table 20-8 lists many of these tools.

Readers are encouraged to consult fellow newsmasters and the various newsgroups and Web sites for other maintenance tools and ideas.

Table 20-8 Other Useful Tools

Tool	Source	Description
Gfilter (INN)	http://www.landfield.com/usenet/usenet-software.html	Logs and deletes specified articles. Good for tagging and eliminating articles from a particular poster.
Arbitron (INN)	http://www.landfield.com/usenet/usenet-software.html	Produces a readership survey of your news server.
Expirectl (INN)	INN Distribution	Dynamically modifies the expire rules in the expire.ctl file.
Darchive (DNEWS)	DNEWS distribution	Archives articles to a file.
Purge_binaries (INN)	http://www.landfield.com/usenet/usenet-software.html	Purge_binaries scans news postings, purging those it determines to be binary files.
GUP (INN)	http://www.landfield.com/usenet/usenet-software.html	Allows remote management of a news feed.
Tally (INN)	ftp://ftp.math.psu.edu/pub/INN/contrib	For logging size information on all incoming news.

21 Intranet Considerations

On the surface there appears to be little difference between private (Intranet) and public news. Both use the same NNTP transport mechanism, both can use the same netnews and reader software, and both employ articles organized in newsgroup hierarchies.

The difference is in the domain in which they exist. Public news can flow virtually anywhere, limited only by the Distribution header and the propagation rules and sensibilities of newsmasters; in contrast private newsgroups are propagated within a defined area. Whereas public news adheres (at least in theory) to certain broadly agreed-to conventions and protocol, such as newsgroup creation, Intranet news can have its own set of rules designed to match company or organization policy, with little if any influence from the outside.

Collaborative Workgroups

Intranet news is among news areas experiencing the largest growth. Apart from enhancing corporate communications in a general way, it allows project teams, committees, and departments to set up collaborative workgroups where people can communicate effectively. "Collaborative workgroups" is a $100 name for what people have been doing for years—

working together—but corporate LAN/WAN networks and network applications have made possible a radical change in how this takes place.

In traditional team structures, members were mostly located under the same roof, often within the same design lab. Information exchange was face to face, through reports, meetings, or paper memos. This mode of working has given way to a more distributed model. Today it is not uncommon to find design teams scattered around the country or around the globe, each able to contribute to the collaborative effort even though the group members seldom or never meet in person. Electronic mail has certainly helped this trend, but Intranet news is rapidly becoming an alternative, especially for large teams.

MIME ATTACHMENTS AND FILE TRANSFER

The news article format was built on the original mail message format defined in RFC 822. MIME, which stands for Multipurpose Internet Mail Extensions, is an upward-compatible set of extensions to RFC 822 currently defined in RFC 1341 and 1342. Using MIME extensions, users can send and receive virtually any file type by encoding and then incorporating the file in a news article. Although this sounds complex, the news reader software handles most of the details. The news server normally transports articles unaltered, but if necessary the newsmaster can configure the system to insert missing MIME headers.

A SAMPLE MIME ATTACHMENT

Here's a portion of a news article accompanied by an encoded Excel file:

```
Path: news.us.pcgbase.com!news.pcgbase.com!jmcd.pcgbase.com
From:"James E. McDermott" <jmcd@pcgbase.com>
Newsgroups: alt.test
Subject: test ignore
Date: Sun, 24 Nov 1996 14:12:49 -0500
Organization: Alermax Entertainment Inc.
Lines: 193
Message-ID: <32989E27.82A@pcgbase.com>
Reply-To: jmcd@pcgbase.com
NNTP-Posting-Host: news.pcgbase.com
Mime-Version: 1.0
Content-Type: application/ms-excel; x-mac-type="584C5333"; x-mac-
creator="584345
4C"; name="test.xls"
```

Content-Transfer-Encoding: base64
X-Mailer: Mozilla 3.0 (Macintosh; I; 68K)
Content-Description: Microsoft Excel Document
Content-Disposition: inline; filename="test.xls"
Xref: news.us.pcgbase.com alt.test:378328

CQIGAAAAEAD2BVwAIAANTWFyam9yeSBCcnljZSAgICAgICAgICAgICAgICAgIAsCF
ACjAwAAAAA9AAQEAACTBgAA9hYAAEIAAgAAgAwAAgBkAA0AAgABAA4AAgABA
A8AAgABABAACAD8qfHSTWJQPxEAAgAAACIAAgABACoAAgAAACsAAgAAAF8AA
gABAIIAAgABAIMAAgAAAIQAAgAAAIAACAAAAAAAAAAAACUCBAAAAAQBjAAE
AAEAAQCNAAIAAACBAAIAwQQbAAQAAQApADECDQDIAAAA38GR2VuZXZhM
QINAMgAAQDfwZHZW5ldmExAg0AyAACAP9/BkdlbmV2YTECDQDIAAMA/38G

The MIME extensions are shown in **boldface.**

Corporate Standards and MIME Attachments

By agreeing on corporate standards for applications and filename extensions, users can seamlessly transfer files among workgroups. If news reader software is set up correctly, client helper applications will automatically decode and display the file.

If you plan to send large articles, the news reader software must be able to support MIME multipart support, otherwise the file may be truncated by the news server.

Maintenance of the Intranet

Control messages provide an easy method of controlling the USENET environment, but, unfortunately, they are very easy to forge. One solution is PGP, a program written by Philip Zimmerman. PGP, which stands for Pretty Good Privacy, is used primarily to encrypt, or "hide," text in electronic files and messages. It can also be used for authentication—making sure that a message is genuine and that the sender is who he says he is. PGP provides newsmasters with a method of sorting the valid control messages from the deliberate or accidental forgeries.

PGP uses a public key system, whereby users have a private key, which is kept secret, and a public key, which the user makes available to anyone who wants it. For authentication purposes a sender encodes a message using his or her private key, and the recipient uses the sender's public key to verify not only that the message came from that certain sender but also that the message has not be altered.

Figure 21-1 illustrates how the process works. Here John is assured not only that the incoming message is from Tara but also that it arrived unaltered.

Figure 21-1 Public key system.

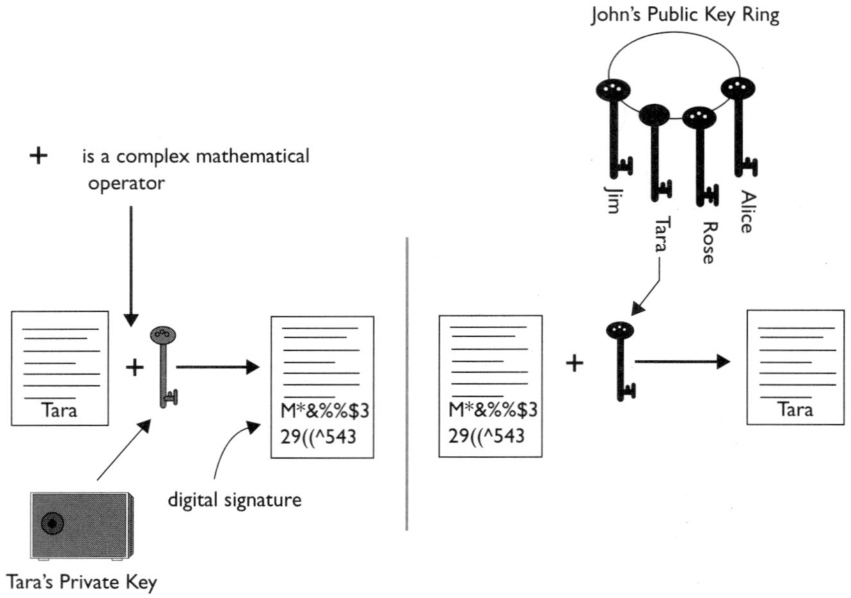

Table 21-1 shows PGP's functions.

Table 21-1 Key Management Functions

K function	Description
-kg	To generate your own unique public/secret key pair.
-ka keyfile [keyring]	To add a key file's contents to your public or secret key ring.
-kr userid [keyring]	To remove a key or a user ID from your public or secret key ring.
-ke your_userid [keyring]	To edit your user ID or password.
-kx userid keyfile [keyring]	To extract (copy) a key from your public or secret key ring.
-kv[v] [userid] [keyring]	To view the contents of your public key ring.
-kc [userid] [keyring]	To check signatures on your public key ring.
-ks her_userid [-u your_userid] [keyring]	To sign someone else's public key on your public key ring.
-krs userid [keyring]	To remove selected signatures from a user ID on a keyring.

PGP software and information can be found at several Internet sites, including the following:

http://web.mit.edu/network/pgp.html (non-commercial)

http://www.viacrypt.com (commercial)

http://www.ifi.uio.no/pgp/ (outside the U.S)

1. Get PGP.

   The distribution includes setup.doc and should be followed closely as there are many subtleties. The installation of PGP for the INN server follows.

2. Install PGP using the following commands:

   news# **cd /local/usr**
   news# **mkdir pgp-2.6.2** [required since tar file doesn't create its own subdirectory]
   news# **mv pg*gz pgp-2.6.2**
   news# **ftp pgp-2.6.2** [2.6.2 is the most current version at time of writing]
   news# **tar xvzf pgp*gz**

   news# **tar xvf pgp262si.tar**
   news# **tar xvf rsaref.tar** [some RSA libraries are required]
   news# **cd rsaref/install/unix**
   news# **make**

   news# **cd.. /../../src**
   news# **arch -k** [extract system information]
   news# **make sun4sunos5gcc** [compile and install]

   To see the list PGP K functions at any time type:

   pcg% pgp -k

3. Create your keys.

   First you need to create a subdirectory somewhere in your home directory hierarchy to hold your public and private key rings and anything else PGP might need (like the language.txt file). The default name PGP assumes is *~/.pgp*. If you want to use a different name, you must set the environment variable *PGPPATH* to point to this place before you use the system. Do so using the following commands:

   news# **su -news** [become the *news* user]
   news# **mkdir .pgp**

   Touch the file .pgp/secring.pgp or PGP will complain.

   news# **touch .pgp/secring.pgp**

   Create your own unique public/secret key pair:

```
news# pgp -kg

Newsmaster@pcgbase.com
```

Follow the on-screen instructions to create your keys.

4. Add public keys.

   Now add the public keys that came with the distribution. This will allow you to validate most control messages regarding the big eight hierarchies.

```
news# cp PGPKEYS /tmp/key
news# pgp -ka /tmp/pgpkeys
```

   PGP may tell you, "One or more of the new keys are not fully certified," and ask you if you would like to "certify any of these keys yourself." Answer **no** twice.

```
news# cd
news# pgp -ka /tmp/key
N
N
```

   To view the public keys use the following command:

```
pgp -kv
```

5. Test PGP.

   To test the PGPverify system, use the sample control message that came with the distribution (sample.control). This message was signed by *tale@uunet*, a trusted source for control messages and was asking newsmasters to create (*action=doit*) a new group called *news.announce.newsgroups.*

```
news# cd /usr/news/bin/control
news# ../pgpverify < sample.control
```

   The system should respond with *news.announce.newsgroups.*

   Now test Parsecontrol. Parsecontrol is the INN program that extracts the key information from the control message and uses PGP.

```
news# cd ../etc
news# ls pa*
parsecontrol  passwd.nntp
news# sh
$ PROG=newgroup
$ set -- tale@uunet.uu.net "" /tmp/sample.control
$ (. ./parsecontrol "$@"; echo $ACTION)
doit [this was the extracted action echoed to the screen]
$
```

Edit the sample.control file and change all occurrences of *newusers* to *newgroups*. Then repeat the Parsecontrol and echo lines. This time verification should fail.

If your system passed these tests, it's ready to handle control messages safely and automatically. The parameter that controls the inclusion of PGP verification is PGPverify in the INN config.data file. This was set to *do* during the construction phase.

As mentioned, PGP can be used for all sorts of things from encrypting the body of a message to verifying the authenticity of a questionable host. The bibliography lists additional reference material on PGP under the heading "Security."

KEEPING INTRANET NEWSGROUPS INSIDE

A company-confidential article intended for internal posting only can inadvertently leak onto the Internet even though you've set the newsfeeds.conf file (DNEWS) or the newsfeeds file (INN) correctly. Because the Newsgroups field in the article header allows cross-posting, a user, posting to a private newsgroup can also cross-post to additional newsgroups, including public ones. Therefore, some form of filtering is required in order to ensure that private messages are not cross-posted to the Internet. There are a number of ways to keep private messages inside your company.

ISOLATE INTRANET NEWS

One simple way to keep news inside is to put an air gap between your Intranet news and public news by using separate servers. With no outside feed there is no chance of internal messages leaking out through cross-posting. Of course, this forces readers who want access to the Internet newsgroups as well to point to another public news server when they want to access the public groups. The Intranet news server software could be built on the same hardware platform as this public news server, but to ensure isolation it's better to build either INN or DNEWS on an entirely separate platform (perhaps a low-end Pentium).

INN—PERL Cross-Posting Filter

The last section of the config.data file covers PERL support. If PERL support is selected when the system is compiled, both INNd and NNRPd will support some amount of PERL filtering. A PERL subroutine will be invoked on every article received by INNd from a peer host or by NNRPd from a reader. Complete details and sample filters are included in the Readme.PERL file included in the distribution.

The sample filter presented below prevents the posting of any article from an internal newsgroup to an outside newsgroup—in this case *pcg*. It is meant only as a guide. Please rework the filter to match your own configuration and requirements and test it thoroughly. This filter is included on the CD-ROM in /opt/local/src.

```
#
#
# Sample perl filtering code for nnrpd hook.
# This script will not allow any articles posted to a pcg group to be
# cross-posted to any other group.
sub filter_post
{
   my($rval) = '';

   # Get a list of all the newsgroups the article is posted to
   my(@groups) = grep(/\S/,split(/,/,$hdr{'Newsgroups'}));

   if ( grep(/^pcg\./,@groups) && grep(!/^pcg\./,@groups) ) {
      $rval = "Article cross-posted between local and non-local groups."
   }

   return $rval;
}
```

To use this PERL script, replace filter_nnrpd.pl in the $INN/site/ directory with this script. Then use the Make utility to install it.

DNEWS—Disallow Cross-Posting Entirely

The optional Maxcount parameter, used in the newsfeeds.conf file allows newsmasters to specify the level of cross-posting allowed. Setting the Maxcount parameter to 1 prevents any cross-posting—period! Unfortunately this restriction would then apply to all newsgroups, not just internal ones. Although this is not necessarily a bad idea, some might find this practice overly restrictive.

HELPFUL PROGRAMS

DNEWSWEB

DNEWSWEB is a Common Gateway Interface (CGI) program that allows World Wide Web surfers to read news using their browser. This is especially useful for news newbies because the interface is familiar and obviates the need to learn a new application. Follow these steps to get DNEWSWEB up and running.

1. Install DNEWSWEB.

   DNEWSWEB comes with the DNEWS distribution and must be installed in the directory that contains CGI programs. An example CGI program directory is: /opt/www/Daemon/sun4-sol2.

   news# **cp dnewsweb /opt/www/Daemon/sun4-sol2**
   news# **cp dnewsweb.ini /dnewsweb.ini** [copy initialization file to root]

   In some instances you will have to place the .ini file in a different directory, depending on your server software. Your HTTP administrator should be able to help you determine the correct location.

2. Edit initialization file.

   Now edit dnewsweb.ini and define three things: the IP number of your DNEWS server, newsgroups to appear on the front page, and newsgroups that you are allowing people to access.

   newshost **205.233.33.5** [IP number of the DNEWS server]
   groups **rec.humor,rec.humor.funny,rec.guns** [groups to index]
   allow * [# Groups to actually let people read]

   Caution: If you don't limit the newsgroups people can access, you may find everyone in the world reading news via your Web pages.

3. Test DNEWSWEB.

   Then try it out; point your Web browser to the CGI directory. In the book example this would be

   http://news.us.pcgbase.com/opt/www/Daemon/sun4-sol2

   You should now be able to search the newsgroups you specified in dnewsweb.ini.

FULL TEXT SEARCHING (FTS) ENGINE FOR DNEWS

The DNEWS distribution comes with FTS, a search engine that provides textual search capability for the spool directory.

Installation and configuration are straightforward, but you will have to ensure that you have enough free disk space. To build a really complete index requires free space up to 50 percent of your spool area. FTS can also gobble up significant processor and memory resources.

To implement FTS, complete the following tasks:

1. Configure FTS.

   In the dnews.conf file define the directory in which to store indexes.

   news# **mkdir /var/spool/dnews/fts** [make the directory]

   The file fts.conf allows you to define how many words of each article are indexed. This is important because it helps you conserve space and allows you to exploit the fact that most salient information in an article (for searching) is generally contained in the top of the message. Edit the fts.conf file.

```
#This file is space sensitive, don't use tabs, don't use extra spaces
# and don't leave trailing blanks either.
#The format is
#       'keyword' 'space' 'value' 'endofline'

# Headers to add to index
headers Subject:,Keywords:,From:,Summary:,Newsgroups:

# Number of words to read from each article, if you want to
# index a full feed then you probably want a value like 100
# But if you are just doing 5 or 10 news groups then you could set
# this value at 10,000 and index the entire article.
item_words 100

#This is the number of times a single word can occur before
# it is considered to be so common that it has no value as a
# searching tool.This number is a percent of items.
word_max 10%
```

   news# **cp fts.conf /var/spool/dnews/fts** [copies fts configuration file here]

2. Create a news feed for FTS.

   FTS is fed articles over a news feed as if it were a news server. Therefore, the newsfeeds.conf file has to be modified to add the FTS feed. This method of feeding FTS news allows the newsmaster to easily restrict what newsgroups get indexed. In this case allow everything but internal and *alt* groups.

   site ftsfeed [defines fts as a news feed, sends articles to XMIT process]
   groups *,!alt,!pcg [no alt or internal groups will be indexed]

Set up the Xmit process to run every 10 minutes at 05, 15, 25 . . . minutes after the hour and in the background.

news# **chmod u+x ./xmit** [make <u>xmit</u> executable]
news# **nohup ./xmit ftsfeed -fts -at "*5" "*" &** [start <u>xmit</u> daemon]

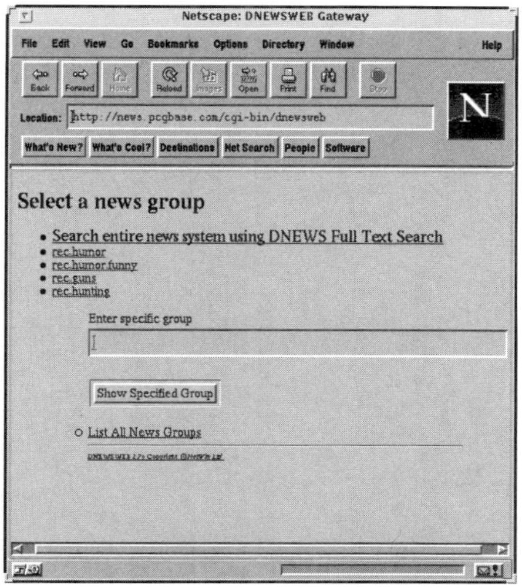

Figure 21-2 DNEWSWEB

3. Turn on FTS.

   In <u>dnewsweb.ini</u> enable FTS by adding the following line:

   search true

   When any DNEWS configuration files are modified, you have to reload them using the Tellnews command Reload.

   news# **tellnews reload**

   The FTS database is accessed through DNEWSWEB. If the installation of FTS is successful, you should see the FTS option available for use. Figure 21-2 shows the DNEWSWEB screen with FTS enabled.

COMPANY.POSTED SCRIPT

Company.posted is a PERL script that was graciously written by Russell McOrmond from an idea supplied by Marc Boucher. It will make a copy of outbound articles posted on the local server. Specified newsgroups can be included or excluded by the associated entry in the <u>newsfeeds</u> file. As previously mentioned, Company.posted can be very useful in regulating employee posts to the Internet. This file is included on the CD-ROM in <u>/opt/local/src</u> and is also listed below.

```
#!/opt/gnu/bin/perl
#
# You need to list the names of your uplinks in the newsfeeds file to exclude postings from these sites
# from being sent to your Company.posted. You also need to exclude  postings to local newsgroups.
#
# Here is a sample newsfeeds entry
#
#posted/news.isp.com!\
#        :*,!pcg.*,!local\
#        :Tp,H2:/usr/news/bin/posted
#
```

```
$localgroup = 'pcg.posted';
$inews = '/usr/news/bin/inews -h';

$newsgroups = '';
while (<STDIN>) {
   if (/^Newsgroups: (.*)\s*$/) {
         $newsgroups = $1;
   }
   if (/^From: (.*)\s*$/) {
         $from = $1;
   }
   if (/^Subject: (.*)\s*$/) {
         $subject = $1;
   }
   if (/^\s*$/) {last};
   push (@headers,$_);
}

if ($newsgroups =~ /(^|,)$localgroup(,|$)/) {
   # Already posted to group
   exit 0;
}

if ($subject eq '') {
   $subject = '<No Subject given>'
}

if ($from eq '') {
   $from = 'unknown.person@nowhere.net'
}

open (NEWS, "|$inews") || die ("Cannot run Inews!!");

print NEWS <<EOF;
From: $from
Subject: $subject
Newsgroups: $localgroup

EOF
while ($line = shift(@headers)) {
   print NEWS $line;
}

print NEWS "\n";

while (<STDIN>) {
   print NEWS $_;
}
```

To use this script place it in the /usr/news/bin directory and make the appropriate entries in the newsfeeds file.

22

The Future of News: Trends and Extrapolations

Predicting the future of anything is problematic at best, ludicrously wrong in the extreme worse cases. Consider the editorial in an early eighties magazine that forecast that home computers would need no more than 1K of RAM. Or a more recent assertion that 640K would probably be okay. This book is being written on a Macintosh computer with 24MB of RAM, and now even that doesn't seem like enough.

The best anyone can hope to do is extrapolate existing trends and make an educated guess at what the future might hold. Unless dramatic changes take place, both in the way News is transported and in the way it is used, one is led to some inescapable conclusions. There will be

- an ever expanding number of News participants and servers,
- more Internet congestion owing to News,
- a lower signal-to-noise ratio,
- increased spamming, and
- more court cases regarding illegal content, spamming, and other detrimental activities.

All this points to News becoming less and less effective as a mean of mass communication, but as in Dickens's *Christmas Carol*, this is only a possible future; there is time to change.

SOME SOLUTIONS

Put binaries where they belong. No, not "where the sun don't shine," but on anonymous FTP sites where USENET won't have to propagate them. All that would be carried on the news server would be a link or URL pointing back to the file.

Create smarter readers. If no one sees a spam article, does it exist? As mentioned in Chapter 9, "Client Software," news readers may soon begin to implement the NoCeM feature, which will automatically hide spam from the reader. This feature could possibly be incorporated into the news server itself to reduce bandwidth and storage before ever hitting the news readers.

Use more moderators. If all newsgroups had moderators, then the only place you would see "$50,000 a WEEK!!!" is in *alt.illegal.scams.* Moderators intercept articles and approve them before post is allowed, thereby preventing garbage and inappropriate cross-posts from cluttering up the newsgroup. Traditionally this sometime thankless job has been handled by a person who was appointed or who volunteered. This job can be time-consuming for the person doing the moderating, and if he or she is overburdened, postings will be delayed.

A program called STUMP (which stands for "Secure Team-based Usenet Moderation Program") Robomoderator by Igor Chudov can help automate the task and promises to make moderated newsgroups more practical and therefore more prevalent.

Here are some feature highlights of STUMP Robomoderator:

- Load sharing for human moderators whereby articles for approval are randomly distributed among a group of moderators. This lowers the burden on any one moderator and raises the likelihood that people will volunteer tò be moderators.
- Automatic rejection of nonconforming messages; for example, megacross-posts and encoded binaries are rejected automatically without human intervention.
- Support of a preapproved list of posters whose posts are presumed to be good and do not need human review. This strategy can reduce the number of articles the moderator or moderator team has to review and will speed

posting for articles from approved posters. It is estimated that about 80 percent of moderators' time can be saved with this feature.

- Automatic archive of articles.
- Exchange between human moderators and the STUMP Robomoderator program is secured by PGP encryption and signatures. This prevents any "spoofing"—when malicious users try to simulate fake moderators' approvals.
- Elimination of articles that have cross-posting. This is useful for private newsgroups where it may be crucial that no article gets inadvertently or otherwise cross-posted to public groups. This can also be essential for small, private, cultural or religious newsgroups that offer freedom of speech but do not want any cross-posted flames.

STUMP Robomoderator is available at the following World Wide Web site:

http://www.algebra.com/~ichudov/usenet/scrm/robomod/robomod.html

NEWS ROUTING USING TRANSIT HUBS

The traffic on USENET has grown substantially in the last several years. Because of the increase in traffic, news administrators have adopted a number of changes to News architectures to increase the performance of their portion of USENET.

Transit hubs have proven to work well for high-volume USENET sites. A transit hub is a News machine configured solely to route news. The news software on the machine operates using only the server-to-server portions of the NNTP protocol. Dedicating machines to be transit hubs has greatly increased the speed of News in some sites, and widespread adoption of this technique could be beneficial to all of USENET.

Operating a transit hub with INN is difficult, although INN is a powerful general purpose news system. The volume of news and the importance of maintaining high availability on a transit hub multiply the challenges of running a reliable News system a thousandfold.

One commercial program on the market today designed specifically to act as a transit hub is Cyclone by HighWind Software, Inc. (www.highwind.com). The biggest difference between Cyclone and INN is that Cyclone is a newsrouter. In a fashion similar to a conventional router, Cyclone doesn't store articles for any significant amount of time, but merely sends them to all interested peer servers. As a result a transit hub running Cyclone requires much less system resources than a transit hub implemented with more conventional news software.

Here are some features supported by Cyclone:

- Uni- and bidirectional feeds,
- Partitioned feeds,
- Inbound and outbound content filtering,
- Anti-spam controls, bidirectional NNTP streaming,
- A Web-based GUI tool to reconfigure feeds,
- The ability to prioritize the transmission of newsgroups (for example, more bandwidth allocated to *comp* than to *alt*).

For large USENET installations, a news architecture consisting of a transit hub, a number of larger regional servers, and several smaller leaf-node machines can support tens of thousands of users. See Figure 22-1.

Figure 22-1 News routers deployed for corporate news network.

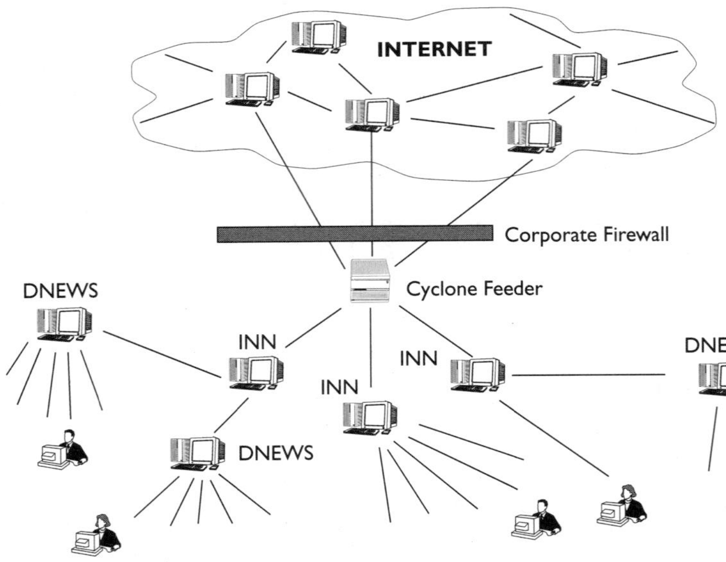

By using a transit hub as the entry point into this news network, this site can connect with numerous sites on the Internet without impacting the performance to its end users. In addition, a large peering relationship will increase reliability and throughput of this site's messages to the Internet at large.

The key point is that the difficult job of routing the messages to the Internet has been given solely to the transit hub machine. This allows the other machines to concentrate on servicing news browsers.

For companies that provide USENET feeds to other companies, using transit hubs (like Cyclone) could be critical. Here a "hub and spoke" News architecture is effective.

In this architecture, several interconnected "hub" machines provide the USENET backbone. These machines are usually geographically dispersed throughout the ISP's physical network. The hubs typically connect with each other, with internal "feeder" machines, and with transit hubs run by other Internet Service Providers.

The feeder machines in this architecture are deployed to gather and explode News to all the companies that this Internet Service Provider serves. See Figure 22-2.

Figure 22-2 Transit hubs create news backbones.

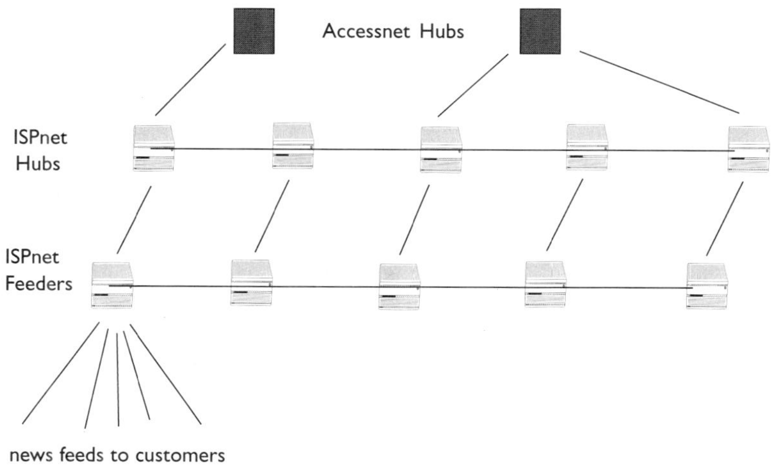

Considering that a reasonably sized workstation running Cyclone can feed hundreds of sites, this architecture can expand to serve many thousands of companies, which in turn service millions of news browsers.

PROTECTIVE LEGISLATION

With freedom comes responsibility. Because of the lack of responsibility shown in the areas of spamming and pornography, legislation will unfortunately be put in place in the future to protect News users. Legislation will come from Net-Police (spams) and from government (content).

THE END OF USENET NEWS?

It's entirely possible that News as we know it today will disappear altogether and be replaced by some form of distributed pay-as-you-use messaging application. News databases, similar to Dejanews, will moderate and organize content in exchange for a usage or monthly fee. There are some precedents for this in both the Internet and other forms of media. Some of you reading this book will remember the early days of the Internet when the system was small, experimentation was rampant, and access was free for the asking. Today it's monstrously large and getting more regulated and commercial by the moment. Radio went through a similar change from a scattered collection of small unlicensed stations, many experimental, to a few tightly regulated, highly commercialized broadcast networks intimately entwined with the business community.

On the other hand, consider the fate of Internet search services such as Infoweb. They initially charged for searching the Internet—so much per search, or a monthly fee—then had to shift gears when free search engines came online. Now, like most others, Infoweb derives revenue from advertisements.

Who knows, someday you may see your posting stamped with an ad for Spam—the luncheon meat, that is.

A The Newsgroup Hierarchy

The following list of all the top-level hierarchies was created and is currently maintained by Lewis S. Eisen in order to help readers locate a newsgroup of interest without having to plod through to 20,000+ newsgroups. Still, there are over 400 entries, and the list is ever growing. The main criteria for inclusion on the list is that the hierarchy must be carried on systems other than the host that created it.

At the time of writing, the list was at version 4.04; it is liable to change significantly with time. The Master List of Newsgroup Hierarchies is posted every second Monday to

news.answers,
news.admin.hierarchies ,
news.groups.

The list is also available by anonymous FTP from:

ftp://ftp.magmacom.com/pub/misc/Master_List.txt

and on the World Wide Web at

http://home.magmacom.com/~leisen/master_list.html

THE MASTER LIST OF NEWSGROUP HIERARCHIES

ab.	Alberta, Canada
acadia.	Acadia University, Nova Scotia, Canada
acs.	University of Calgary, Computer Science, Alberta, Canada
ak.	Alaska, USA
akr.	Akron, Ohio, USA
alabama.	Alabama, USA
alt.	USENET alternative newsgroups
aol.	America Online, ISP
apana.	Australian Public Access Network Association
apk.	APK Net, Ohio, USA (ISP)
at.	Oesterreich (Austria)
athena.	MIT, Cambridge, Massachusetts, USA
atl.	Atlanta, Georgia, USA
aus.	Australian and Australasian newsgroups
austin.	Austin, Texas, USA
av.	Antelope Valley, California, USA
az.	Arizona, USA
ba.	San Francisco Bay area, California, USA
balt.	Baltimore, Maryland, USA
bburg.	Blacksburg, Virginia, USA
bc.	British Columbia, Canada
bcs.	Boston Computer Society, Massachusetts, USA
be.	Belgique/Belgïe/Belgien (Belgium)
bermuda.	Bermuda
bionet.	Biology Network
birmingham.	Birmingham, England
bison.	Manitoba, Canada
bit.	originating from BITNET (IBM mainframe)
biz.	USENET business newsgroups
blgtn.	Bloomington, Indiana, USA
bln.	Berlin, Germany
bnr.	Bell-Northern Research
bocaraton.	Boca Raton, Florida, USA
bofh.	sysop gripe sessions (Bastard Operator from Hell)
bologna.	Bologna, Italia
boston.	Boston, Massachusetts, USA
boulder.	Boulder, Colorado, USA
brasil.	Brazil
bremen.	Bremen, Deutschland
brocku.	Brock University, Ontario, Canada
byu.	Brigham Young University, Utah, USA

ca.	California, USA
cabot.	Cabot College, St. John's, Newfoundland, Canada
calgary.	Calgary, Alberta, Canada
calstate.	California State University, USA
caltech.	California Institute of Technology, USA
cam.	Cambridge area, England
can.	Canada
canb.	Canberra, Australia
capdist.	Albany (Capital District), New York, USA
carleton.	Carleton University, Ottawa, Ontario, Canada
ccc.	Contra Costa County, California, USA
cern.	Cern, Geneva, Switzerland
ch.	Switzerland
chi.	Chicago, Illinois, USA
chile.	Chile
chinese.	China and Chinese language newsgroups
christnet.	Christian Network
cityscp.	Cityscape Internet Services, UK (ISP)
cl.	/CL-Netz (German language newsgroups)
clari.	Clarinet News Service (commercial)
cle.	Cleveland, Ohio, USA
cmh.	Columbus, Ohio, USA
co.	Colorado, USA
comp.	USENET computer newsgroups
compuserve.	CompuServe (ISP)
computer42.	computer42, Deutschland
concordia.	Concordia University, Quebec, Canada
conn.	Connecticut, USA
cor.	Corvallis, Oregon, USA
cornell.	Cornell University, New York, USA
courts.	United States court decisions
cov.	City of Coventry, West Midlands, UK
covuni.	Coventry University, West Midlands, UK
cs.	University of British Columbia, computer science, Canada
csn.	Colorado SuperNet, USA
ct.	c't (German computer magazine)
cu.	University of Colorado, USA
cz.	Czech Republic newsgroups
dal.	Dalhousie University, Halifax, Nova Scotia, Canada
dc.	Washington, D.C., USA
ddn.	Defense Data Network, USA
dds.	Dutch Freenet language groups

de.	International German language newsgroups
delaware.	Delaware, USA
demon.	Newsgroups from the Demon network, UK
denver.	Denver, Colorado, USA
det.	Detroit, Michigan, USA
dfw.	Dallas–Ft. Worth, Texas, USA
dk.	Danmark (Denmark)
dod.	Department of Defense, USA
dsm.	Des Moines, Iowa, USA
duke.	Duke University
dut.	Delft Institute of Technology, Nederland
easynet.	Easynet, UK (ISP)
ed.	Edinburgh, Scotland
edm.	Edmonton, Alberta, Canada
es.	España and Spanish language newsgroups
eug.	Eugene/Springfield, Oregon, USA
eunet.	European Networks
eye.	eye WEEKLY Newspaper, Toronto, Ontario, Canada
fido.	originating from Fidonet
finet.	Finland and Finnish language alternative newsgroups
fj.	Japan and Japanese language newsgroups
fl.	Florida, USA
fnet.	originating from Fnet (France)
fr.	international French language newsgroups
francom.	groupes de discussion en français
fras.	German language binaries
freenet.	Groups originating from freenets
ga.	Georgia, USA
gay-net	German language Gay and Lesbian newsgroups
gay.	Gay and Lesbian newsgroups
geometry.	discussions about geometry
git.	Georgia Institute of Technology, USA
gnu.	GNU operating system
hacktic.	Dutch/English hackers' newsgroups, Nederland
halcyon.	Halcyon Corporate newsgroups
hamburg.	Hamburg, Deutschland
han.	Hangul language newsgroups (Korean)
hannet.	Hannover, Deutschland
hannover.	Hannover, Deutschland

harvard.	Harvard University, Massachusetts, USA
hawaii-online.	Hawaii-Online (ISP)
hawaii.	Hawaii, USA
hebron.	Hebron, Israel
helsinki.	Helsinki, Finland
hepnet.	High Energy Physics Network
hfx.	Halifax, Nova Scotia, Canada
hiv.	HIV-related issues
hk.	Hong Kong
hna.	Hunter Network Association, Australia (ISP)
hookup.	Hookup, Canada (ISP)
houston.	Houston, Texas, USA
hr.	Croatian newsgroups
hsv.	Huntsville, Alabama, USA
hum.	Humber College, Etobicoke, Ontario, Canada
humanities.	discussions about Humanities
hun.	Hungarian newsgroups
ia.	Iowa, USA
ibm.	IBM-based newsgroups
idirect.	I-Direct (ISP)
ie.	Ireland
ieee.	IEEE standards
iij.	IIJ (ISP)
iijnet.	IIJ (ISP)
il.	Illinois, USA
in.	Indiana, USA
info.	Internet technical information
inforamp.	Inforamp, Canada (ISP)
interlog.	Interlog, Canada (ISP)
israel.	Israel
it.	Italia
ithaca.	Ithaca, New York, USA
jaring.	Jaring network, Malaysia (ISP)
k12.	international educational network
ka.	Karlsruhe, Deutschland
kanto.	Japanese language newsgroups
kc.	Kansas City, Kansas/Missouri, USA
kiel.	Kiel, Deutschland
kingston.	Kingston, Ontario, Canada
knox.	Knoxville and surrounding area, Tennessee, USA

ks.	Kansas, USA
ksu.	Kansas State University, USA
kw.	Kitchener–Waterloo, Ontario, Canada
ky.	Kentucky, USA
la.	Los Angeles, California, USA
laurentian.	Laurentian University, Sudbury, Ontario, Canada
leeds.	Leeds, England
li.	Long Island, New York, USA
linux.	Linux operating system
lon.	London, England
lou.	Louisiana, USA
lv.	Latvian newsgroups
man.	Manitoba, Canada
maus.	originating from MausNet (Deutschland)
mcgill.	McGill University, Montreal, Quebec, Canada
mcmaster.	McMaster University, Hamilton, Ontario, Canada
md.	Maryland, USA
melb.	Melbourne, Australia
melbpc.	Melbourne PC User Group, Australia
memphis.	Memphis, Tennessee, USA
mex.	Mexican newsgroups
mi.	Michigan, USA
miami.	Miami, Florida, USA
microsoft.	Microsoft newsgroups
midlands.	English midlands, UK
milw.	Milwaukee, Wisconsin, USA
misc.	USENET miscellaneous newsgroups
mistral.	Brighton, England
mit.	Massachusetts Institute of Technology, USA
mn.	Minnesota, USA
mo.	Missouri, USA
ms.	Mississippi, USA
mtl.	Montreal, Quebec, Canada
muc.	Munchen, Deutschland
mun.	Memorial University, Newfoundland, Canada
mv.	MV Communications, Inc. (ISP)
mx.	Mexico
nanaimo.	Nanaimo, British Columbia, Canada
nasa.	National Aeronautics and Space Administration, USA
nashville.	Nashville, Tennessee, USA

nb.	New Brunswick, Canada
nbn.	North Bay Network, California, USA
nc.	North Carolina, USA
ncf.	National Capital Freenet, Ottawa, Ontario, Canada
ncle.	Newcastle (and Hunter Valley), Australia
ncsc.	North Carolina SuperComputing, USA
nctu.	National Chiao-Ting University, Taiwan
nd.	North Dakota, USA
ne.	New England area, USA
near.	Nat. Centre for Atmosph. Research, Colorado, USA
nebr.	Nebraska, USA
netz.	originated by Netz e.V., Deutschland
nevada.	Nevada, USA
neworleans.	New Orleans, Louisiana, USA
news.	USENET news
nf.	Newfoundland, Canada
nh.	New Hampshire, USA
niagara.	Niagara Peninsula, Canada/USA
nj.	New Jersey, USA
nl.	Nederland
nlnet.	Nlnet (ISP)
nm.	New Mexico, USA
no.	Norge (Norway)
north.	Weser-Ems Region, Deutschland
ns.	Nova Scotia, Canada
nu.	Newcastle University, Australia
nv.	Nevada, USA
nwt.	Northwest Territories, Canada
nwu.	Northwestern University, Illinois, USA
ny.	New York State, USA
nyc.	New York City, New York, USA
nyu.	New York University, USA
nz.	New Zealand
oau.	Orlando, Florida, USA
oc.	Orange County, California, USA
ogi.	Oregon Graduate Institute, USA
oh.	Ohio, USA
ok.	Oklahoma, USA
okinawa.	Okinawan newsgroups
ont.	Ontario, Canada
or.	Oregon, USA
osu.	Ohio State University, USA
ott.	Ottawa, Ontario, Canada

pa.	Pennsylvania, USA
pdaxs.	Portland Metronet, Oregon, USA
pdx.	Portland, Oregon, USA
pei.	Prince Edward Island, Canada
pgh.	Pittsburgh, Pennsylvania, USA
phl.	Philadelphia, Pennsylvania, USA
phoenix.	Phoenix, Arizona, USA
phx.	Phoenix, Arizona, USA
pi.	Planet Internet, Nederland (ISP)
pinnacle.	Pinnacle, UK (ISP)
pipex.	Pipex (ISP)
pitt.	University of Pittsburgh, Pennsylvania, USA
pl.	Poland and Polish language newsgroups
pnw.	Pacific Northwest (USA/Canada)
prima.	Prima e.V., Dortmund, Deutschland (ISP)
princeton.	Princeton University, New Jersey, USA
prodigy.	Prodigy (ISP)
psi.	PSINet (ISP)
pt.	Portugal and Portuguese newsgroups
pubnet.	Public Access Systems network
purdue.	Purdue University, Indiana, USA
qc.	Quebec, Canada
queens.	Queens University, Kingston, Ontario, Canada
rabbit.	Rabbit Network (ISP)
rain.	RAINnet (ISP)
realtynet.	Real estate network
rec.	USENET recreational newsgroups
region.	Mittlehessen, Deutschland
relcom.	Relcom, Commonwealth of Independent States (ISP) (Cyrillic)
rg.	Rio Grande Valley, New Mexico, USA
rhein.	Rhein area (Cologne and Bonn), Germany
ri.	Rhode Island, USA
rmii.	Rocky Mountain Internet (ISP)
roanoke.	Roanoke, Virginia, USA
ru.	Rutgers University, New Jersey, USA
ruhr.	Ruhrgebiet, Deutschland
rv.	Rogue Valley, Oregon, USA
rye.	Ryerson University, Toronto, Ontario, Canada
saar.	Saarbruecken, Deutschland
sac.	Sacramento, California, USA
sacramento.	Sacramento, California, USA

sanet.	SAnet (South Africa)
sat.	San Antonio, Texas, USA
sba.	Santa Barbara, California, USA
sbay.	South Bay region, California, USA
schl.	newsgroup echo of KidLink mailing-lists
schule.	German language school newsgroups
sci.	USENET science newsgroups
scot.	Scotland
scruz.	Santa Cruz, California, USA
sd.	South Dakota, USA
sdnet.	San Diego, California, USA
sea.	Seattle, Washington, USA
seattle.	Seattle, Washington, USA
sfnet.	Suomi-Finland, Finland and Finnish language newsgroups
sfu.	Simon Fraser University, British Columbia, Canada
sg.	Singapore
sgi.	Silicon Graphics, Inc.
shamash.	Jewish newsgroups
si.	Slovenian newsgroups
simcoe.	Simcoe County, Ontario, Canada
sj.	Saint John's, Newfoundland, Canada
sk.	Saskatchewan, Canada
sk.	Slovakian newsgroups
slo.	San Luis Obispo, California, USA
slonet.	SLONET (ISP)
soc.	USENET social issues newsgroups
socs.	McGill University School of Computer Science, Quebec, Canada
solent.	Solent, U.K. (ISP)
sonoma.	Sonoma County, California, USA
spk.	Spokane, Washington, USA
srg.	Swiss Broadcasting Corporation
srjc.	Santa Rosa Junior College, California, USA
stgt.	Stuttgart, Deutschland
stl.	St. Louis, Missouri, USA
stmarys.	St. Mary's University, Nova Scotia, Canada
su.	Stanford University, California, USA
sudbury.	Sudbury, Ontario, Canada
surfnet.	Dutch university newsgroups, Nederland
sw.	Sverige (Sweden)
swnet.	Sverige (Sweden)
t-netz.	German language newsgroups (obsolete)
tacoma.	Tacoma, Washington, USA

talk.	USENET talk newsgroups
tamu.	Texas A & M University, USA
tba.	Tampa Bay, Florida, USA
tdw.	Tidewater, Virginia, USA
thur.	Thuringia, Deutschland
tn.	Tennessee, USA
tnn.	Japanese newsgroups
tor.	Toronto, Ontario, Canada
torfree.	Toronto Freenet, Ontario, Canada
toulouse.	Toulouse, France
tp.	Toppoint, Kiel, Deutschland
trentu.	Trent University, Ontario, Canada
triangle.	Research Triangle Park, North Carolina, USA
trumpet.	discussions of Trumpet programs
tulsa	Tulsa, Oklahoma, USA
tvontario.	TVOntario, Ontario, Canada
tw.	Taiwan
tx.	Texas, USA
u3b.	discussions on AT&T 3B systems
ualberta.	University of Alberta, Canada
uark.	University of Arkansas, USA
ubc.	University of British Columbia, Canada
uc.	University of California, USA
ucalgary.	University of Calgary, Alberta, Canada
ucb.	University of California at Berkeley, USA
ucd.	University of California, Davis, USA
ucsb.	University of California at Santa Barbara, USA
ucsc.	University of California at Santa Clara, USA
udes.	Université de Sherbrooke, Quebec, Canada
uf.	University of Florida, USA
uiuc.	University of Illinois, Urbana–Champaign, USA
uk.	United Kingdom
ukr.	Ukraine and Ukrainian language newsgroups
uky.	University of Kentucky, USA
ulaval.	Université Laval, Quebec, Canada
um.	University of Maryland, USA
umiami.	University of Miami, Florida, USA
umich.	University of Michigan, USA
umn.	University of Minnesota, USA
umoncton.	University of Moncton, New Brunswick, Canada
umontreal.	Université de Montreal, Quebec, Canada
unb.	University of New Brunswick, Canada
uo.	University of Oregon, USA

upenn.	University of Pennsylvania, USA
uqam.	Université de Quebec à Montreal, Canada
us.	United States
usask.	University of Saskatchewan, Canada
usf.	University of South Florida, USA
ut.	University of Toronto, Ontario, Canada
utah.	Utah, USA
utcs.	University of Texas, Computer Science, USA
utk.	University of Tennessee, Knoxville, USA
utexas.	University of Texas, USA
uunet.	originating from UUNet (UNIX)
uvic.	University of Victoria, British Columbia, Canada
uw.	University of Waterloo, Ontario, Canada
uwa.	University of Washington, USA
uwarwick.	University of Warwick, UK
uwash.	University of Washington, USA
uwindsor.	University of Windsor, Ontario, Canada
uwisc.	University of Wisconsin, Madison, USA
uwm.	University of Wisconsin, Milwaukee, USA
uwo.	University of Western Ontario, London, Canada
va.	Virginia, USA
van.	Vancouver, British Columbia, Canada
vegas.	Las Vegas, Nevada, USA
vic.	Victoria, British Columbia, Canada
vmsnet.	originating from Digital VAX network
vpro.	VPRO TV-station newsgroups, Nederland
vt.	Vermont, USA
vu.	Vanderbilt University
wa.	Western Australia
wash.	Washington, USA
wgtn.	Wellington, New Zealand
wi.	Wisconsin, USA
wimsey.	Wimsey, British Columia, Canada (ISP)
wny.	Western New York, USA
wpg.	Winnipeg, Manitoba, Canada
wyo.	Wyoming, USA
xs4all.	Xs4all, Nederland (ISP)
yakima.	Yakima, Washington, USA
yale.	Yale University, Connecticut, USA
yk.	Yellowknife, Northwest Territories, Canada

yfn.	Youngstown, Ohio Free-Net, USA
yolo.	Yolo County, California, USA
york.	York University, Ontario, Canada
ysu.	Youngstown State University, Ohio, USA
z-netz.	originating from Z-Netz (German newsgroups)
za.	South Africa and Afrikaans newsgroups
zer.	German language newsgroups (obsolete)

B DNEWS Technical Information

Configuration Files

The DNEWS .conf files are used to configure the DNEWS system. Table B-1 lists the six .conf files and a brief description of each. Following that, the configuration parameters for each of the .conf files are listed in Tables B-2 through B-6.

Table B-1 DNEWS Configuration Files

File Name	Description
dnews.conf	Main configuration file
access.conf	Controls NNTP access to your server
expire.conf	Specifies how long to keep news items
newsfeeds.conf	Defines feeds out of your news system up the line of news servers
moderators.conf	Defines where to send e-mail to a moderated newsgroup
control.conf	Defines how to process control messages for autocreation and deletion of newsgroups

Dnews.conf

This file is the main configuration file for DNEWS. Entries have the following format:

```
<symbol> <value>
```

Table B-2 lists the numerous configuration options for the dnews.conf file.

Table B-2 Configuration Parameters—dnews.conf

Parameter	Example	Description
Active_static	true	Stops new groups from being added by the sucking feed. Use this if your feed site has lots of groups you never want added into your active file.
Auth_case	true	Tells DNEWS to be case sensitive when testing usernames and passwords.
Body_chunk	20000	Sets the size of chunks to read from disk when a user reads an article; the default is 20000.
Cachedall	true	Pretends all groups are cached; use this if you are taking a full Ihave feed in.
Cachedonly	true	Only accepts items into groups that are cached; this is used for the hybrid feed where items are sent by a feed but only taken if users are reading that particular group.
Cancel_anyone	true	Allows cancel messages to work even if they are not from the original poster.
Cancel_users	me@here	Only allows cancel messages from this person.
Chan_nobuff	true	Use to help the Mosaic news reader to work.
Config	dnews_top:	Directory for configuration files (*.conf).
Confirm	*.this.place	Sends e-mail confirmation to postings from these addresses (set this to match your local e-mail addresses).
Db_index	2000	Sets how many index files to keep in memory; each one is 1200 bytes; the default is 200. If you have memory to burn, then increase this to 3000 for better performance.
Db_max	200	Sets how many files DNEWS should attempt to keep open to increase performance. On Windows NT you can safely set this value to about 200; on most other systems a value of 30 or 40 is about as high as you can go. You can use the command Tellnews test_files to see how many free file handles DNEWS has.
Debug	chan_read:chan_write:	Use to set which debug lines should be printed to the log file. The parameters cannot be separated by spaces. The default setting is control:db:cancel:file:lib:,warn:,fatal:,post:,chan:,feed:,hist:,nntp:,str:,err:,debug:,expire:,info:,item:,group:,suck:,cmd:,ncmd:,init:,db:,mem:,");
Debug_rotate	10000	Automatically rotates log files (renames and deletes the oldest one) if more than 10,000 lines are written). This is good if you have turned on debugging, as you always have the last few thousand lines if a problem develops, but you don't run out of disk space owing to the huge log file.
Db_flush_every	1	How many seconds to wait before closing some more files (default 60).
Db_flush_n	10	How many files to flush when the Flush_every timeout occurs. Increase this to make sure all files are closed; decrease it to improve performance. (Default 1.)

Table B-2 Configuration Parameters—dnews.conf (Continued)

Parameter	Example	Description
Debug_store	100	Stores the last 100 items as files; the items are stored before they are processed. This was used for finding items that crashed DNEWS. The last stored item was the problem. It is not an official setting (that is, it may be removed).
Df	/usr/bin/df -Pk	Define the Df command to use on UNIX systems, where to find it if necessary, and the switches to use if needed.
Diskspace	100	Total disk space in megabytes a dynamic feed needs 20–200MB. A full feed needs approximately 1000MB.
Expire_at	5 23,3	Run an expire job at 11:05 and 3:05 in the morning.
Expire_bits	true	Allows the expire to run more smoothly by stopping partway through large files to allow DNEWS to respond to users' requests. (Not generally needed.)
Expire_chunk	100000	Sets how many lines from the history file to expire in one go.
Expire_delay	3	The maximum delay before DNEWS will expire some more items even if it is flat-out answering user requests. (Not generally needed.)
Expire_fast	true	Increases priority of expire job to get it done fast in the night. (Not generally needed.)
Expire_minutes	true	Used to make DNEWS use the minutes setting in the expire_at rule.
Expire_small	1000	When DNEWS is using more than 89 percent of the available disk space, there is a danger of it deleting too many items in one go. This setting is used to limit how many it deletes before checking to see if the disk is still almost full.
Feed_reader	true (default)	Sends the Mode reader command when connecting to a feeding site. This is the default. You will probably never have to change this setting.
Fts_dir	d:\dnews\fts	Sets the directory where the FTS index files are being stored. (See the section on FTS for more details.)
Fts_expire	true	Automatically set if fts_dir is true. This tells DNEWS to write a list of all expired articles so that the FTS system can remove them from the FTS database.
Groups_at	20 2	Sets when DNEWS should check for newly created newsgroups on the site that it is sucking news from. (Not needed with an Ihave feed, where the control news items perform this function.)
Head_cache	200	How many item headers to keep in memory. If you have memory to burn, then a setting of 3000 will improve performance of some NNTP commands
Head_limit	2000	Limits the size of headers to keep in the cache. The default is about 2000.
Hide_queue	true	Stops the list of groups being sucked from being shown in the "Downloading . . ." message.
History	\dnews\spool	Directory for history file. This could grow to 40MB for a full feed (80,000 blocks).
History_min	5	Pause if less than *n* megabytes are free.
Item_max	100000	Sets the maximum size for any article that DNEWS can deal with. The default is 1,000,000. A smaller number will save memory.

Table B-2 Configuration Parameters—dnews.conf (Continued)

Parameter	Example	Description
Life	30	Number of days to keep caching a newsgroup after someone reads an item in it.
List_min	300	How many groups need to be cached before the update method switches to the technique that works best for large numbers of groups.
Log_inline	false	Stops logging of all the "item ok" messages inside the dnews.log file.
Log_nntp	false	Stops logging all the NNTP commands sent to DNEWS.
Logdir	\dnews	Directory to write log files.
Logdir_min	5	Pause server if less than 5MB is left free on logging disk.
Loglvl	info	One of: error, warn, info, debug, flush. There are four levels of error reporting: "error" includes serious errors, "warn" includes possible problems, "info" includes general information messages, and "debug," which is used for tracing bugs. "Flush" is the same as "debug," but the log file is flushed with every single line written. This is useful if the system is crashing but not providing a stack dump.
Loguse	true	Write a log of every item body read by users in the file used.log.
Mail	smtp	This is only used on VMS systems. The name of the foreign e-mail system on VMS—typically in % or smtp% (don't include the %).
Mail_from	system@your. domain	Sets the From address used when DNEWS sends a report or e-mail confirmation to a user. This is sometimes needed by SMTP servers, which require a valid return address.
Manager	system@here. this.place	E-mail address of the news manager.
Max_out	10000	Limits the speed at which any channel can read news articles in characters per second.
Max_speed	10000	Limits the speed at which any channel can send news into DNEWS.
Myname	news.this.place	Your full Internet name, if left out. This may be picked up from the system. It's best to put it in by hand to make sure it's right.
Nntp_block	true	Sets all the sockets as blocking. We don't know why you would want to do this.
Nntp_feeder	news.feeder.site	The news site where you are going to suck a feed from. You need NNTP reader access to this site. If you are not sucking a feed, then comment this line out. If you need to specify a port other than the default one (119), then add it on the end of the name; for example, feeder.site.edu:2021
Nntp_logoff	"You are not one of our users"	Specifies the message to give to users who are not granted connect access via access.conf.
Nntp_pass	mysecretword	Use this if the site you are sucking from requires a username and password to access it.
Nntp_suck2, 3, 4	second.feeder alt.irc.* myuser mypassword	Get *irc* groups from another news server every 10 minutes. The user/passwords are optional. (Also see update_groups.)
Nntp_user	jbloggs	Use this if the site you are sucking from requires a username and password to access it.
Nntp_xposting	true	For a posting feed. This lets you add a header that will identify any user that attempts to post spam through your server.

Table B-2 Configuration Parameters—dnews.conf (Continued)

Parameter	Example	Description
No_newnews	true	Disables the Newnews command.
Nocontrol	true	Prevents automatic creation of the *control* newsgroup.
Nodns	true	Stops DNEWS from doing reverse DNS lookups every time a user connects. You will have to put IP numbers into access.conf if you use this feature, but if your DNS is faulty or slow, then this can improve connection times.
Nospacecheck	true	Stops DNEWS from attempting to find out how much disk space is free. If this test is failing, your server may pause itself, so this setting gets it working again. This is quite safe as the test is used only as a backup check.
Nostream	true	Tells DNEWS to pretend it cannot take a streaming incoming feed.
Nwserver	hostname	Use on netware servers if NetWin suggests it should be used.
Open_block	true	Makes NNTP open calls block the news server.
Open_retry	5	How long to wait after failing to open an NNTP connection before retrying.
Org	NetWin Ltd	Sets the name to be added to local posts that do not have the organization header set.
Org_replace	true	Forces local posts to have your organization name even if the news posting software attempted to put some other name in.
Out_size	4000	Sets the size of packets to be sent in one Write operation to a socket.
Pident	true	Enables Pidentd checking (a way of authenticating users on multi-user UNIX systems).
Port	119	The TCP port at which DNEWS should listen for incoming connections.
Post_log	true	Logs every local message to a post.log file
Post_route	true	Enables routing of incoming Ihave messages to outgoing posting feeds.
Postonly	true	Stops items from being posted locally until they echo back from the feeder site. This gives a very clear confirmation that the message has been passed upstream. You cannot do this if you want to have local groups that are not on the site you are sucking from.
Replicate	true	Makes DNEWS use the same item numbers for each item as are used on the server it's sucking from. The result is a second server that mirrors the first.
Report	no	Stops the daily e-mail report from being sent to the manager after every expire run.
Send_at	*5 *	Send messages upstream when the time matches. This would do it every 10 minutes; for example, at 1:05, 1:15 ...
Send_later	true	Stops DNEWS from attempting to send a post immediately. Useful if you are using a dial-up connection. You can trigger this by hand using Tellnews requeue.
Sendmail	/usr/ucb/sendmail	Path to Sendmail or equivalent software with switches. (Used only on UNIX.)
Spool	\dnews\spool	Disk name (or logical name) for news articles.
Spool_min	5	Pause if less than *n* megabytes free.

Table B-2 Configuration Parameters—dnews.conf (Continued)

Parameter	Example	Description
Suck_batchn	100	Maximum number of items to get from one group before going on to the next group.
Suck_batchsize	1000000	Maximum bytes to get from one group before going on to the next group. Use this to stop DNEWS spending all day just on binary groups.
Suck_requeue	true	Tells DNEWS to requeue a group that is not finished.
Suck_stream	true	Makes DNEWS suck much faster. Don't set this unless you need to, since it hurts the server you are sucking from.
Suck_timeout	300	How many seconds a sucking feed can be idle before DNEWS should close the connection to try to get it unstuck.
Suck_uucp	/uucp_in/*.bag	Directory and filenames of incoming UUCP files. Every minute DNEWS will scan this directory and read in any files it finds and then delete them. They should be in standard Rnews format.
Tcp_nodelay	true	Sets the socket to send data immediately. This may solve problems with buggy news readers; for example, Mosaic news reader.
Timeout	30	Defines how long to wait after a channel becomes idle before disconnecting it. The default is 120 minutes.
Timezone	EST	Time zone hh:mm or time zone name.
Too_old	50	Refuses items that were created more than this many days in the past. This prevents old items from being redistributed when a machine dumps old news items onto the network.
Update_at	*0,*5 *	Checks for new items every time the minutes end in a 5 or a zero and at any hour; for example, every 5 minutes.
Update_at2, 3, 4	10 *	Updates setting for second, third, and fourth feeds. Checks less frequently, every hour at 10 minutes past.
Update_groups 1, 2, 3	*binary* 45 1	A way of getting specific groups more frequently. Works only with the main feed. For example, gets binary groups once a day at 1:45. This is in addition to the update_at setting, not instead of.
Uucp_crlf	true	Writes UUCP files as MSDOS text files instead of proper UNIX format.
Workarea	\dnews\spool	Directory for work files (active.dat, *.feed, and so forth).
Workarea_min	5	If less than *n* megabytes are free on this disk, then pause the news system (stop accepting new articles).
Xover_cache	4000	How many Xover records to cache. This is the best way to improve performance if you have spare memory. Set it as high as 15000.

Access.conf

This file controls access to your system. You can control access by IP name, by IP number, or even by an individual user using password protection. Entries have the following format:

<host>:<perm>:<user>:<pass>:<groups>

Table B-3 contains further information on the contents of the access.conf file.

Table B-3 File Contents—access.conf

Parameter	Example	Description
host	161.29.23.*	A wildcard name or number. This rule is used only if the connection matches this address.
perm	Read, Post	Allow any combination of reading, posting, or Ihave feeding from this site.
user	jep	Some news readers can send a username. If so then it will be matched here, and the password can be checked.
pass	cos67	The password in plain text.
groups	*,!*.binaries.*	Allow access to groups matching this wild card.

Unlike other news implementations, you can permit reading and posting to different combinations of newsgroups; for example, you may wish to allow students to read all groups but post only to local newsgroups.

The last matching line in the file is used. This file can be tricky to set up. If it doesn't work as expected, check that you have the entries in the right order so that the last matching IP name does what you want.

Expire.conf

The expiration file used in DNEWS is very different from that used in INN and CNEWS implementations. Rather than a simple set of rules, the DNEWS expire rules match both newsgroup names and current disk usage. So as use increases, the rules can be automatically modified to become more stringent. In addition rules can specify minimum or maximum numbers of items. This allows a single rule to apply to newsgroups that get 20 items a day or 20 items a month.

Each line of the file has the following format:

UPTO x GROUPS x KEEP x DEFAULT x PURGE x MAXITEMS x MINITEMS x

Table B-4 contains further information on the contents of the expire.conf file.

Table B-4 File Contents—expire.conf

Parameter	Example	Description
upto	20%	This rule applies if less than 20 percent of the disk space is full.
groups	alt.*,comp.binaries.*	This rule applies if the group matches this list.
keep	2	Keep items for this many days even if they have already expired (dated from the expire date in the article header).
default	10	Keep items this long and then delete them unless the expiration date says to keep them longer.
purge	35	Delete after this many days even if the expire header says to keep it longer. This should be set long enough to keep FAQs and no longer to prevent abuse.
maxitems	1000	Delete old items if the group has more than this many items in it. Good for controlling high-volume groups.
minitems	10	Don't apply any other rules if the group has less than this many items in it. This is good for making "low volume" groups usable.

As in the case of the access.conf, the order of the lines in the file is significant.

Newsfeeds.conf

This file controls feeds to other sites. It also controls the feed into DNEWS.

Table B-5 contains further information on the contents of the newsfeeds.conf file.

Table B-5 File Parameters—newsfeeds.conf

Parameter	Example	Description
site	me	The name of the site to feed to. Usually it's the full Internet name defined by $*nntp_feeder*. The *me* feed must be *my.leaf.site*, the first one in the file.
builtin	(flag, no value)	Specifies the built-in feeding mechanism that should be used. This is intended only for sending local postings upstream. It is not fast enough to send a full feed on to another site.
posting	(flag, no value)	Specifies that the NNTP Post command should be used to send items upstream. This gives your feeder site the job of deciding how to e-mail postings to moderated groups.

Table B-5 File Parameters—newsfeeds.conf (Continued)

Parameter	Example	Description
exclude	feeder.real.name,feeder.third.name	Use this if your feeder site is "name stamping" articles with a name other than its IP name. This MUST be right or DNEWS will attempt to echo everything it gets back to the feeder site. (check the Path header)
smtp	(flag, no value)	Specifies that this is not really a feed, but on a VAX it is actually the e-mail queue used to send articles to moderated groups. This is needed only on VMS, and then only if you are not using the Posting mechanism to feed upstream.
maxcross	50	Throw away items that are cross-posted to more than 50 newsgroups. This is good for preventing spamming, which is where people post adverts and moneymaking schemes to inappropriate newsgroups.
maxsize	100000	Limit items to 100K. The default is 1MB. If you want to make it larger than 1MB, then you must also increase *ITEM_MAX* in dnews.conf. Personally I think 100K is too big. FTP sites and the Web should be used for larger items.

Moderators.conf

This file allows a moderator to be designated for a particular moderated newsgroup. Articles destined for the newsgroups are intercepted and e-mailed to the moderator for consideration. You normally won't need to touch this file unless you want to add a local group and designate that it will be moderated. In that case, add your groups at the top of the file as the first match is used.

Format:

```
<newsgroup>:<email-address>
```

If the e-mail address contains a "%s" then that is replaced by the newsgroup name with the dots changed into dashes.

Example:

```
local.gossip.moderated:chrisp@marc.cri.nz
gnu.*: %s@tut.cis.ohio-state.edu
*:%s@uunet.uu.net
```

Control.conf

This file controls the action taken when control messages are received. For each type of control message, you can specify an action based on who sent it and the group being affected.

All control messages have the following format:

```
message-type:e-mail-address:action
```

Table B-6 lists the three control messages currently supported by DNEWS and their effect.

Table B-6 Control Messages

Message Type	Explanation
newgroup	Create a new newsgroup
rmgroup	Delete an existing newsgroup
version	Netnews software version

DNEWS Server Actions

Table B-7 lists the possible actions that can be taken by the server.

Table B-7 Actions Taken by DNEWS

Action	Description
drop	Discard the control message.
log	Just log the control message.
mail	E-mail the administrator.
doit	Perform the action specified by the message.
doit,mail	Perform the action specified by the message and e-mail the administrator.

TELLNEWS COMMANDS

Tellnews commands are used to control and communicate with the DNEWS server (see Table B-8).

Table B-8 Tellnews Commands

Command	Syntax and Description
Addlost	Syntax: tellnews addlost Description: A very useful command. Used when the history file and the database get out of sync. It reenters into the history file items that are not indexed, and also corrects the range of items for each group (as stored in the active.dat file). This command runs as a background task, like an expire. It will take several hours per gigabyte of news. So a large system may take 10–24 hours to complete.
Cached	Syntax: tellnews cached group_wildcard n_days Description: Causes the group or groups listed to be cached on the server for the number of days specified.
Checkgroups	Syntax: tellnews checkgroups check_news_item.txt Description: Processes the given file as if it had been received as a "checkgroups" message. A "checkgroups" message is a list of real newsgroups in a given news hierachy; for example, all the *rec.** newsgroups. Any newsgroup that is not in the "checkgroups" messages is deleted; any newsgroup that is missing is added.
Clear_cache	Syntax: tellnews clear_cache Description: Clears some of the internal caches used for reading item files.
Crash_now	Syntax: tellnews crash_now Description: Very dodgy command used to simulate the behavior of other companies' news servers.
Debug	Syntax: tellnews debug [chan_read:chan_write:...] Description: Used with *loglvl, debug,* or *flush,* to control which debugging messages are sent to the log file. The list of options must not contain spaces.
Disconnect	Syntax: tellnews disconnect n (where *n* is the number of the channel to disconnect) Description: Used by the DNEWS newsmaster to disconnect a single channel. Select the number *n* by doing a Tellnews status command first.
Dns_clear	Syntax: tellnews dns_clear Description: Used by the DNEWS newsmaster to clear DNEWS's cache of IP numbers and names. Very rarely necessary. If you change the names or numbers of local machines, this command should be used.
Dns_show	Syntax: tellnews dns_show Description: Used by the DNEWS newsmaster to inspect DNEWS's internal cache of IP numbers and names. Very rarely useful for normal operation unless you are having trouble granting access to a particular IP name and you need to see what name DNEWS is finding for that computer in the DNS
Doupgrade	Syntax: tellnews doupgrade Description: NEVER use this command. It was for converting the DNEWS database from version 1.0 to 2.0. It will also be used to force an upgrade from version 2.0 to version 3.0. Since this process is automatic, there is never any need to use this command.
Exit	Syntax: tellnews exit Description: Shuts down the DNEWS server cleanly.

Table B-8 Tellnews Commands (Continued)

Command	Syntax and Description
Expire	Syntax: tellnews expire Description: Used by the DNEWS newsmaster to force an expire run during the day. This is occasionally necessary if something has prevented normal expire runs from working and after fixing the problem you wish to start an expire run immediately to free up disk space. The expire run will begin as soon as the current entry in the sucking queue has completed.
Fileonly	Syntax: tellnews fileonly Description: Used by Netwin support staff to test DNEWS performance. NEVER use this command.
Fixnames	Syntax: tellnews fixnames Description: Used by DNEWS newsmaster to fix the active.names file. This command will check that the file is internally consistent, and it will remove any duplicate entries. This command should be used every few months to keep the system clean.
Fixrange	Syntax: tellnews fixrange Description: Tells DNEWS to forget how many items it thinks each group contains and actually checks the next time a user enters the group. This is sometimes useful if Winvn is crashing because DNEWS has lost track of how many items exist in a particular group.
Fixtimes	Syntax: tellnews fixtimes days_old Description: Tells DNEWS to rewrite the active.times file and pretend that all groups were created "days_old" ago. This command should be used once every six months to clean out old groups from the active.times file.
Getgroups	Syntax: tellnews getgroups [n] Description: Used with a sucking feed to get the list of groups from the provider. If there are more than 300 groups cached, DNEWS will do this automatically every Update_at period. If there are less than 300 groups cached, it will do this command automatically once per day. It can also be used to get the groups lists from additional feeds by specifying 2, 3, or 4 as *n*. This has to be used to add an additional feed to DNEWS. When you first start up DNEWS, it will also try to get the full list of groups, but if it fails on the first attempt (owing to some temporary problem; for example, you forgot to plug in the Ethernet cable), then use this command to force it to fetch the list again.
Getnames	Syntax: tellnews getnames Description: Gets the list of newsgroup names from the news server you are sucking from and stores them in the active.names file. Very few news readers display these full names, so it is not critical to get this.
Getold	Syntax: tellnews getold <group wildcard> n Description: DNEWS keeps track of the latest item number for every group on the site it is sucking from. This command lets you adjust this counter downward by *n* for every matching group. This can be useful as a way to refetch items that were somehow missed previously. This command will not result in duplicate articles. Because of the history file, DNEWS will not refetch an article if its message id is stored in the history file.
Group_age	Syntax: tellnewsgroup_age Description: Age all groups. This command emulates the passing of each day. Each cached group has a counter of how many days it should remain cached for, and this command will reduce every counter by one and will then uncache any group whose counter has reached 0.

Table B-8 Tellnews Commands (Continued)

Command	**Syntax and Description**
Group_merge	Syntax: tellnews group_merge Description: Merge a file called active.add (in the workarea directory) with the existing active.dat file. This is the correct way to update your active list to include groups from a new site that is now sending you items via Ihave. Don't edit the active.dat file by hand :-)
Group_nodup	Syntax: tellnews group_nodup Description: Checks the active file and removes any duplicates. This command should never be necessary. It was added during an early version of DNEWS that had a bug that could allow duplicate groups to get into the active file.
Hist_test	Syntax: tellnews hist_test Description: Shows in the log file every time an actual history file read is necessary. This was used to confirm that history lookups were as rare as possible while accepting an Ihave feed.
Key	Syntax: tellnews key Description: Enter a license key to the server. The key is letter-number-letter- . . . and all of the letters are lowercase. There are a few different responses this command may give that indicate whether the key has been entered successfully.
Killgroup	Syntax: tellnews killgroup <group wildcard> Description: Removes the specified group(s) from the active file. You must shut down and restart DNEWS after using this command. This command does not attempt to delete the items related to the group. This command is intended for use only when you know best. To cleanly remove a newsgroup use the Rmgroup command (which is reversible) and then wait several days or weeks for the expire process to delete the items in the now deleted group.
Killitem	Syntax: tellnews killitem <group name item number | "message id"> Description: Delete an item in a group. The item is defined either by its message id or by a combination of its number and the group it is in. This information can be found by using a news reader such as WinVN that shows the article numbers. Usually used for removing inappropriate postings from private local groups.
Log	Syntax: tellnews log Description: Display the last 50 lines of the dnews.log file.
Loglvl	Syntax: tellnews loglvl <debug | flush | info | warn | error> Description: Set the level of messages to be recorded in the dnews.log file. Can be used in conjunction with the Tellnews debug command. This command is very useful for enabling a higher level of debugging for a brief period while testing some problem system.
Matchfeed	Syntax: tellnews matchfeed Description: Marks all groups that don't match the groups entry under site me in the newsfeeds.conf file as deleted. This is typically used to change the me feed to allow groups that were previously blocked (in conjunction with Tellnews undelete) or to set newly blocked groups to be deleted.

Table B-8 Tellnews Commands (Continued)

Command	Syntax and Description
Newgroup	Syntax: tellnews newgroup <groupname> [y |m][creator][description] Description: Add a new group to the group list. This can be a local group or a new group from another feed site or a group from the upstream feed. The optional Y or M field is used to set the group as normal (y) or moderated (m). The optional creator field is a one-word name for the group's creator. The optional description field is a few words describing the group.
Purgelost	Syntax: tellnews purgelost Description: Removes all of those articles in DNEWS's database that don't have an entry in the history file. Very useful if the system has become very full owing to some condition that caused it to lose a number of entries from the history file. Generally speaking, Addlost is a better choice to fix a mixed-up DNEWS database.
Purgegroups	Syntax: tellnews purgegroups Description: Actually remove and forget about groups that have been marked for delete. You must stop and start DNEWS after using this command. If you use this on a sucking feed and the deleted groups exist on the site you are sucking from, then the groups will reappear.
Purgelinks	Syntax: tellnews purgelinks Description: Similar to the Addlost command, this command checks the integrity of the DNEWS database. For each cross-posted article it checks that the actual article still exists. If it does not, then the cross-post is deleted. This command should be necessary only if you have corrupted the database by deleting item files by hand.
Refeed	Syntax: tellnews refeed feed.name Description: This command will resend all current articles to a particular news feed. This command is fairly CPU intensive since the entire history file (maybe 80MB) must be parsed. Also, it does not apply all the rules associated with the feed you have specified; it only checks that the group name matches. This command is particularly useful when setting up the FTS system on a running server. It allows you to reindex all existing items.
Reindex	Syntax: tellnews reindex Description: In theory this command is like Addlost, but instead of working off the .idx files it reads the .itm files and recreates the .idx files. In practice it does not yet work correctly except to fix up problems caused by a bug in 3.0a. In future it will be modified to rebuild the .idx files under any conditions.
Reject	Syntax: tellnews reject "<message@id.host>" Description: Tells DNEWS to immediately reject the specified item if it is offered by an Ihave feed. This command is very rarely useful if a particular item is blocking an incoming feed for some unexplained reason.
Reload	Syntax: tellnews reload Description: Reloads the .conf files. Necessary to make any changes to the files take effect. If not done the changes will not take effect until you restart DNEWS.
Reload_FTS	Syntax: tellnews reload_fts Description: Tells DNEWS that the FTS index has changed and should be reloaded from disk. This command is not usually needed. The index is normally reread fairly often automatically.

Table B-8 Tellnews Commands (Continued)

Command	Syntax and Description
Report	Syntax: tellnews report Description: Forces DNEWS to generate the expire report and mail it to the manager address set in DNEWS .conf. Very useful if you are not getting these reports. It allows you to check the log file and see why the report isn't successfully sent.
Reque	Syntax: tellnews reque Description: Puts all outgoing feeds into the sucking queue and attempts to send them. Again this is useful if a built-in outgoing feed or SMTP feed is not working. It allows you to trigger a retry and watch to see why it fails.
Resetall	Syntax: tellnews resetall Description: Use with care; this resets all of the article counts in the active.dat file. The main use for this commnad is to clear an active file that has been sent from someplace other than your provider via FTP and the numbers are meaningless. NEVER, NEVER, NEVER use this command on a working DNEWS server. It is intended only for use during the initial installation to clear out an active file from a UNIX system. To add groups from someone else's active file use the Group_merge command described earlier.
Rmgroup	Syntax: tellnews rmgroup <group name> Description: Flags the specified group(s) as deleted. This is the clean way to delete a group, and if you make a mistake, you can undelete the groups.
Rotate	Syntax: tellnews rotate Description: Manual command to rotate the log files and remove the oldest one. There is an automatic setting for doing this in the dnews.conf file (*debug_rotate n*). Moves dnews.log to dnews2.log, dnews2.log to dnews3.log, and so forth.
Setused	Syntax: tellnews setused <n Mb> Description: Set the disk space used to *n* MB; *n* has to be manually calculated and should be the actual amount of news on the system. Used to correct problems caused if the actual disk usage gets out of sync with what DNEWS thinks it has used. Related to the disk space setting in dnews.conf, and displayed in the output of tellnews.status. For example, if the expire process is not removing much from the system because DNEWS thinks it has used only 10 percent of the available disk space, but the feed is stopped because there is no space left. Setused can be used to tell DNEWS that it has used all of the space, and the expire process will then take care of removing articles until the system is functioning normally again.
Showcached	Syntax: tellnews showcached Description: Displays a list of the groups that are cached on the system and the number of days that they will continue to be updated for. At the end of the update time no more new articles will be fetched for the group, and the expire process will gradually remove the items from the group. The cached life of the group is reset to the value specified for the life parameter in dnews.conf each time an article from the group is read.
Showmem	Syntax: tellnews showmem Description: Shows how much memory DNEWS is using in great detail. Note: the value under Strdup is not accurate. The output of this command is useful to NetWin support staff if you are having a problem with memory use. (See also the related command Test_mem.)

Table B-8 Tellnews Commands (Continued)

Command	Syntax and Description
Showqueue	Syntax: tellnews showqueue Description: Displays a list of groups waiting in the queue to be updated.
Speed	Syntax: tellnews speed Description: Shows how fast articles are arriving. Use in conjunction with Tellnews speed_reset for performance testing.
Speed_reset	Syntax: tellnews speed_reset Description: Resets the counters for testing how many articles are arriving per second.
Speed_test	Syntax: tellnews speed_test Description: This command acts as a toggle. It is used to test how fast articles would arrive if DNEWS didn't have to store them on disk. The items are thrown away. Use at your own risk Normally used in conjunction with Tellnews speed to determine if DNEWS is slowing down the incoming feed or if it is limited by some external bottleneck (for example, the network or the sending machine).
Stats	Syntax: tellnews stats Description: Returns a listing of statistics showing which NNTP commands have been used and how long DNEWS has taken to process each command.
Stats_in	Syntax: tellnews stats_in Description: Returns a report about what DNEWS has sucked/accepted since the last expire.
Stats_groups	Syntax: tellnews stats_groups Description: Shows the top 40 groups by the number of times they have been read by users and by the volume of articles received into that group. This allows you to spot groups that are gobbling up disk space and bandwidth but are not being read by significant numbers of users.
Status	Syntax: tellnews status Description: Returns a report about the status of the system,
Test_files	Syntax: tellnews test_files Description: Used on UNIX systems for checking on memory problems. Checks to see how file handles DNEWS can allocate.
Test_mem	Syntax: tellnews test_mem Description: Used for checking on memory problems. Checks to see how much memory DNEWS can allocate. If it cannot allocate at least 20MB or 30MB, then your page file is probably not big enough. You MUST restart DNEWS after using this command to allow the memory to be freed.
Test_sleep	Syntax: tellnews test_sleep n Description: Locks up DNEWS for *n* seconds (works only on Windows NT). This is used to the test behavior of DNEWS under certain load conditions.
Test_sockets	Syntax: tellnews test_sockets Description: Tests how many sockets DNEWS can open.

Table B-8 Tellnews Commands (Continued)

Command	Syntax and Description
Trimgroups	Syntax: tellnews trimgroups n Description: Similar to the Getgroups command, but instead of adding missing groups, this command removes groups that no longer exist on the site you are sucking news from. Groups will not be deleted if they don't match the wild card in dnews.conf for that feed. In this way local groups will probably not be deleted :-)
Uncached	Syntax: tellnews uncached <group wild card> Description: Sets the specified groups as not cached.
Undelete	Syntax: tellnews undelete <group wildcard> Description: Mark a previously deleted group as undeleted.
Update, Update2, Update3, Update4	Syntax: tellnews update[n] Description: Cause an update from the specified feed to be queued. Used only for sucking feeds. New items in any cached groups will be fetched.
Update_clear	Syntax: tellnews update_clear Description: Clear the update queue.
Updateone	Syntax: tellnews updateone <group wildcard> [n] Description: Add the specified group or groups from the feed [n] in the update queue; *n* is an optional value from 1 to 4; it will default to the main feed if no *n* is specified.

ERROR MESSAGES

Table B-9 lists common error messages and what they mean.

Table B-9 Error Messages

Error Message	Meaning
411 License key expired, sorry	This error is returned to users when your license key has expired. NetWin is always happy to provide a temporary license key to get things going until the paperwork can be sorted out, or until you have finished your testing process. See *netwin@netwinsite.com*
411 no such newsgroup	This means the newsgroup does not exist in the active.dat file on this server.
411 no permission to read that group	This means that users do not have permission to read the group. See the file access.conf.
411 group did exist but has been deleted	This means that the group has been deleted with the Rmgroup Tellnews command. It can be undeleted with Tellnews if necessary.
Read error on group %d:%d, offset %d wanted %d got %d	This usually means that the index file .idx for the specified group was corrupt. An Addlost is probably a good idea if these error messages happen too often.
Error reading index file {%s}	Ignore this error. DNEWS will often look for files that don't exist, this is considered normal. :-)

Table B-9 Error Messages (Continued)

Error Message	Meaning
Syntax error in expire.conf expire: syntax error in expire.conf line %d Syntax error in expire.conf {%s}	This means that one of the lines in your expire.conf file did not make sense. Check the file carefully and make sure you are editing it with a text editor.
active.times is too big, please use command: tellnews fixtimes -100	This means the active.times file that grows slightly every day is getting a bit too large. You must issue the suggested command. You'll need to do this every six months or so.
Discarding incoming data due to big error above %d	This may occur if you run out of space in the work area directory. Basically look above this error to find the real cause of the problem.
Nntp: Socket closed, errno=%d	This means that an NNTP connection from a reader or another server closed in an unusual way. Normally this can be ignored. You can look up the error number in a UNIX errno.h file to see if that gives more help, but it is unlikely to.
socket_read failed	Often this occurs when a news reader closes a connection unexpectedly. It can usually be ignored.
Socket newchan accept() call failed	This means someone tried to connect to your server, but when DNEWS tried to accept the connection the user had gone, or something prevented the connection from being accepted. This is an unusual error and may be significant if you are having other problems.
socket_write error	Ignore this. It's usually just caused by a connection closing unexpectedly.
wsock: (%s) The virtual circuit was reset by the remote side.	This usually means that the other end closed the connection.
wsock: (%s) Connection Refused	This usually occurs when you try to connect to a news server that isn't running at all. It doesn't mean that you were refused access by the access.conf file.
wsock: (%s) Address in use	This often means that you have some other news server or port mapper running that has a hold on port 119.
last error: NNTP open of {%s} failed, check dnews.log	This error often can be ignored, but it implies that the sucking feed may be down briefly. If you stop getting new news, this would indicate something is wrong with the place you are sucking news from.
suck: BAD status code returned {%s} {%s} {%s}	Read the error message inside the brackets carefully. This error probably came from the site you are sucking from, not DNEWS itself, so if the error in the brackets said "You have no permission to talk," then the problem is that the place you are trying to suck from has not given you permission to talk.

C INN Technical Information

Configuration Files

The site directory contains the files and scripts used to configure INN. Table C-1 lists each file or script and gives a brief description of each. The descriptions that appear in Table C-1 were extracted—with minor modifications—from the man pages, associated Readme files, or comments within the files themselves. (The most prominent source of information is listed in column 3 of the table.)

Table C-1 INN Files and Directories

File or Directory Name	Description	Source
Makefile	Used by the Make utility to install changed files.	file
RCS	Directory used to store RCS archives.	file
actsync.cfg	Configuration file that controls the behavior of Actsync(8), which permits one to synchronize, compare, or merge two active(5) files.	file, Actsync(8)
actsync.ign	Actsync ignore configuration file.	Actsync(8)
Checkgroups	Checkgroups control-message handler.	file
config	This file contains the date of the last configuration done with the Make utility.	file
control.ctl	Specify handling of USENET control messages.	control.ctl(5)
Default	Default control-message handler script.	file

Table C-1 INN Files and Directories (Continued)

File or Directory Name	Description	Source
distrib.pats	Specify default Distribution header for newsgroups that match the patterns in this file.	distrib.pats(5)
Do-subst.sh	Script to run Subst over a list of files. It will get files in and out of source control if present.	file
Docheckgroups	Script to execute Checkgroups text. The results are sent Stdout.	file
expire.ctl	The default control file for the Expire(8) program.	expire.ctl(5)
Expirerm	Expirerm is a script that removes a list of files.	Expirerm(8)
filter.tcl	A TCL procedure that will be run over every article.	Readme
filter_innd.pl	Sample PERL filtering file for the INNd hooks. This file gets loaded at INNd process startup, and everytime a Reload PERL xxx or a Reload all xxx is done.	Readme
Filter_nnrpd.pl	This PERL script is loaded when NNRPd starts up. If it defines a sub named "filter_post" then that function will be called during processing of a posting.	Readme
Getsafe.sh	Script to safely get a file from the samples directory.	file
hosts.nntp	Contains list of hosts that feed us NNTP news.	hosts.nntp(5)
hosts.nntp.nolimit	File containing list of hosts that will be permitted to connect past the limits set up by the "-i" and "-X" flags to INNd(8).	file
Ihave	Script to handle Ihave control messages.	file
inn.conf	Contains configuration data for InterNetNews programs.	inn.conf(5)
Inncheck	Script to check INN configuration and database files.	Inncheck(8)
Innlog.pl	PERL script to summarize INNd and NNRPd log files.	Innlog.pl(8)
Innshellvars	Script to set up any and all shell variables that an INN shell script might need. Also sets umask.	file
innshellvars.csh	Csh version of Innshellvars.	file
innshellvars.pl	PERL version of Innshellvars.	file
innshellvars.tcl	TCL version of Innshellvars.	file
Innstat	Script to print a snapshot of the INN system including the operating mode of the server, as well as disk usage and the status of all log and lock files.	Innstat(8)
Innwatch	Script normally started by Rc.news to periodically examine the load average, the number of free blocks and inodes on the spool partition, as described by its control file, innwatch.ctl(5).	Innwatch(8)
innwatch.ctl	File used to determine what actions are taken during the periodic supervisions by Innwatch.	innwatch.ctl(5)
moderators	The GetModeratorAddress(3) routine reads this file to determine how to reach the moderator of a newsgroup. This is used by Inews(1) when an unapproved local posting is made to a moderated newsgroup.	moderators(5)
Newgroup	Script to handle Newgroup control messages.	file

Table C-1 INN Files and Directories (Continued)

File or Directory Name	Description	Source
News.daily	Script that performs a number of important USENET administrative functions. This includes producing a status report, removing old news articles, processing log files, rotating the archived log files, renumbering the active file, removing any old socket files found in the firewall directory, and collecting the output. This program should be run under the news administrator's ID, not as root.	News.daily(8)
newsfeeds	File that specifies how incoming articles should be distributed to other sites. It is parsed by the InterNetNews server INNd(8) when it starts up, or when directed to by CTLINNd(8).	newsfeeds(5)
nnrp.access	File that specifies the access control for those NNTP sites that are not handled by the main InterNetNews daemon INNd(8). The NNRPd(8) server reads it when first spawned by INNd.	nnrp.access(5)
Nntpsend	Front-end script that invokes Innxmit(1) to send USENET articles to a remote NNTP site.	Nntpsend(8)
nntpsend.ctl	File that specifies the default list of sites to be fed by Nntpsend(8).	nntpsend.ctl(5)
overview.fmt	File specifies the organization of the news overview database. Blank lines and lines beginning with a number sign "#" are ignored. The order of lines in this file is important; it determines the order in which the fields will appear in the database.	overview.fmt(5)
Parsecontrol	Script to perform the initial parsing of control messages.	file
passwd.nntp	File to contain passwords for connecting to remote NNTP servers.	file
Pgpverify	PERL script to verify PGP signatures on control messages.	file
Rc.news	News boot script. Runs as "news" user and requires Inndstart to be *setuid* root.	file
Rmgroup	Script to handle Remove group control messages.	file
sample.control	Sample control message with PGP signature for testing purposes.	file
Scanlogs	Script that summarizes the information recorded in the INN log files (newslog(5)). By default, it also rotates and cleans out the logs. It is normally invoked by the News.daily(8) script.	file
Scanspool	Script that will scan first the active file, noting problems such as malformed line; group aliased to a nonexistent group; group aliased to a group that is also aliased. Then it will examine all articles under your news spool directory, looking for articles in which the basename starts with a leading 0; the basename is out of range with the active file; it does not contain a Newsgroups line; there is an article that is all header and no text; an article is in a directory for which there is no active group; there is an article that is in a group to which it does not belong.	file
Send-ihave	Script to send Ihave batches out.	file
Send-nntp	Script to send NNTP news out.	file
Send-uucp	Script to send UUCP batches out.	file
Sendbatch	Script to send UUCP batches out.	file

Table C-1 INN Files and Directories (Continued)

File or Directory Name	Description	Source
Sendme	Script to handle Send-me control messages.	file
Sendsys	Script to handle Sendsys control messages.	file
Senduuname	Script to handle Send-uuname control messages.	file
startup.tcl	TCL program to process filters. If you compile with TCL support enabled, then this file (even if empty) must exist in location defined in the config.data.	file
startup_innd.pl	Sample startup code for PERL hooks in INN. This file, after it's installed in the right spot, will be loaded when INNd starts up.	file
Tally.control	Script to tally/update the Newgroup/Rmgroup control log. This script will also merge in a log that contains Newgroup/Rmgroup control messages so that the control.log file is updated to contain the new counts of how often each group has been newgroup'd or rmgroup'd. This is run by Scanlogs, which prepares this from the control-message handlers if control.ctl specifies logging.	file
Tally.unwanted	Script to tally/update the unwanted newsgroup log. It will read an INNd log on Stdin, scan it for articles that were unwanted because the newsgroups were not in our active file. Update unwanted.log to have the new count of unwanted groups, and how often they were used.	file
update	File that contains the last date and time the News system was updated.	file
Version	Script to hand Version control messages.	file
Writelog	The Writelog script is used to write a log entry or send it as mail. The Name parameter specifies the name of the log file where the entry should be written. If it is the word *mail* then the entry is mailed to the newsmaster. The data that is written or sent consists of the text given on the command line, followed by standard input indented by four spaces. Shlock(1) is used to avoid simultaneous updates to a single log file.	file

CTLINND—CONTROLLING THE INTERNETNEWS DAEMON (INND)

Ctlinnd is used to control INNd. Table C-2 lists the CTLINNd options and commands. (The following information was extracted from the Ctlinnd(8) man page.) Note that all commands have a fixed number of arguments. If a parameter can be an empty string, then it is necessary to specify it as two adjacent quotes: " ".

Table C-2 CTLINNd Information

Command or Option	**Description or Syntax**
-s	If the "-s" flag is used, then no message will be printed if the command was successful.
-t	The "-t" flag can be used to specify how long to wait for the reply from the server. The Timeout value specifies the number of seconds to wait. A value of zero waits forever, and a value less than zero indicates that no reply is needed. When waiting for a reply, CTLINNd will try every two minutes to see if the server is still running, so it is unlikely that "-t0" will hang. The default is "-t0."
-h	To see a command summary, use the "-h" flag. If a command is included when CTLINNd is invoked with the " -h" flag, then only the usage for that command will be given.
Addhist	addhist <Message-ID> arr exp post paths Add an entry to the history database. This directs the server to create a history line for Message-ID. The angle brackets are optional. *Arr, exp,* and *post* specify when the article arrived, what its expiration date is, and when it was posted. All three values consist of a number representing the number of seconds since the epoch. If the article does not have an Expires header, then *exp* should be zero. *Paths* is the pathname within the news spool directory where the article is filed. If the article is cross-posted, then the names should be separated by white space, and the paths argument should be inside double quotes. If the server is paused or throttled, this command causes it to briefly open the history database.
Allow	allow reason Remote connections are allowed. The reason must be the same text given with an earlier Reject command, or an empty string.
Begin	begin site Begin feeding site. This will cause the server to rescan the newsfeeds(5) file to find the specified site and set up a news feed for it. If the site already exists, a "drop" is done first. This command is forwarded; see below.
Cancel	cancel <Message-ID> Remove the article with the specified Message-ID from the local system. This does not generate a Cancel message. The angle brackets are optional. If the server is paused or throttled, this command causes it to briefly open the history database.
Changegroup	changegroup group rest The newsgroup group is changed so that its fourth field in the active file becomes the value specified by the Rest parameter. This may be used to make an existing group moderated or unmoderated, for example.
Checkfile	checkfile Check the syntax of the newsfeeds file and display a message if any errors are found. The details of the errors are reported to Syslog(3).

Table C-2 CTLINNd Information (Continued)

Command or Option	Description or Syntax
Drop	drop site Flush and drop the site from the server's list of active feeds. This command is forwarded; see below.
Feedinfo	feedinfo site Print detailed information about the state of the feed to the site or more brief status of all feeds if the site is an empty string.
PERL	PERL flag Enable or disable PERL news filtering. If flag starts with the letter *y*, then filtering is enabled. If it starts with *n*, then filtering is disabled.
Flush	flush site Flush the buffer for the specified site. The actions taken depend on the type of feed the site receives; see newsfeeds(5). This is useful when the site is fed by a file and batching is going to start. If the site is an empty string, then all sites are flushed, and the active file and history databases are also written out. This command is forwarded; see below.
Flushlogs	flushlogs Close the log and error log files and rename them to have an .old extension. The history database and active file are also written out.
Go	go reason Reopen the History database and start accepting articles after a Pause or Throttle command. The reason must either be an empty string or it must match the text that was given in the earlier Pause or Throttle command. If a Reject command was done, this will also do an Allow command if the reason matches the text that was given in the Reject command. If a Reserve command was done, this will also clear the reservation if the reason matches the text that was given in the Reserve command. Note that if only the history database has changed while the server is paused or throttled, it is not necessary to send it a Reload command before sending it a Go command. If the server throttled itself because it accumulated too many input/output errors, this command will reset the error count. If the server was not started with the "-ny" flag, then this command also does a Readers command with "yes" as the flag and reason as the text.
Hangup	hangup channel Close the socket on the specified incoming channel. This is useful when an incoming connection appears to be hung.
Help	help [command] Print a command summary for all commands, or just one command if specified.
Logmode	logmode Cause the server to log its current operating mode to Syslog.

Table C-2 CTLINNd Information (Continued)

Command or Option	**Description or Syntax**
Mode	mode Print the server's operating mode as a multi-line summary of the parameters and operating state.
Name	name nnn Print the name of channel number *nnn* or of all channels if it is an empty string.
Newgroup	newgroup group rest creator Create the specified newsgroup. The Rest parameter should be the fourth field as described in active(5); if it is not an equal sign, only the first letter is used. The Creator should be the name of the person creating the group. If the newsgroup already exists, this is equivalent to the Changegroup command. This is the only command that has defaults. The Creator can be omitted and will default to the empty string, and the Rest parameter can be omitted and will default to "y." This command can be done while the server is paused or throttled; it will update its internal state when a Go command is sent. This command updates the active.times (see active(5)) file.
Param	param letter value Change the command-line parameters of the server. The combination of defaults makes it possible to use the text of the Control header directly. Letter is the INNd command-line option to set, and Value is the new value. For example, "i 5" directs the server to allow only five incoming connections. To enable or disable the action of the "-n" flag, use the letter *y* or *n*, respectively, for the value.
Pause	pause reason Pause the server so that no incoming articles are accepted. No existing connections are closed, but the history database is closed. This command should be used for short-term locks, such as when replacing the history files. If the server was not started with the "-ny" flag, then this command also does a Readers command with "no" as the flag and reason as the text.
Readers	readers flag text Allow or disallow news readers. If the flag starts with the letter *n*, then news reading is disallowed, by causing the server to pass the text as the value of the NNRPd(8) "-r" flag. If the flag starts with the letter *y* and text is either an empty string, or the same string that was used when news reading was disallowed, then news reading will be allowed.
Reject	reject reason Remote connections (those that would not be handed off to NNRPd) are rejected. The reason for the rejection is explained.

Table C-2 CTLINNd Information (Continued)

Command or Option	Description or Syntax
Reload	reload what reason The server updates its in-memory copies of various configuration files. What identifies what should be reloaded? If it is an empty string or the word *all*, then everything is reloaded; if it is the word *history*, then the history database is closed and opened; if it is the word *hosts.nntp*, then the hosts.nntp(5) file is reloaded; if it is the word *active* or *newsfeeds*, then both the active and newsfeeds files are reloaded; if it is the word *overview.fmt*, then the overview.fmt(5) file is reloaded. If it is the word *filter.perl*, then the filter innd.pl file is reloaded. If a PERL procedure named "Filter_before_reload" exists, it will be called prior to rereading filter.tcl. If a PERL procedure named "Filter_after_reload" exists, it will be called after filter.pl has been reloaded. Reloading the PERL filter does not enable filtering if it is disabled; use filter to do this. The reason is reported to Syslog. There is no way to reload the data inn.conf(5) file; the server currently uses only the Pathhost parameter, so this restriction should not be a problem.
Renumber	renumber group Scan the spool directory for the specified newsgroup and update the low-water mark in the active file. If Group is an empty string, then all newsgroups are scanned.
Reserve	reserve reason The next Pause or Throttle command must use reason as its text. This "reservation" is cleared by giving an empty string for the reason. This command is used by programs such as Expire(8) that want to avoid running into other instances of each other.
Rmgroup	rmgroup group Remove the specified newsgroup. This is done by editing the active file. The spool directory is not touched, and any articles in the group will be expired using the default expiration parameters. Unlike the Newgroup command, this command does not update the active.times file.
Send	send feed text... The specified text is sent as a control line to the exploder feed.
Shutdown	shutdown reason The server is shut down, with the specified reason recorded in the log and sent to all open connections. It is a good idea to send a Throttle command first.
Signal	signal sig site Signal sig is sent to the specified site, which must be a channel or exploder feed. Sig can be a numeric signal number or the word *hup*, *int*, or *term*; case is not significant.

Table C-2 CTLINNd Information (Continued)

Command or Option	Description or Syntax
Throttle	throttle reason Input is throttled so that all existing connections are closed and new connections are rejected. The history database is closed. This should be used for long-term locks, such as when Expire is being run. If the server was not started with the "-ny" flag, then this command also does a Readers command with "no" as the flag and reason as the text.
Trace	trace item flag Tracing is turned on or off for the specified item. Flag should start with the letter *y* or *n* to turn Tracing on or off. If Item starts is a number, then tracing is set for the specified INNd channel, which must be for an incoming NNTP feed. If it starts with the letter *i*, then general INNd tracing is turned on or off. If it starts with the letter *n*, then future NNRPds will or will not have the "-t" flag enabled, as appropriate.
Xabort	xabort reason The server logs the specified reason and then invokes the Abort(3) routine.
Xexec	xexec path The server gets ready to shut itself down, but instead of exiting it executes the specified path with all of its original arguments. If the path is "INNd" then /usr/news/bin/innd is invoked; if it is "INNdstart" then /usr/news/bin/inndstart is invoked; if it is an empty string, it will invoke the appropriate program depending on whether or not it was started with the "-p" flag; any other value is an error.

D NNTP Information

NNTP Commands

NNTP has its own unique command language as tabulated in Table D-1.

Table D-1 NNTP Commands

NNTP Command	Description
Article	Display the message header and text of the specified article
Body	Display only the body of the specified article
Group	Sets the "current" newsgroup
Head	Display only the header of the specified article
Help	Prints a summary of all valid commands
Ihave	Indicates that specified article is available
Last	Sets article point to previous article in current newsgroup
List	Returns list of all valid newsgroups on server
Newgroups	Returns list of newgroups created since specified time/date
Newnews	Returns list of all read/posted articles for specified newsgroup
Next	Sets article point to next article in current newsgroup
Post	Indicates a posting is requested, if accepted then sends article
Quit	Terminates session
Slave	Indicates interaction with a slave server
Stat	Displays only the status of the specified article
Xhdr	Lists the requested header of all articles for the range of specified articles
Xover	Returns information from an overview database for the range of specified articles

NNTP RESPONSE CODES

Most of the problems with the INN server can be traced to NNTP exchanges. The NNTP response codes from the upstream news host can shed a great deal of light on a problem and should be examined closely when problems occur. The NNTP response code is divided into three parts: R, F, and I. The digit in the hundreds place corresponds with R, or Response; the digit in the tens place corresponds to F, or Function; the digit in the ones place corresponds to I, or Information. Following is the key to the numbers in each digit place.

R (Response)

1xx	Informative message.
2xx	Command ok.
3xx	Command ok so far; send the rest of it.
4xx	Command was correct but couldn't be performed for some reason.
5xx	Command unimplemented or incorrect or a serious program error occurred.

F (Function)

x0x	Connection, setup, and miscellaneous messages.
x1x	Newsgroup selection.
x2x	Article selection.
x3x	Distribution functions.
x4x	Posting.
x8x	Nonstandard extensions (AUTHINFO, XGTITLE).
x9x	Debugging output.

I (Information)

There are no defined semantics for information.

Table D-2 lists the set of NNTP response codes as defined in RFC 977 and elsewhere.

Table D-2 NNTP Response Codes

Code	Description
100	help text follows
111	date value follows
190	debug output
200	server ready, posting allowed
201	server ready, no posting allowed
202	slave status noted
203	streaming supported
205	closing connection, goodbye!
211	group okay
215	list of newsgroups follows
220	article follows
221	header follows
222	body follows
223	nothing follows
224	overview follows
230	list of new articles follows
235	article transferred okay
238	I want this article (specified by ID#)
239	article received okay (specified by ID#)
240	article posted okay
335	send article to be transferred
340	send article to be posted
400	service discontinued
411	no such newsgroup
412	no newsgroup selected
420	no current article has been selected
421	no next article in this group
422	no previous article in this group
423	bad article number
430	no such article found
431	resend ID later
435	article not wanted
436	transfer failed, try again later
437	article rejected, do not try again
438	got ID, do not send
439	transfer of ID failed
440	posting not allowed
441	posting failed
500	command not recognized
501	command syntax error

Table D-2 NNTP Response Codes (Continued)

Code	Description
502	permission denied
503	program fault, command not performed
504	server overloaded, try later
505	connection rejected—too many calls by this user

Bibliography

USENET

Pfaffenberger, Bryan. *The USENET Book.* Reading, Mass.: Addison-Wesley Publishing Company, 1995.

Podner, Tom. USENET and Internetnews. Online paper, 1995.

http://ace.alleg.edu/~cortes/Postscript/nntp.ps

Todino, Grace and Dale Dougherty. *Using UUCP and USENET.* Sebastopol, Calif.: O'Reilly & Associates, 1996.

Todino, Grace, and Tim O'Reilly. *Managing UUCP and USENET.* Sebastopol, Calif.: O'Reilly & Associates, 1996.

Security

Cheswick, William, and Steven Bellovin. *Firewalls and Internet Security.* Reading, Mass.: Addison-Wesley Publishing Company, 1995.

Garfinkel, Simson. *Pretty Good Privacy.* Sebastopol, Calif.: O'Reilly & Associates, 1994.

Kent, Peter. *The PGP Companion for Windows.* Research Triangle Park, N.C.: Ventana, 1995.

Stallings, William. *Protect Your Privacy—A Guide for PGP Users.* Upper Saddle River, N.J.: Prentice-Hall, 1994.

Zimmermann, Phil. *The Official PGP User's Guide.* Cambridge, Mass.: MIT Press, 1995.

———. *Source Code and Internals.* Cambridge, Mass.: MIT Press, 1995.

RFCs

RFC 822. Standard for ARPA Internet Text Messages.

RFC 934. Proposed Standard for Message Encapsulation.

RFC 977. Network News Transfer Protocol.

RFC 1034. Domain names—concepts and facilities.

RFC 1035. Domain names—implementation and specification.

RFC 1036. Standard for Interchange of USENET Messages.

RFC 1123. Requirements for Internet Hosts—Application and Support.

RFC 1153. Digest Message Format.

RFC 1341. MIME (Multipurpose Internet Mail Extensions): Mechanisms for Specifying and Describing the Format of Internet Message Bodies.

RFC 1344. Implications of MIME for Internet Mail Gateways.

RFC 1437. The Extension of MIME Content-Types to a New Medium.

RFC 1521. MIME (Multipurpose Internet Mail Extensions) Part One: Mechanisms for Specifying and Describing the Format of Internet Message Bodies.

RFC 1522. MIME (Multipurpose Internet Mail Extensions) Part Two: Message Header Extensions for Non-ASCII Text.

RFC 1563. The text/enriched MIME Content-Type,
"Son of 1036," "News Article Format and Transmission" (proposed).

Index

Building Net Sites with Windows NT™

Jim Buyens
ISBN 0-201-47949-4, $39.95 w/CD-ROM

Building Net Sites with Windows NT provides the essential tools and information to build a full Internet site offering Web pages, e-mail, FTP and more on Windows NT. It covers site planning, security, site maintenance, and Microsoft's Internet Information Server. It also explores advanced Web techniques including clickable image maps, CGI programs, Server Side Includes, Java, database interfaces, and more. The CD-ROM contains server, client, and utility software.

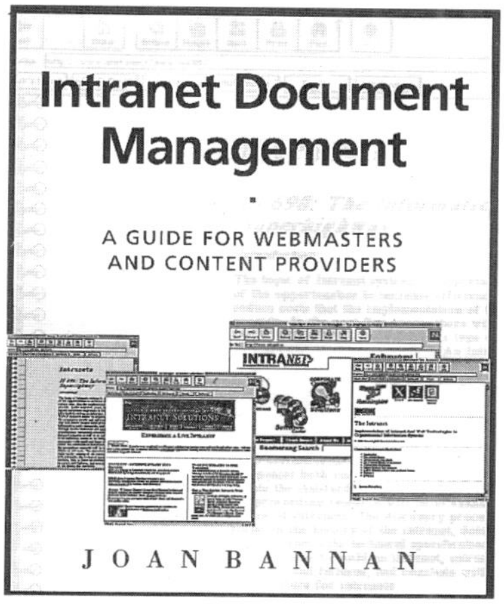

Intranet Document Management

A Guide for Webmasters and Content Providers

Joan Bannan
ISBN 0-201-87379-6, $29.95

Intranet Document Management is the first book to address the most important considerations in designing and maintaining a large organizational Intranet. Web site implementers who want to transform document and information management by instituting an intranet "Web" within their organization will learn how to manage extensive collections of Web documents, handle very large documents, convert legacy documents, and access databases.

CGI Programming in C & Perl

Thomas Boutell
ISBN 0-201-42219-0, $34.95 w/CD-ROM

This book shows you how to create interactive, dynamically-generated Web pages with CGI programming in two practical languages: C, which has distinct performance advances, and Perl, one of the most popular choices for CGI today. You'll learn how to generate HTML pages and images on the fly, parse form submissions directly, and much more. The CD-ROM contains a complete range of CGI software libraries in both C and Perl, ready to plug into your Web site.

Addison-Wesley warrants the enclosed disk to be free of defects in materials and faulty workmanship under normal use for a period of ninety days after purchase. If a defect is discovered in the disk during this warranty period, a replacement disk can be obtained at no charge by sending the defective disk, postage prepaid, with proof of purchase to:

Addison Wesley Longman (CEPUB)
Editorial Department
One Jacob Way
Reading, MA 01867

After the ninety-day period, a replacement will be sent upon receipt of the defective disk and a check or money order for $10.00, payable to Addison-Wesley Longman.

Addison-Wesley makes no warranty or representation, either express or implied, with respect to this software, its quality, performance, merchantability, or fitness for a particular purpose. In no event will Addison-Wesley, its distributors, or dealers be liable for direct, indirect, special, incidental, or consequential damages arising out of the use or inability to use the software. The exclusion of implied warranties is not permitted in some states. Therefore, the above exclusion may not apply to you. This warranty provides you with specific legal rights. There may be other rights that you may have that vary from state to state.